Discovering
sociology

By the same author

Key problems of sociological theory
Race, colonialism and the city

John Rex

Professor of Sociology
University of Warwick

Discovering sociology

studies in sociological theory and method

RECEIVED

JUN 6 1974

MANKATO STATE COLLEGE LIBRARY
MANKATO, MN

Routledge & Kegan Paul
London and Boston

First published 1973
by Routledge & Kegan Paul Ltd
Broadway House, 68–74 Carter Lane,
London EC4V 5EL and
9 Park Street,
Boston, Mass. 02108, U.S.A.
Printed in Great Britain by
Western Printing Services Ltd, Bristol
© John Rex 1973
No part of this book may be reproduced in
any form without permission from the
publisher, except for the quotation of brief
passages in criticism

ISBN 0 7100 7411 5

HM24
.R45

For Margaret, Kate, Helen,
Freddie and David

361559

The paradox of Sociology lies precisely in this, that though we are compelled by forces external to ourselves, these forces are nonetheless made by men and can be changed by men.

Contents

Acknowledgments

Most of the essays which are included in this volume have been given as lectures or broadcasts or published as papers before. Chapters one, three and seven were broadcasts in the BBC Third Programme. Chapter two first appeared in the *Yorkshire Bulletin for Social and Economic Research* in July 1959. Chapter four was given as an address to the meeting of the Sociology Section of the British Society at its Southampton meeting in 1964. Chapter five was a seminar paper given to the new Sociology Department at Durham University, and Chapter six was my inaugural address at that university. Chapters eight, ten, eleven, fourteen and fifteen have appeared in *New Society*, and Chapters ten, eleven and fourteen have been re-published in Timothy Raison (ed.), *The Founding Fathers of Social Science*, Penguin Books, 1969. These essays are reproduced by permission. Chapter twelve is a revised version of a broadcast in the BBC Third Programme on the occasion of the one hundredth anniversary of the publication of *Das Kapital*. Chapter sixteen appeared as the preface to the German edition of my book *Key Problems of Sociological Theory*, and Chapter twenty appeared in the *Sociological Review Monograph*, number 16, entitled 'The Sociology of Sociology' in September 1970. Chapter nineteen was given as a paper to the annual conference of the British Sociological Association in April 1971. Chapters nine, thirteen, seventeen and eighteen are published here for the first time.

My thanks are due to Margaret Bass and Lesley Crone for typing the typescript and to Ivan Oliver for sorting out the footnotes.

Introduction

The essays which form the twenty chapters of this book have been written over a period of nearly fifteen years, but they have a certain consistency about them which, I hope, justifies their being collected in a single book. So far as the development of my own thought goes they may serve to bridge the gap between my first and very tentative book *Key Problems of Sociological Theory* (1961) and a more comprehensive and up-to-date work on which I am now engaged. I hope that they are also of much wider interest in that they exhibit a growing confidence in a non-positivist type of sociology, as this non-positivist approach has gained widespread recognition since 1960.

When I wrote *Key Problems* it was still necessary to fight for the existence of sociology as a subject in British universities. Such sociology as there was, tended to be merged with other disciplines and with various ideologies, which were sufficiently acceptable to have been given house-room in the universities. Today this is no longer the case. As universities have expanded, new and old alike have created sociology departments, and although some appointments have been about as appropriate as appointing Durkheim to a Chair in Obstetrics, growing acquaintance with the literature of the subject by senior non-sociologists who were appointed, as well as by their more eager younger colleagues, has produced some degree of consensus as to what the subject is about. There is no absolute agreement, it is true, but there is sufficient overlap of interests, sufficient understanding of one school by another, to say that there is something called British sociology. In such circumstances (i.e. when one finds that one does have an actual public for one's views amongst one's colleagues), one feels less insecure and more willing to make one's own individual contribution more distinctive.

The original statement of my views brought two favourable

responses, one less important than the other. The less important response was from Marxists and other radicals who saw in my recognition of the importance of disruptive conflict a line of thought which had been missing in British sociology. When, however, a wide variety of other sociological positions opened on the 'left' or the 'conflict' end of the political continuum, the theoretical perspective which my book advocated lost its uniqueness. Moreover, some of the new varieties of Marxism which took hold amongst student opinion were opposed to sociology as such, and my own approach, based as it was on one of the mainstreams of the sociological tradition, namely that of Weber, came to command less support on purely political grounds.

The more important favourable response, however, came from those who saw my approach as 'phenomenological' rather than 'positivist'. This led me to take a much deeper interest than I had done previously in the work of Alfred Schutz and his successors, such as Berger, Cicourel and Garfinkel in the United States, and in the anti-positivist tradition in Germany. The work of the American authors mentioned, greatly enriched my understanding of problems of sociological conceptualization, but I remained stubbornly convinced that, in two respects, the work of Weber aspired to two goals, which some of those interested in the phenomenology of everyday life were inclined to abandon. One was his insistence that a distinction could be made between the relative objectivity of the ideal types of action, formulated by sociologists, and the observed actor's definition of the situation. The other was his use of his typologies, in a politically serious way, to draw comparisons between the structural features of major socio-economic and political systems in history. Because he stuck consistently to these goals, Weber never trivialized sociology and was not subject to the criticism which Marxists sometimes make of phenomenological sociology, namely that it deals only in 'false consciousness'.

To say this, of course, is not to say that Weber gave a satisfactory account of the way in which his hypotheses could be given objectivity. Certainly there is strong reason to doubt whether he was right in suggesting that the sociologist should use causally adequate explanations in an attempt to supplement explanations adequate on the level of meaning. But many of those who have criticized Weber for doing this have failed to show what is meant by defining the objective of the human studies as giving an account of rule-governed behaviour, or as discovering the rules of the games which people play, when they speak to one another and interact with one another. What the critics seem to do, having seen that total objectivity is impossible, is to accept a total subjectivity of approach. There are simply a number of different ways of looking at any situation and all of them have equal validity. Not surprisingly, many of them are followers of Wittgenstein, who, having spent the earlier part of his career seeking the one true language with which to speak about the world, concluded, in the long run, that many language-games were possible.

My own position on these questions is clear enough. With Weber, I accept that there are many different points of view from whence social reality can be studied, but these points of view, and the 'rules of the game' which they imply, can be shown to be operative or not operative in any situation by the objective examination and comparison of cases[1]. The account which we give of them is probably not, in literal scientific terms, a causal account, but it is not 'any old account'; it is not, in Weber's words, merely a plausible story. It is an account of the motivation of actors and the consequences of one actor orienting his conduct to the action of others and to norms, which can be demonstrated as actually operating in the world. Thus, while I do from time to time use the notion of the rules of the game myself, I always argue that it is possible to prove or disprove that this rather than that game is being played. It is this that enables me to take an interest in the 'forced-labour game' which is the key to colonialism or the 'urban-leap-frog game' (see Rex, 1968 and 1970) which is crucial to the understanding of race relations problems in metropolitan contexts. It is not necessary for me to reduce sociology to a mass of individual biographies.

Friendly responses to my work were to be expected from anti-positivists in Germany, and it was from German friends that I first heard that my work was of interest to them. But the philosophic waters of Frankfurt and Berlin run deep and dark. I had, it is true, emphasized the anti-positivist aspects of Weber's work

[1] In the earlier chapters of this book I continually commend the practice of social anthropologists because at their best they have intuitively chosen to do what sociologists should be doing.

and I had seen in Mannheim's *Ideology and Utopia* a statement of the problem of objectivity which was acceptable. More than this, I had seen both Mannheim and Weber as too much inclined to come to terms with positivism and its causal account of human behaviour. I had not however even tried to come to terms with Hegel and the German enlightenment.

Since political events, particularly amongst students, forced me to come to terms with this tradition,[1] I have come to have the greatest respect for it. But I do not think that it is simply a sociology. It is both more and less than a sociology: more, in that it concerns itself with positing an institutional order in which human self-fulfilment is possible, and less, in that it does not regard sociological theory as testable except in terms of practical political action. For my part, while I find such speculations and the political exhortations which underly them very close to my own, I still see the object of sociology as that of giving a comparative account of social structures which exist and through the theory which such comparisons generate, showing what might be. Thus while the work of Lukács or Goldmann, or Adorno or Marcuse or Habermas is of great interest to me as one politically involved in his times, I see it as part of my role as a sociologist to remain agnostic about the futures which they posit, and the objective truths which they profess to see. Amongst other things, this means that my own political positions are more pessimistic than theirs. I can describe social structures and evaluate them as repressive and exploitative, but see no ground for assuming that because they are repressive and exploitative, they will in the long run be transcended. I believe that the repressive structures which lead to the denial of rights to America's black population, to the maintenance of various sorts of colonialism, settler-domination and neo-colonialism, as well as the more sophisticated forms of class exploitation evident in Europe and America, have a great deal of resilience, and that the sociologist who wants to make his sociology relevant to his political action would do well to contemplate these structures in their full complexity, before rushing off in the quest of some unobtainable Utopia. In this, of course, I depart from Max Weber, whose great anxiety was that the Western European institutional

---

[1] In Chapter seven I go beyond sociology to explore the prospects of social change in a more speculative way.

order would break down, rather than that it should survive. On the other hand, I retain an unfashionable respect for the work of C. Wright Mills, because he had the courage, both to be thoroughly pessimistic about the future, yet to give his life to promoting those social changes which he thought desirable.

The layman reading this book may find these disagreements and arguments remote from the day-to-day dilemmas which he faces, and from which he hopes science might save him. They are, however, far from irrelevant, as I hope the first part of my book shows. What has to be dispelled, above all, is the conception of the sociologist as a man who can deduce moral and political injunctions from a foolproof procedure of questionnaire design, data-processing and statistical calculation. Sociology has no capacity to do this. What it can do, and should do, is to exhibit the principles which underly the social structures within which we live, and of the social movements which seek to change them. Sociology does not render the exercise of moral and political judgment unnecessary. It makes clear what the practical choices are, but thereafter the choice lies with men as political individuals and political groups. Moreover, very often clarification is better achieved by stating a complex problem in a qualitative rather than a quantitative form.

I realize full well that there are some of my colleagues and students who will argue that what I have just said involves an abdication of political responsibility by the sociologist. All I can say to this is that for me sociology is an agonizing vocation, because by its very restraint in making value judgments, it opens up the full horror of the kinds of structural change and structural stability which face us in the last years of the twentieth century. The real problem which the sociologist has to face responsibly is this: does he foreshorten his analysis of social relations and structures in order to enable himself to give immediate policy-advice, or does he treat the actions of the powerful as up for analysis and as variable elements, as much as he does the actions of those over whom they exercise authority? For my part, I have always refused to do narrowly-defined, policy-oriented research in the field which interests me most. What I have done is to describe the interlocking patterns of motivation which exist, and to avoid the pretence that this or that politician's proposals can alter the political and economic order within which he works merely by wishing them away or by declaring some political change to be scientifically necessary.

The first part of this book consists of lectures which I have given to lay audiences. Chapter one, written as early as 1958, defines in simple language what I believe sociologists should be doing, and I am surprised on re-reading it how much it has withstood the test of time. One might today have chosen other examples of good sociological work, but the defining character of what is good and bad, which is given in this essay, remains. Chapter two shows how statistics might be put to sociological use if the right questions are asked of them, Chapter three argues the case for theoretical models in the analysis of quite simple social and political situations and Chapter four explores the relation between such theory and what is called 'understanding'. The fifth and sixth chapters, foreshadowing the second part, discuss the relative merit of some of the major sociological and semi-sociological traditions in dealing with methodological questions. The seventh establishes a relationship between literary and sociological concerns, while the eighth, written eight years after the first, shows how sociologists are coping and might cope with their new-found popularity.

The aim of the second part is best defined by disputing the criticism, made by Hubert Blalock, that sociological theory is too much concerned with the ideas and teachings of certain great men (see McKinney and Tiryskian, 1970, p. 274). In my view, sociological theory as such has been produced by relatively few men, and these have been men who were deeply involved in trying to come to terms with their own times. Standing head and shoulders above all others are Durkheim, Marx and Weber. My own approach has been based especially upon the work of Weber but, as other essays show, I am seeking all the time for the convergences between his theory and the theory of Durkheim and Marx. It is this which leads me to the view that there is, in the classical tradition of sociology, a broadly shared methodological approach. Chapter fifteen on C. Wright Mills is added to remind my readers and myself that it is possible for sociologists to make structural analyses of the problems of our day, as surely as the founding fathers of sociology did of theirs.

Sociological theory, however, is not merely the history of sociological writing in the past. What we have derived from the past is a legacy which lives on today in the best work and is too little discussed. What I have done, therefore, is to include three major pieces. One relates my own work to that of Weber; another sets out in a pre-emptory way thirty theses which do not claim to be the final truth about sociological theory and method, but which do at least indicate some of the main areas in which the debate should lie. Lastly there is an essay which shows that one important debate about an area of research turns upon the issues which these thirty theses pose, and one on the dangers inherent in the institutionalization of sociology.

I hope that what emerges here shows a certain unity and that it will stand as a general statement of my own position until I am able to complete a new systematic statement. I do not expect all my readers to accept what I argue for, because there is a sense in which each sociologist makes his own sociology (cf. Durkheim, Marx and Weber). What I do hope is that those who are morally committed to the politics of their society will find here some of the intellectual tools through which they may overcome the sense of impotence which too often besets us as we strive to cope with the slick world-views which are prescribed to us by the media and which stand in for sociology, in the absence of adequate sociological criticism.

Sociology and the layman

1 Towards a significant sociology

One of the greatest American teachers of sociology recently remarked that nearly all sociological research took place under one of two banners. One of these reads, 'We don't know whether what we are saying is true, but it is at least significant'; the other, 'This is demonstrably so, but we cannot indicate its significance' (Merton, 1957). There is little need in England, with its traditions of historical scholarship and its emphasis upon empirical detail in sociological investigation, to point out the dangers of putting significance before truth. What I wish to do here, therefore, is to put in a plea for a more significant sort of sociological research.

Let me begin by saying that I regard sociology as an attempt to understand and explain the kinds of social relations which exist among people and the changes which occur from time to time in those relations. Another way of saying this is that sociology seeks to understand the nature of our social structure. I believe that a scientific study of this sort can do much to clarify both our political conflicts and more intimate personal conflicts which take place between individuals and small groups. But I believe that sociology in Great Britain is not doing this job and is prevented from doing so by its empiricist traditions.

The earliest empirical research undertaken by people calling themselves sociologists in Great Britain was not concerned with the study of social relations as such, but with the incidence and distribution of primary poverty. Thus, from the beginning, sociology was not merely contributing to the advancement of knowledge for its own sake, but was providing essential information for political reformers. Of course, there were those like Hobhouse and Westermarck who continued in the older Spencerian tradition with their comparative studies of social institutions on a world scale, but the major emphasis was upon the study of the

3

socio-economic characteristics of the population, and its significance was to be found within a framework of reformist political beliefs.

This tradition still lives on today. Apart from developing more and more precise measures of poverty, it has collected a wider range of information about the social conditions of the British people. The census has been affected by these researches, and now seeks to discover some of the more subtle characteristics of the population; and, outside government departments, sociologists have directed their attention especially to the occupational distribution and to the distribution of educational facilities. Indeed the most characteristic studies in post-war sociology were concerned with the correlation between the educational opportunities of children and the occupation of their parents. Professor Glass's book *Social Mobility in Britain* (1954) brought together some of the best of these studies.

Now I do not wish to dispute the value of work such as this in itself. One can only admire the degree of refinement of some of the measures of mobility which have been evolved. Moreover it is clear that, by ruthlessly excluding preconceived ideas and paying attention solely to what numbers come up, our statisticians have presented us with new and surprising data. What I want to ask, however, is, 'What do these facts mean?' And here, as a rule, I find it difficult to get a clear or convincing answer.

Despite what I have already said, I would sometimes be happier if those who write and talk about social mobility would confine themselves more rigorously to the facts. If they did, and I asked the question, 'What does the statement "there is such-and-such a degree of mobility" mean?' they would be bound to answer that it meant only that there was a certain likelihood that children will, at some point in their lives, be working in a different group of occupations from their parents. If this was the answer, I do not think that I should be considered rude if I replied, 'So what?'

But the issue is made less clear by the fact that our empiricists often go beyond the facts and suggest that what they are talking about is mobility between classes. I suspect that it would be considered rude to ask what exactly they mean by class, because there is a suppressed premiss that 'everyone knows what classes are and mobility between classes is a good thing'.

Nonetheless, at the risk of discovering what sociologists are fighting for, I should like to press the point and ask what class membership is supposed to imply in contemporary Britain. Does it mean that upwardly mobile boys and girls will renounce their parents' values? Does the fact of mobility have political implications? If so, what are they? What truth, if any, is there in Marx's predictions about the behaviour of the various social classes? And, if there is none or little, what are the factors which have led to their invalidation? I am asking, in fact, what we mean by class.

But here again we are on barren ground if we turn to the teachers of sociology. How familiar the arguments are. And how singularly unilluminating. We are told that it is impossible to find an objective criterion of class, and that subjectivism can only lead to work like that of Lloyd Warner in Yankee City, which is said to miss the point with its emphasis upon snobbery and status classes. Finally, avoiding all the difficulties, we are asked to be content with an occupational-status classification, because there is widespread agreement on the subjective status rating of occupations.

What are the questions, then, which these mobility studies leave unanswered? I suggest that they give us no knowledge or understanding at all of those sorts of social relations which we call class relations. They do not tell us, for example, what the implications are for the manual worker of membership of the working class. They do not tell us how he is likely to feel towards his fellow workers, or towards the manager of the firm which employs him, or towards the employing class as a whole. They tell us nothing of how he would behave in the case of an unofficial strike, or how he spends his leisure and why. Nor do they tell us anything about the equivalent problems of middle-class membership.

Similar problems arise in connection with the study of educational opportunity. Is there not a danger of assuming that grammar, technical and modern education are the first, second and third prizes of the scholastic world, and that the only problem is that of how the prizes are shared? Is it not time that someone tried to find out what the various sorts of education mean in terms of later group affiliations and the adoption of attitudes and ideologies? What we need to know is not how the population may be classified, but how it acts in groups, and what the relation is between one group and another.

The sort of research which I have in mind has been undertaken far more by people calling themselves social anthropologists than by sociologists, and I think that the best hope for the future lies in a careful and considered application of the anthropologist's techniques to the analysis of the problems of large-scale societies.

I say 'careful and considered application' because I can see relatively little that can be gained from studying one village, district, town or street community after another, as though they were likely to be as excitingly different from one another as the Trobrianders and the Andamanese. I think that the emphasis should be upon communities which *prima facie* seem to have a special importance for our larger national society, such as the mining communities, which have played so large a part in shaping our political ideologies and organization, or upon special features of community life which illustrate processes widespread in industrial areas, as was the case with the family relationships of Bethnal Green investigated by Michael Young and Peter Willmott (1957) and reported in their book *Family and Kinship in East London*.

But far more important than purely local studies, it would seem to me, are studies undertaken on a national scale in order to understand the nature of some of the larger social groupings to which we belong. One of the best examples of this kind of study in the immediate post-war years was Ferdinand Zweig's (1950) *The British Worker*.

It is no criticism of this book that, instead of giving statistical proofs, Zweig tells us what he heard in a pub in Scunthorpe. The fact remains that he is telling us important things about the working class, how they feel about pools and pubs, as well as about socialism, trade unionism and religion. Even if one doubts Zweig's veracity, one will still find in his work a mine of hypotheses well worthy of investigation.

But, to be more explicit, we must ask what the anthropologist's methods are in studies of this kind. The pity is that so few of them are clear as to what the logic of their procedures is, and that those who have attempted to formulate it have been quite gravely misleading.

Thus I cannot accept the formulation which says that the anthropologist's task is to explain social activities in terms of the contribution which they make to the maintenance of the 'social structure'. I feel that it is this so-called 'social structure' which needs explaining, and that the merit of some of the anthropologists is that they have tried to do this. The first great proponent of structural-functionalism, Radcliffe-Brown, failed to get beyond metaphor and analogy when he sought to explain his method (Radcliffe-Brown, 1952), and, later, Talcott Parsons (1952) produced such a complex theory, that unravelling it could leave little time for empirical research. I do not think that the problem is nearly as difficult as either Radcliffe-Brown or Parsons make it out to be, and I think that, in order to understand the nature of what they do we should watch the anthropologists at work, rather than in reflective contemplation years afterwards.

I think that the key to the anthropologist's method is simply close first-hand observation, even to the point of participant observation, coupled with the interpretation of what is observed in terms of the purposes and the meanings of the observed culture. Surely the great achievement of Malinowski was that he came back from the Trobrianders to say to those he liked to call 'museum-moles', 'Go out and live with the native and try to understand how he looks at his world. If you do, you may find that he is not the fool you take him for, either in his agriculture or in his magic.'

If indeed the revolution of method which the anthropologists propose is as simple as this, I would suggest that what they are saying today has its precedents in German historiography and sociology of the late nineteenth and early twentieth centuries, and I should like to conclude this chapter by suggesting that this German tradition has much of importance to contribute to contemporary sociology. If some of its methods were used to supplement the purely empirical studies currently carried on, we might find a way in Britain of blending truth with significance.

Probably the outstanding figure in the German tradition to which I refer was Wilhelm Dilthey (see Hodges, 1944). Just as Malinowski revolted against the misuse of the comparative method by sociologists seeking to establish an evolutionary pseudo-science, so Dilthey revolted against the positive sociology of Comte and Spencer. Malinowski called on the anthropologist to understand the native mind. Dilthey called on the historian for what he called 'self-surrender' which, as he said, would make 'The inner being of the time-born historian into a universe which mirrors the whole historical world'.

Now, of course, no self-respecting sociologist could accept this as a complete account of method, any more than he would feel that the methods of the sociologist of working-class life were adequately explained by the sentence, 'I went boozing with them.' Fortunately, however, there is no need to stop there. It is perfectly possible to go beyond this to the precise formulation of hypotheses about the motivation of typical participants, which can be used with something of the same degree of accuracy as any other scientific hypothesis used to interpret observed data. It was the primary contribution of Germany's greatest sociologist, Max Weber, that he made the logic of this procedure explicit. Today many people pay lip service to Weber, I think it is time that we started to apply his methods. How very few pieces of research there are today which explain human behaviour to us in the illuminating way which Weber did in his analysis of the social structure of capitalism, in terms of the life orientation of the typical Calvinist.

It is interesting to notice that nearly all the important socio-logical works which survive and are actually read today are, in fact, ideal typical accounts of some society or some system of social behaviour. Such a work for example is Veblen's *Theory of the Leisure Class* (1931).

Veblen's sketch of conspicuous consumption was more than an ironic pillorying of upper-class values. It was also an illuminating interpretative theory which helped a generation of Americans to understand themselves and their society better. More recently the work of C. Wright Mills on *The Power Elite* and William Foote Whyte on *The Organization Man* has continued the Veblen tradition, while at the other end of the political spectrum, Lloyd Warner (Warner and Lunt, 1941) has used similar methods in his nostalgic account of the status system of old New England. The most stimulating passage in all the Yankee City reports is to be found in the hundred pages of composite portraits of Yankee City people.

Equally the great value of Marx's work was that it was

precisely an ideal typical account of capitalism. There is one beautiful point in *Capital* where Marx, having outlined the processes at work in the enclosure movement, goes on, 'Let us now cull a nosegay of examples.' From the point of view of scientific methodology, how scandalous! But, from the point of view of understanding social reality, how important!

I suggest that British sociology would profit greatly if it would get down to the imaginative task of framing ideal types which might help to explain some of the data which our empirical studies turn up. Let me just mention examples of what I have in mind. I think that one of the key problems of contemporary social structure is that of the attitudes, ideologies, and political behaviour of the new middle classes. It is time that academic sociologists stopped regarding them as nasty little Poujadists and tried to discover the sources of their motivation. Again, we know little or nothing about the motivation of the new youth culture, whose emergence was one of the key phenomena of the fifties. On a wider scale, we know little if anything about the varieties of colonial nationalism, with which it is necessary to live.

Compared with sociological studies of the time, how illuminating Thomas Hodgkin's *Nationalism in Colonial Africa* was. This was a really path-breaking little book which gave a precise yet sensitive formulation of the political behaviour and motivation of the new Africans with whom the author had talked on his West African journeys. Reading it, one was able to foresee and understand much that was important in the processes and structures involved in decolonization and neo-colonialism.

There are many other topics which cry out for analysis by a Weber or a Veblen. I think that what prevents their being tackled is the fear that such work might be controversial and less than scientifically respectable. And, of course, it never will have the same exactness and precision as analyses of the numbers of boys and girls who failed the eleven plus last year. In urging that it should be undertaken, however, I would suggest that there are ways in which studies of this kind can be tied down to empirical fact and rendered relatively scientific.

To begin with, I would suggest that the first step in the procedure of constructing ideal types should be the study of the attitudes and ideologies of the group for whom an ideal type is to be constructed. My own bias would be in favour of the relatively unstructured interview to find these out, but all types of attitude studies could contribute something. At all events, here is a field of empirical study in which precious little is being done at present.

It is the second stage of type-construction, however, which is the more controversial. Here we must proceed beyond mere reports on motives of particular persons to formulate typical cases. And this does not merely mean the construction of averages or any sort of inductive generalization. It means the highlighting, the special emphasis, even the caricature of certain aspects of the subject's behaviour. Such studies are bound to be controversial because what one puts into the type may well depend upon how well disposed one is to one's subject. But this is no insuperable objection, since the type is merely a hypothesis which must be shown to have predictive value before it becomes, even in a limited sense, an explanatory principle or theory. Indeed no harm would come from a dash of malice in the formulation of types. This would inevitably lead to the emergence of counter-hypotheses and the testing of alternatives in a healthy atmosphere of controversy. We fear controversy too much in sociology. It need not be the enemy of accurate testing of hypotheses. It could be its guarantor.

I come back, finally, to my original definition of sociology as the science which seeks to understand and explain the sorts of social relations which exist between people. Though such relations may not depend upon the motives of those who immediately participate in them, ultimately they do depend upon motives of some sort. Social structures do not exist without people. Our sociology will be more significant when it explains them in terms of human motivation and action.

2 The uses of social statistics

This chapter was first published as a discussion of *A Survey of Social Conditions in England and Wales* (Carr-Saunders, *et al.*, 1958). Unfortunately there has been no subsequent book of this kind. The questions which are asked here, however, are as relevant now as they were then.

Sociologists often exasperate their colleagues by their apparent concentration on theoretical speculation, and their failure to undertake what, to common sense, would appear to be the first task for a science of society, namely, the accurate description and classification of contemporary societies. It has been pointed out with some justice that British sociologists know more about Trobriand or Andamanese society than they do about modern Britain. Yet there are better reasons for this state of affairs than the critics of sociology will allow. The methods of the anthropologist are not really relevant to the investigation of the larger social structures of an industrial society, and it is usually necessary to glean what information one can about them by inference from the available statistics. These statistics, however, will not have been collected necessarily with a view to describing society. For the most part, they are gathered in order to throw light on some administrative problem, or with a view to promoting social reform by throwing light on the inequalities of opportunity currently existing. If they are to be sociologically useful, then it is essential that the sociologist should confront each new compilation with the questions which theoretical considerations suggest are important in the description of industrial societies.

There are four important sets of questions which must be answered if a useful description of contemporary British or any other industrial society is to be given. Each set may be grouped under a general question as follows:

1 What are the social relations which exist between the

11

various roles in industrial production, and between the dependants of those who participate, as a result of their participation?

2   What are the processes whereby individuals are recruited, selected and trained for the fulfilment of key roles in the industrial system?

3   In what ways do members of the society behave in their leisure time?

4   What is the extent and the manner of deviance from the social norms assumed in the answers to questions 1, 2 and 3?

The last attempt which was made at a comprehensive account of the social statistics of contemporary Britain was that by Carr-Saunders, Caradog Jones and Moser in 1957. It is interesting to see how far it answers our questions. We shall be concerned here with the contribution which it makes to answering our first and second questions and we shall deal rather more shortly with the third and fourth questions where the book's answers are much more limited in scope.

1   The social structure of industry

Our first question may now be broken down into six questions as follows:

1   What is the size of the labour force and what proportion of the total, the male and female, single and married population does it represent?

2   How is this labour force divided between industries and occupations?

3   What status differences exist between different occupational roles, and what is the size of the various status groups?

4   What income differences exist between different occupational and status groupings?

5   What are the differences in property ownership between the participants in the industrial system and, in particular, who owns and controls the means of production?

6   What is the size of the various groups in industry, classified according to their relationship to the means of production?

It may be said at once that these statistics are least useful in answering questions 5 and 6, and that their weakness here results, sociologically speaking, in a lack of direction in answering most of the others. However, we would do well to begin reviewing the statistics presented, by considering the answers which they provide to the first four questions.

There were 14,063,542 men and 6,272,876 women gainfully occupied in England and Wales in 1951. This represented 88 per cent of the male and 35 per cent of the female population over fifteen years of age. A large part of the remaining 12 per cent of the males would be taken up by boys at school and old-age pensioners. The interesting point here lies in the degree of participation of females in the labour force. Although the over-all percentage of the female population in employment had hardly changed, the percentage of married women occupied had increased from 10·4 per cent to 22·5 per cent since 1931. The percentage is greatest among wives aged fifteen to nineteen and decreases with each age group up to the group thirty-five to forty-four. At this age there is a slight increase again, and 26·7 per cent of wives go to work. These figures draw attention to the important sociological fact that the married woman in industry, and therefore absent from home, is an increasingly common phenomenon.

There is also a noticeable return to work after the earlier stages of child-rearing have been completed, even if Mrs Average Woman has not fully recognized the possibilities of a second career at forty to which, as Professor Titmuss tells us, the 'demographic revolution' entitles her.

Figures which show the distribution of the occupied population by industry are sociologically important in so far as they help us to recognize the percentages of the total who are involved in social systems of various kinds (e.g. an insurance official moves in a very different social world from a factory worker). Perhaps the workers whom we think of as most completely engaged in industry (with a capital 'I') are the miners, those in manufacturing industry, in the building trade, or in the gas, electricity and water supply industries. It is important to recognize that these constitute only 49·4 per cent of the occupied population. Agriculture, forestry and fishing provide 4·8 per cent, transport 7·7 per cent and the distributive trades 12·1 per cent. The remaining industrial groups, including insurance and banking, local and central government, and professional services, as well as a small miscellaneous group, make up 26 per cent. If we add the figure for the distributive trades to this, we have a total of 38·1 per cent engaged in what we might call white-collar industries. But contrary to a popular impression, these figures do not show a Britain becoming more and more white-collared. The distributive trades have shrunk in relative importance, and the most noticeable expansion is in manufacturing industry, especially in engineering, electrical goods and vehicle building. The one white-collar group to have expanded is the professional services group.

We might be justified in concluding from these figures that the system of social relations of production has become relatively complex, and that a fairly large proportion of the population is engaged in industries not directly concerned with basic industrial production, but we should not be entitled to conclude that our industrial system has a continually shrinking industrial base. The figures for 1931 and 1951 suggest that this base was expanding.

When we pass beyond classification of the population by industry to classification by occupation and status, the significance of the statistics becomes less clear. In the census classification of the population by occupation, for example, the largest group consists of those in manufacturing occupations, but the use of another heading, 'administrators, directors, managers, not elsewhere specified', indicates that there is some doubt as to whether the category headed 'manufacturing' is not really an 'industrial' rather than an 'occupational' one. In fact, it probably falls between the two. Perhaps, however, it can be agreed that the percentage of the population in manufacturing occupations remains the largest single group. Much clearer is the continued growth in the percentage of workers in clerical occupations. Less than 1 per cent in 1850, their percentage rose to 6·8 per cent by 1931 and no less than 10·5 per cent by 1951.

The significance of such a growth in size of the clerical population clearly lies in its impact upon the status and class situation in industry. But the attempts of the Registrar-General to distinguish the various status groups in industry still seem unsatisfactory. Three separate classifications are quoted by Carr-Saunders and his colleagues. These we state summarily in Table 1.

Table 1   *Classifications of status groups in industry*

I Industrial status		II Type of income		III Social class	
	%		% %		%
Employers	2·1	Salaries	22	Professionals,	
Managers	3·7	Managerial	7	administrative, etc.	3
Operatives	86·9	Technical and		Intermediate	15
Own account	5·3	professional	6	Skilled occupations	53
Unemployed	2·0	Clerical	9	Partly skilled	16
		Wages	78	Unskilled	13
		Industrial	65		
		Non-industrial	8		
		Agricultural	5		

It is figures like this which drive the theoretically oriented sociologist to something like despair. Is the classification of the population into status groups meant solely as a statistical exercise, or are these classifications meant to refer to groups who might act as groups, or who might be thought of by their fellows as sharing a common way of life and meriting a characteristic degree of esteem? Clearly there does seem to be some claim that these represent real groups rather than statistical classifications. Section III of Table 1 is said to be a classification according to social class. But the implications of this term are left open to be filled in by the reader according to his own ideological pre-conceptions. Surely it would be more valuable if statisticians who continually claim to be using sociological concepts, were to find out what groupings were of real sociological importance and then seek to describe these, rather than the groupings which are of little importance but which happen to be easily measurable.

One of the facts we should like to know about a status group or a social class (terms which are carefully distinguished from each other by major sociological theorists like Weber and Tönnies[1]) is what the 'life-chances' (to use Weber's term) of its members are. In particular, we should like to know what their income level is. Unfortunately, the statistics of income which we have are mainly collected for other purposes, and are, for the most part, classified in terms of arbitrary statistical levels. The one potentially useful section of Table 1, from the point of view of a sociologist,

[1] See their essays in *Class Status and Power*, Reinhard Bendix and S. M. Lipset (eds), Routledge & Kegan Paul, 1954.

is that which shows the distribution of income according to type of income. Both pre-tax and post-tax income tables show 'rent, dividends and interest' to have lost ground to salaries and wages. Curiously, salaries appear to have improved their position since the war, but this is largely due to the definition of the salariat so as to include the salaries, and even some fees, of directors, as well as the salaries of top management.

Comparison of the pre-war spread of incomes with those of 1956 suggests a considerable degree of equalization. After adjusting the groupings to take account of the changed value of money, the bottom group had shrunk from 88 per cent in 1938 to 65–70 per cent in 1956, while the top group had shrunk from about 0·5 per cent to 0·25 per cent. But there is one omission from these figures. They take no account of either expense allowances or capital gains. We do not know how large a difference incomes from this source would make, but we may reasonably conclude that, if account were taken of them, the income figures would show a lesser degree of redistribution away from the highest group (if not, as many people believe on the basis of their own observations of continuing conspicuous consumption, showing them to be actually maintaining or improving their position), and a greater relative share of the burden falling on the middle income groups and on the lower orders among the salariat. It is perhaps unfortunate that the possible effect of these factors is not mentioned, for students reading the book might easily jump to too glib conclusions about the extent of equalization which has gone on in our society.

That the figures given for the distribution of incomes may be misleading can readily be seen by turning to the chapter on personal property. Before the war, 1 per cent of the population owned 56 per cent of total property. In the period 1946 to 1950, 1½ per cent owned 54 per cent. At the other end of the table, pre-war, 75 per cent owned 5 per cent, post-war, 62 per cent owned 3 per cent. This does not suggest a society in which there has been a dramatic and revolutionary change in property ownership. It shows that the property-owning classes have exhibited a remarkable resilience in the face of the egalitarian atmosphere of the post-war world.

The mere facts of unequal property distribution, however, do not tell the whole story, or provide the answer to significant sociological questions. The sociologist is interested not merely in who owns property in an economic sense. He wants to know what kind of property different groups hold, because one kind of property puts its owner into a different social setting from another. At the bottom of the scale, estates consisted mainly of money savings, furniture and houses (one in five households owned their house, outright or with a mortgage), while industrial shares counted for nothing. In the £2,000 to £3,000 range, shares still only accounted for 4 per cent of estates, but in the £100,000 to £500,000 range they accounted for 50 per cent. Land also became an increasingly important type of property among the highest groups.

These are the only figures which are given about the ownership of industrial property, and, from a sociological point of view, the failure to analyse the nature of groups owning and controlling industry represents an unfortunate omission. It is the more unfortunate that the authors failed to discuss this matter because it is, at the moment, the subject of much controversy. The detached analysis of a group of statisticians would have done much to clarify the issues. At the time of the publication of *A Survey of Social Conditions in England and Wales*, the best sources were probably Hargreaves Parkinson (1951) arguing against the possibility of a minority of shareholders gaining control of a large joint-stock company, and Professor Sargant Florence (1953) arguing that our present system is one of 'oligarchic minority owners' control'.

Real groups in industry operate under the direction of those who control the means of production, whether managers or minority owners. But what are the real groups among the non-owners? The Marxian view was that they would all be driven to unite into a single class, the proletariat, who, faced with the prospect of 'increasing misery', would unite to overthrow existing forms of ownership. Professor G. D. H. Cole (1955) has analysed the census figures for industrial and occupational distributions in order to test this hypothesis. He distinguishes between those whom Marx claimed were creators of 'surplus value' and the remainder, and shows that the number of the former has shrunk to less than 50 per cent of the total population. He then goes on to discuss in an illuminating way the structure of the middle-class groups who, to Marx, could only be parasitic and of temporary significance, showing that there have emerged in our population new groups with new relationships to the means of production and new sorts of motivation, who are unlikely to become 'proletarianized' in the future.

Among the groups which do have significance in the changing pattern of our contemporary society, we may distinguish between those actually engaged in basic industries, and those only indirectly engaged. Amongst the latter we should have to include shopkeepers and others working on their own account, civil servants and local government officers, and a variety of new professional types, both in the scientific and technical spheres, and also in such spheres as journalism, broadcasting and so on. The way in which groups of this kind might be expected to behave socially and politically in our society is important because of the increase in their numbers, to which Cole draws attention. Older models, such as Marx's, which see them as destined to join the ranks of the proletariat, seem to be quite inapplicable in the present situation. We need careful studies of the motivations and the role of these groups. But in the meantime it would be well worth while if statisticians would classify them separately so that we can follow the fluctuations in their size.

Similarly, we need to study the changing social relations of production within our basic industries, distinguishing between the strict managerial hierarchy, the experts standing outside the 'line-organization' of industry, the clerical workers, and the workers who are more strictly of proletarian status because they are expected to sell their labour as a commodity.

What I am appealing for here, is the presentation of statistics of the industrial population in a new form. We should spend less time in trying to make classifications according to some highly elusive criterion of status, and direct our attention to the description and measurement of those social groups who, because of the distinctive way in which their motivations are bound into the industrial system, do tend to behave, and to be regarded as, groups. Cole's *Studies in Class Structure* points the way to what might be done in this sphere. It might have been hoped that *A Survey of Social Conditions in England and Wales*, published, as it was, some years after Professor Cole's book, would have followed up some of Cole's insights and presented the industrial and occupational statistics in a less pedestrian and more enlightening fashion.

2 The recruitment, socialization, training and selection mechanisms of an industrial society

The statistics discussed above, from which we have been trying to deduce some picture of the social relations of industry, are mainly what we should call economic statistics. They are preceded in the book, however, by demographic and educational statistics. We now turn to these statistics to ask what they tell us about the mechanisms employed by our society for the recruitment, socialization, training and selection of future participants in our industrial system.

The family may perhaps be looked upon as making a threefold contribution to the functioning of industry. First, it contributes its male head as a worker in nearly all cases. Second, as we have seen, it contributes 22·5 per cent of its female heads as well. In both these cases we might notice that the goals of family life provide perhaps the most important incentive to work in industry. But it is the third part of the family's recruitment function, namely the procreation of children, which is of the greatest long-term importance. Some of the older indices for measuring the extent to which the population was replacing itself have apparently fallen into disrepute (notably the net reproduction rate), but the Family Census conducted for the Royal Commission on Population still led to the conclusion that the child-bearing of women born between 1895 and 1899 was 26 per cent below the replacement level. The rates among those married between 1926 and 1943 were likely to attain replacement level, but it was too early to say in 1959 whether this upward trend would be maintained (later statistics do appear to confirm this trend).

The demographic revolution was signalized by falling death rates, especially for women, and a contraction of the period during which child-bearing takes place could do a great deal to revolutionize the family. The widely accepted model of the 'isolated conjugal family' which has been developed by such theorists as Mead (see Landis, 1953) and Parsons (see Parsons and Bales, 1956) emphasizes the segregation of the adult sex roles within the family. The husband is thought of as moving within the impersonal world of industry, and the wife within the affective world of family relations. In many studies of established working-class communities in Britain (Young and Willmott, 1957; Bott, 1957) a similar pattern has been described. The husband is seen as looking to his home for certain basic services and for a sense of status and security, but at the same time spending much of his leisure time with friends of his own sex. The mother, on the other hand, is seen as moving within her own kinship network. Family life in Bethnal Green, we are told, turns out to be matrilocal, and the wife's 'mum' is an all-pervading figure in the young family. This pattern, however, is already changing rapidly as families are rehoused in new areas, and any large-scale increase in the percentage of married women going to work would do much to accelerate the process of change. The tendency will be increasingly towards a merging of the sex roles.

The increase in the number of divorces, the figure for which, having reached a peak of 60,254, settled in the 1950s at about 28,000, nearly four times the pre-war number, would probably serve to facilitate this merging of roles since, with an increasing willingness to seek divorce, there is likely to go a rejection of rigidly segregated sex roles.

But it should not be supposed that these trends have yet reached a point at which it could be said that family life is becoming unstable. Despite women's work and increasing divorce the vast majority of families continue to seek a secure private family life. Some interesting statistics regarding the structure of households given by Carr-Saunders and his colleagues show that over eleven million out of just over thirteen million households consisted of a single family nucleus. In the remaining composite households there was usually simply an extra young couple with children or about to have children; who it might be assumed would be eager to leave as soon as possible and set up on their own. As we have seen, one in five households owned its own house or was buying it, and this further emphasizes the desire for independent family life.

The normal child then, will be born into a small family unit in which the process of socialization will be begun. The smallness of the family undoubtedly creates the possibility that this will be more skilfully done, but the greater possibilities of this situation may well be offset by the difficulties arising from the social isolation of the parents and the confused conception of the female role. Less than 10 per cent of all children are receiving any sort of training outside the home between the ages of two and four, so that a great deal depends upon the parents. Whether the child is fortunate enough to be successfully socialized will depend to a large extent upon the personal qualities of the mother, on the income of the father and, a consequence of these other two factors, on the physical and social environment of the home.

The very great differences in property and income which still exist mean that, by the time children enter primary school at the age of five, some measure of inequality of opportunity has already been allowed. The primary school provides an equalizing environment which may do something to correct this, for 95 per cent of all children will go to LEA or direct grant private schools. At the age of eleven-plus, however, the educational system becomes intertwined with the selection machinery whereby boys and girls are selected to fulfil the major social roles. The statistics which have been collected in this sphere in recent years are of absorbing interest and serve to tell us much about the nature of our society.

Of all children aged thirteen, 9·5 per cent went to direct grant and independent schools and 90 per cent to state schools. Less than 1 per cent of all boys admitted to secondary schools went to the twenty major public schools. Of those at state schools, 10 per cent were still in all-age schools in 1956 and, presumably, did the secondary modern course, 65 per cent were in modern schools, 20 per cent in maintained grammar schools, 4 per cent in technical schools and 1 per cent in comprehensive schools.

Those who go to grammar schools and technical schools were encouraged to stay on after the age of fifteen, but the percentages actually staying were only 84 per cent in grammar schools and 54 per cent in technical schools. Moreover, many of those who did leave were the children of manual workers. Of those entering grammar schools in 1946, the proportion from skilled and semi-skilled workers' homes was approximately equal to the proportion of skilled and semi-skilled workers in the population (58·9 per cent). Only the unskilled workers (12·8 per cent of the population) failed to secure an equivalent number of places for their children (only 5·8 per cent). The proportion of manual workers' children in the top group at the time of the eleven-plus examination was 66 per cent. But by the end of the grammar school course, the proportion of manual workers' children had dropped sharply; among the top group in the final school examinations they numbered only 47 per cent, and among grammar school children going to university only 36 per cent.

University figures show an even greater decline in the proportion of these children, because grammar school children are joined there by boys and girls from the public schools. Only 26 per cent of university students come from the homes of manual workers. At Cambridge, the figure is only 9 per cent, and at Oxford 13 per cent. London has 21 per cent, and the provincial universities 31 per cent. These statistics are interesting for two reasons. First, they tell us how many different sorts of education are being given, and second, they indicate the extent to which schools provide avenues of social mobility through which children can escape from following in their parents' footsteps.

There seem to be four main types of secondary education, that given by the public schools, and that given by the three types of secondary school. The authors of *A Survey of Social Conditions in England and Wales* are remarkably reticent about the public schools and their role, and on practically the only occasion when they mention them, play down their significance. It may be asked, however, whether it is permissible to do so. Less than 1 per cent of boys may go to the major public schools, but their absolute numbers might be quite enough to provide sufficient replacements for the élites who govern British industry and, to a decreasing extent, the higher civil service. There is one really remarkable gap in the statistics of university education. This is the absence of any discussion of the proportion of public school boys at Oxford and Cambridge. Thus, although we know that the proportion of working-class boys at Oxford and Cambridge has increased, we do not know from the figures given whether such an increase has been at the expense of the public school boys or at that of other boys from grammar schools.

The second sort of education provided is that given by the grammar schools; 20 per cent of the children at state schools receive education of this kind. What are the assumptions on which it is based? If it is supposed that children at grammar schools are being prepared for university entry, it is worthy of note that only slightly more than one in nine do go to university, and nearly 75 per cent go into paid employment. It would be interesting to know more about the future careers of both groups. We know surprisingly little about the role of grammar schools in our society. What we should like to know is what roles the students are being prepared for in a society which recruits its élites from the public schools to a very large extent. Or has the expansion of managerial, technical and clerical work been sufficiently large to absorb today one in five of the population?

Technical education with only 4 per cent makes a poor showing, and it is obvious that our industrial system could not rely on the technical schools alone for its supply of technical experts. Finally, there are the modern schools. What assumptions about the future of their pupils are held by modern-school teachers, by parents, and by the children themselves? What are these schools aiming at as they shape the future attitudes of 75 per cent of the population?

The second point revealed by these educational statistics is that there is a limited but significant amount of mobility in our society. There is an educational ladder for the children of working-class parents through the grammar schools and provincial universities. The most significant barriers to advancement appear to be those at Oxford and Cambridge, and those raised by the top people in our society against common children who have graduated. But even more interesting than these barriers is the fact that working people were apparently failing to take full advantage of the opportunities open to their children. The Committee on Early Leaving concluded that it was not financial difficulty which prevented working-class parents from keeping their children at school beyond the age of fifteen. And, though some 2,000 to 2,500 applicants failed to secure places in the English universities, there were also 2,000 to 2,300 places unfilled.[1]

The final question which we must ask in this section concerns the transition from school to work, and from childhood to maturity. Some figures are available here from the records of that most important but most underrated of our social services, the

[1] These trends showed significant alteration in the 1960s when the numbers and proportion of working-class children staying on till the sixth form and seeking higher education increased significantly.

Youth Employment Service. Forty per cent of all school leavers use the service, and of those who did at fifteen, 36·9 per cent entered apprenticeships or training schemes and 5 per cent became clerks. The remaining 58·1 per cent entered other employment. It may be, of course, that the 60 per cent of all school leavers who did not use the service would show a higher proportion receiving further training, but it would be a reasonable guess that about half the modern-school leavers enter industry having received all the education they ever will by the time they reach the age of fifteen.

Figures for further and adult education show a considerable increase in numbers both for day and evening classes since the war, but it is interesting to notice that the old three-year tutorial class has shrunk in the numbers it enrols and, in general, adult education has become a predominantly feminine activity.

We may now summarize the conclusions of this section as follows: a child born into our society finds his first social milieu in a small 'nuclear' family, where he is much more dependent than children in other societies upon the competence and the ability of his parents, even though he may receive more of their attention. Primary schools provide an equalizing environment for nearly all children at the age of five years, and to some extent make up for the inequalities of home background.

At the age of eleven, the emphasis swings away from equalization of opportunity towards selection and differentiation. Five different pathways[1] open up to the child between the ages of eleven and thirteen: (i) to go to a public school and to have a good chance of entering the governing élite; (ii) to enter grammar school, continue to some form of higher education and enter some relatively unrestricted profession; (iii) to enter a grammar school and to go from it to clerical or white-collar work; (iv) to enter a modern or technical school and to go on to an apprenticeship or professional training; and (v) to enter a modern school and to become, on leaving, a 'hand' in industry. Entry to all but the first of these pathways depends upon some objective test of ability, modified by the nature of the home background. Entry to the first

[1] Later figures suggest that a sixth path was very important: namely, that of going to the semi-independent direct grant schools which were more successful than any other in obtaining university places for their children.

depends primarily on the home background either in the sense that wealth is important, or that ancestry is what matters.

The selection system does make a considerable measure of mobility possible within this system, but attitudes of parents are such that all the opportunities available are not taken.

3   Recreation and deviance

Some account of what people do outside their working hours is essential to the sociologist both for its own sake, social relations outside industry being as much a part of the structure of society as the social relations of production, and also because these activities, in one form or another, act as social controls for the sort of behaviour to be found within industry.

Not all of our leisure time activities are easily measurable, but since some of them provide profit for others, and some are considered to be vices, we can rely upon the zeal of businessmen and social reformers to gather some statistics for us. Readership surveys, for example, which serve as a guide to those who wish to place advertisements, are one of the most revealing of all sources of information about modern Britain.

The figures shown in Table 2 of the national expenditure in 1956 on various items provides an interesting introduction to the analysis of our leisure habits.

Table 2   *National expenditure on leisure items in 1956*

Item	£ million
Alcohol	895
Tobacco	935
Books	50
Newspapers	116
Sports and hobbies	128
Cinema	104
Other entertainments	93

(Gambling took £548,000,000, but £478,000,000 came back to the winners. The cost of gambling is therefore about £70,000,000.)

Since, however, these categories are so all-inclusive, football attendance being included in the category of sports and hobbies, and television in the category of 'other entertainments', it is worth looking more closely at the audience and crowd figures for football, cinema and radio, as well as the readership figures for newspapers.

Football attendances have dropped from forty millions in 1949 to 1950 to under thirty-three millions in 1956 to 1957. The cinema had 1,635 million attendances in 1946 but this dropped in the fifties to about two-thirds of this figure. The television public, on the other hand, continued to rise rapidly, and had reached a figure of 14,925,000 in 1955. In 1954, 59 per cent of this public was from the lowest of three income groups. Sixteen million copies of the ten leading daily newspapers were printed on the average day in 1956, and on Sundays the nine leading Sunday papers sold twenty-nine million copies. It might have been added that the number of readers far exceeds this. The *News of the World* has a faithful readership each Sunday of about eighteen millions.

It should be remembered, of course, that the other leisure time activities of people in their homes and their voluntary associations are not reflected in these figures because there are no statistics collected for such activities. Nevertheless, it would accord with one's own observations to accept that participation in mass amusements, which might be said to have a narcotic effect, is the characteristic form of leisure time activity in our society, and these amusements, surely, are the people's opium.

In this respect, the mass press, television, cinema and sporting entertainment seem to have replaced religion. But the statistics for religious participation are themselves interesting. Estimates of the percentage of the population going to church on Sunday vary between about eight and seventeen per cent. Those who do go, moreover, are drawn from particular age groups. The percentage attending falls off sharply in the twenties and rises again in the forties. The reason for this can be guessed at, and indeed, some extremely interesting work has been done on this point by the Rev. W. Pickering (1958) in Scunthorpe and Rawmarsh. Unfortunately, in the book of statistics under review the authors have not been able to find room for material of this kind, which would have served to light up, and render meaningful, some of the figures given. Perhaps, however, we may be justified in concluding from these figures that organized religious practice is on the decline, most especially among young adults.

Approximately 100,000 people of all ages were found guilty of indictable offences in 1955. This represented a rate of about 276 per 100,000 of the population over the age of eight. The fluctuations in this rate since 1914 have been somewhat surprising. When the First World War broke out, the number of offences known to the police fell, but rose after the war and went on rising steadily up till 1938. On the outbreak of the Second World War there was a sharp rise, which went on until 1948, when there was a slight drop, followed by a rise which reached a peak in 1951 and 1952. Since then, figures have declined. The rise in the crime rate after the First World War and at the beginning of the Second was largely due to juveniles, but later rises were more marked among adults. Larceny is still apparently the main offence, but there has been a relative increase in sexual offences and in violence against the person since 1938. No attempt is made in this compilation of statistics to say anything about attempts which have been made to locate the cause of crime.

4 Conclusion

A purely statistical account of our society cannot be expected to leave us with a very clear picture of what its principal structural features are. Indeed, it would be quite possible for sociologists to find evidence here to support the thesis that any of three current models explained our society's working. Some would see in it a picture of a Welfare State, with a national minimum established and the tables of inequality being crushed at both ends. Others would argue that this is a society run by a power élite, secure in their possession of property and power and keeping the masses happy with plenty of bread and the best circuses ever. Others would see in the proliferation of mass amusements, if not 1984, at least something in the early eighties.

By and large one does get the impression of social stability, most especially from the educational statistics, showing as they do the lack of pressure against barriers to mobility. On the other hand, there are other factors such as the increase in adult crime as well as that among juveniles which might perhaps be indicators of impending change.[1]

[1] Twelve years later recurrent political demonstrations labelled as

As a compendium of current British social statistics, *A Survey of Social Conditions in England and Wales* is certainly more comprehensive and useful than anything else previously published. But it suffers both from the general blindness which afflicts all statisticians attempting to describe social structures without understanding their meaning, and from the ideological blindness which leads to the posing of nearly all questions as tests of the amount of welfare in the community rather than in terms of the distribution of power, or some other index. On the other hand, sociologists should welcome any book which brings together reliable social statistics as a means for answering their theoretical questions. It is to be hoped that a sociologist will join the author of a future edition and pose some of the statistical questions in a more significant form.

violent seemed to indicate increasing instability but such facts would not have fallen within the range of this compendium.

One often hears it said nowadays that social research has had enough of theory. What we need to do, so the argument runs, is to abandon empty theoretical speculation and study the facts. It is an argument that has a profoundly common-sense ring about it; and anyone who suggests that you can't really learn very much about our society that way is likely to be dismissed as an arm-chair sociologist who is not much concerned with immediate problems, or, still worse, as a dangerous revolutionary who wants to change everything at once and isn't really interested in social reform.

Unfortunately, however, the 'facts' with which the sociologist has to deal are not of the plain and simple kind which common sense suggests. True, anyone can find out what proportion of the population lives in poverty, is divorced or has council houses. And we have statisticians who are quite clever at guessing these proportions for the population as a whole from quite small samples. But sociology is more than simply a statistical study of the distribution of characteristics of this kind. It is the study of the social relations which hold between men and the nature of these social relations is not given to us by the statistics.

The real difficulty is that we can't observe social relations directly. All that we can observe is the behaviour of individuals. Yet we all know that in our own daily lives we take account of the behaviour of others and that we think of ourselves as belonging to 'groups', 'communities' and 'societies'. The main problem facing the sociologist is that of finding a scientific and objective way of talking about these things.

One way of envisaging the sociologist's problem is to say that he is always in the position of a man who comes across people playing a game. He observes the way that the participants respond to one another and, after watching carefully and for a long time,

MANKATO STATE COLLEGE LIBRARY

Mankato, Minnesota

he says, 'I think the rules of the game they are playing are like this . . .' Once these rules are properly understood, any particular move which a player makes fits naturally into place.

This is, of course, an oversimplification. Social behaviour is usually more complicated than simple game-playing. For one thing, some of the players change the rules from time to time so that several games are being played at once. For another, some people break the rules and cheat. Nonetheless if we hang on to this analogy we will find it useful. What we have to do in sociology is first to discover the basic rules of the game and then to go on to discover the alternative rules and the pattern of cheating.[1]

A further problem, however, is that in living in a society we play games within games. Once the main lines of the game have been set, we work out special rules for dealing with special problems. Thus there may be certain rules of the game for industrial society as such and more particular sets of rules for family life within that society.

The main task which the founders of sociology set for themselves was that of distinguishing the rules of the game of industrial society from those of other societies. Herbert Spencer (1885) argued that the basic difference lay in the individualism of industrial as compared with the authoritarian and hierarchical organization of earlier societies which he calls 'militant'. The greatest of French sociologists drew the contrast between the 'mechanical solidarity' of primitive societies where uniformity was demanded of everyone and the 'organic solidarity' of societies based upon the division of labour (Durkheim, 1933). Karl Marx saw ancient societies as based upon the institution of slavery, feudal society as based upon serfdom, and capitalist society as based upon a free labour market in which all employer-employee relations were based upon the 'callous cash-nexus' (Marx and Engels, 1962b). And Max Weber drew on his rich comparative studies of great civilizations to point to other, more subtle, distinguishing features of Western Capitalism (Weber, 1961).

At the present time sociologists are concerned with spelling out these broad distinctions in more detail, and in showing the nature of the more specialized games-within-the-game which are

[1] This notion of social behaviour is at the heart of 'transactional sociology' and what is called 'ethnomethodology'.

going on. I want to discuss three examples of this kind of theoretical work.

The first of these I take from the work of the American sociologist, Talcott Parsons (1952); and I choose Parsons deliberately because he, more than any other of our contemporaries, is accused of being intolerably theoretical. I want to show, that, despite the admittedly irritating jargon and style of Parsons's work, in it there lie the most acute insights into the 'rules of the game' of industrial society.

Parsons's starting point is a theoretical distinction made by the German sociologist, Ferdinand Tönnies (1955). Tönnies argued that human beings always live in two different kinds of social world which he called 'community' and 'society'. The first of these is characteristic of primitive and rural people and more characteristic of the world of work than that of the home and neighbourhood. The second is to be found in modern urban-industrial conditions and in a form of industrial organization which is sharply differentiated from the world of the family. Parsons set out to clarify these differences between two kinds of social system.

The first difference is between social relations in which emotion comes into play, and those in which it doesn't. The second is between social relations in which people have a large number of ill-defined obligations to one another, and those in which they owe each other quite specific services. The third is between the case in which we regard other people as individuals, and that in which we respond to them as members of categories (for example as employees, as consumers, as students or as voters). And, finally, there is the distinction between cases in which our obligations to an individual are fixed by who and what he is, and those in which they vary according to his performance (for example how well he does in an examination or how much he can pay).

There is no need for us to worry too much about the terms which Parsons uses to describe these differences What matters is that they give us the broad outlines of the rules of the game, in our working life on the one hand, and in our home life on the other At work we must accept the rule that 'there's no sentiment in business'; we must be able to see our colleagues and ourselves as specialists; we must react to others according to the role they are playing and not according to their personal characteristics; and we must not give or expect services except where they are earned by achievement. At home, on the other hand, emotion may have a freer rein. The members of one's family will be seen as general helpmates. They will matter as individuals and we shall not alter our own behaviour towards them according to their education or income.

Naturally it is not always as clear as this. Personal factors do enter into business and some homes are less warm and affectionate than others. Nonetheless, these rather exaggerated pure theoretical types do help us to find our bearings and give us a yardstick by means of which we may measure actual cases. What is even more interesting, however, is what Parsons has to say about the relationship between these two worlds or about the connection between the two games.

The family is dependent upon the world of work for its income, and industry is dependent upon the family for the recruitment of new workers. Thus the family game is affected by the rules of the industrial game. In the first place the father and bread-winner must be capable of playing impersonal roles in the world of work as well as being a good husband to his wife, and a good father to his children. His is essentially a liaison role between the two systems. And, second, the family has to see to it that its children are equipped, by the time they become adults, to enter the world of work themselves. Unlike primitive and rural children, children in industrial society must learn the rules of two games successively. They must first be turned into good family members. Then they must be ejected from the family into the more impersonal world outside. Having clarified the differences between these two worlds, Parsons is able to say some revealing things about the role of the father, the school, and the group of age-mates in making this transition possible.

Another interesting area of study is that which is concerned with the way in which a society of this kind brings deviants back into the fold. Dealing with such people is the task of the medical and social work professions. The organization of these professions has many of the characteristics of the world of work. The social worker or doctor has to be objective and detached. Yet at the same time he has to establish a personal relationship with his client or patient. The efficient performance of the professional role, therefore, demands that some balance be kept between a personal family-type relationship and the element of deliberate control and discipline. Thus a good doctor has to have a 'bedside manner', but his professional ethics debar him from becoming too personally involved with his patient (Parsons, 1952, pp. 58–112, 297–321).

What Parsons does in this kind of analysis is to take some fairly simple principles or rules of the game and show how, if they are taken to their logical conclusion, they explain much of the behaviour and much of the stresses and strains which we observe every day. Another area in which this could be done is in the study of the city as a social unit, although no one has put forward a theory of the city as clear as that which Parsons has developed in relation to the family.

Sociologists at Chicago, however, did try some forty years ago to develop such a theory (Park, Burgess and Mackenzie, 1925). They discovered that industrial cities like their own tended to develop four main industrial zones. The innermost one, around the central business district, was the lodging-house zone inhabited by new immigrants and by the down-and-outs of urban society. The second zone was that of the established working classes. The third was that of the middle classes and the fourth that of the urban commuter. The Chicago sociologists sought to explain this distribution of the population rather inadequately in terms of the result of 'free competition for land use'. A more detailed and closely argued theory is urgently necessary.

What has seemed to me, during my own research, to be the underlying urban process is something like this. In the first place the middle-class way of life, based upon family property, and the working-class way of life, based upon neighbourly mutual aid, become established. Then there emerges an area of larger terrace houses which form the homes of the intermediate lower-middle classes. There emerges within the city a status system based upon these styles of life and it is in the nature of such a status system that the lower groups will come to aspire to the way of life of those above them. So one gets the beginnings of the move to semi-detached suburbia aided first by mortgages and then by public house building. The old homes of the lower-middle classes are abandoned, and become divided up into lodging houses for the newest immigrants to the city. At the same time in the competition for entry into the desired suburban world, the down-and-outs and deviants get pushed to the back of the queue and finish up with the immigrants in the lodging houses.

Given a basic set of rules like this, one would expect to find a number of different styles of life in the city. There will be the semi-detached family life of suburbia, in which families live relatively independently of their neighbours. There will be old working-class areas with obvious neighbourly institutions like chapels, pubs and shops which express the collective nature of working-class community. And there will be the disorganized life of the lodging-house areas, where people on the whole, lack the support of family and other kin-groups, but cling closely to what they have, and where the strange mixture of cosmopolitanism and vice makes life peculiarly fascinating. City life is made up of these various styles of life and of the continual transition from one to the other.

A third area in which sociological theory has helped to illuminate problems of social research is in the study of industrial and government administration. The greatest contributor in this sphere was Max Weber (1968, Vol. I, Chap. 2). Weber recognized that one of the key features of modern society was that it did not entrust the business of economic production to kin or neighbourhood groups but to organizations based upon authority. He therefore asked, 'What is the form of organization in which the will of one man can most reliably be carried out by many agents?' His answer was given in his theory of a perfect bureaucracy.

Bureaucracy involves, according to Weber, the elimination of all irrational personal factors in social relationships. It assumes a form of authority in which it is the legal occupation of an office that matters, rather than an individual's personal qualities or hereditary position. The individual in a bureaucracy must separate his personal affairs and the affairs of his office completely. He must not mix his personal and domestic accounts with those of the office. Nor should his files contain any personal correspondence. On the other hand, his job is not his personal property, and, ideally, there should be a record of all his official acts so that his successor can take over with a minimum of explanation.

The bureaucrat is responsible for taking decisions within his own defined sphere of competence and must give an account of what he has done, to his superior. But his superior may not interfere within that sphere of competence or make any demands upon the private life of his subordinate. All personal and emotional factors must be excluded from the relationship between superior and inferior, and all decisions must be rationally argued from principle and precedent. Ideally, individuals should enter a bureaucracy after passing a competitive examination. They should not owe their office to election or personal influence. Later students of industrial organization have been inclined to argue that no actual organization is completely like this; but Weber never expected that they would be. What he was doing, was indicating what the main rules of the game were and contrasting these with the forms of administration to be found in, say, Chinese, Hindu, or European feudal society. And, however much we may wish to modify Weber's theory in terms of more subtle and complex moves made by modern organization men, it is surely the case that Weber pointed out some of the basic principles of social organization which we take for granted in these more subtle theories.

The three examples which we have given show how sociological research on the family, the city and industrial organization may be illuminated by theory. Clearly we could not have arrived at these theories simply by looking at tables of statistics. At some point, if we are really to study social facts, we have to sit down and think, and try to discover what the rules are which produce people of the kinds shown up in our statistical categories. The danger is that, as we develop more sophisticated ways of counting and calculating with the aid of the computer, we shall lose this capacity to think.

On the other hand, if we do continue to do some theoretical work, we shall be able to take advantage of these new techniques because we shall know what things are worth measuring and counting. Instead of working blind, we shall go to the facts with important questions to ask, and quite often we shall be driven back to think again and revise our pure theories. Theory and empirical research should continually feed on one another. But we shall get very far in sociology, if we try to dispense with theory altogether. The great weakness of English social research is that, too often, this is what it has tried to do.

4 Understanding and sociological theory

In previous chapters we have made some attempt to justify a discussion of theoretical issues separately from ongoing empirical research. For no doubt there will be some, social scientists as well as laymen, who will accuse us of a kind of armchair speculation, which they will say is precisely what inhibits any real advance in the social sciences.

There is no need to reply at length to this accusation. It must suffice to say that the issues which will be raised in this and subsequent papers are issues which have occurred to the more insightful sociologists in the course of actual empirical research, and that they are issues which press for discussion; for sociological phenomena are complex in their nature, and only the naïve would pretend to say anything about them, without first reflecting on what their nature is, how they are to be observed and what kind of questions might be asked about them.

We may, it is true, make some measure of progress in our knowledge of social facts in the immediate future, because of the technological revolution which has taken place in the methods of processing data. But real scientific discovery will not take place through these means alone. If we want to do more than discover a vast number of unconnected correlations between phenomena, if we want to have any kind of continuity in social research, if we really want to find our way about the social world, we must still be prepared to think and to theorize. We need, therefore, if we are going to have fruitful and interesting hypotheses to test, to construct models, albeit on middle levels, and by no means necessarily in the grand Parsonian manner, of those interconnected phenomena which we propose to talk about. What may perhaps be at issue here is the kind of model which we should use.

The two great traditions of sociological theorizing seem to

me to arise from Emile Durkheim and Max Weber, and what I wish to do is to say something about these traditions, and to urge upon you, and perhaps upon British sociology, the superiority of the latter. The fact that Weber's theory has been much discussed since the centenary of his birth in 1964 makes such a discussion particularly appropriate.

The Durkheimian tradition is, of course, an exciting one, and it was Durkheim who first really made sociology into a respectable discipline by his repeated insistence on the irreducibility of social facts. And, even though we may trace this tradition back to the conservatism of Joseph de Maistre, who wanted to oppose all attempts at rational interference with the established social order, it nonetheless remains true that human behaviour is sometimes determined or affected by supra-individual factors, which are not studied adequately within a biological or psychological frame of reference. The individual cannot do what he likes. He is constrained by external factors and not all of these factors are of a physical kind.

The difficulty, however, lies in giving more than a residual definition of social facts. They are external to the individual and they are not simply physical in their nature. What then are they like? Durkheim's own answer to this question is vague, elusive and even sometimes mystical. He can tell us how, or in what degree, social entities affect our behaviour, but when we ask what the entities are like he retracts into metaphor and uses terms like 'collective currents' and 'social solidarity', the definitions of which remain irritatingly obscure.

I should like to emphasize in self-defence, at this point, that I am not asking for a metaphysic of social entities. What I do want is some kind of theoretical model which will enable sociologists who are told that certain observed behaviour, say a particular suicide rate, is due to some social entity (e.g. a kind of solidarity) to go on immediately to put forward other hypotheses about other behaviour which might be observed. When we have some model of how the alleged entities behind the facts work, we are able to argue from their operation in one observed case to how they will operate in other cases not yet observed. If we have clearly understandable models of this kind, we can have some hope that our research will be continuous and cumulative.

One line of approach to constructing such a model was to resort to analogy. And the favourite analogy was that of the animal organism. From Spencer to Radcliffe-Brown, one finds this kind of explanation used quite explicitly, and even among the opponents of 'organicism' one finds an implicit acceptance of this kind of argument. Just as a physiologist might sometimes 'explain' a physiological activity by showing that if its effects were not produced, the organism might die, so the sociologist would explain that a recurrent social activity, such as a funeral ceremony, was necessary in order to maintain the social *status quo*.

But, as Radcliffe-Brown himself saw, societies were not like that. Very often the recurrent activity could cease and be replaced by some new activity. Or alternatively, while the society might cease to exist, or 'die', in its old form, it continued in some new form. As Radcliffe-Brown put it, it was as though, in the life of the animal world, a pig in dire sickness suddenly turned into a hippopotamus (Radcliffe-Brown, 1952).

So the analogy broke down, and happily so, for it forced sociologists to do some thinking on a more detailed and micro-sociological level about the nature of their subject matter. An analogical model, taken over ready-made from another science, could only be conducive to intellectual idleness and dogmatism. To have to work out one's own models appropriate to one's own subject matter meant studying the empirical world and not merely labelling it.

The key term which had to be analysed in the new microsociology was really the term 'social relation'. All other terms like group, association and institution seem to be thought of, if they are not thought of mystically, as networks of social relations. But what are social relations and how do we observe them? This seems to me to be the question which we have to answer before we can begin to study sociology. If we do not answer it, either we do not do any sociology, or we are not sure what we are talking about.

Now the difficulty with this term is that we all feel that we know what we mean by it, because we have all used it long before we become sociologists. Some such term has to be used when we are planning even the most trivial action. To achieve our purposes, we have to take account of how the world is, and what things in it may be used as means and conditions for our action. Amongst these 'things', are the actions of other people. We say that we have a relationship with someone when we can to some extent predict and rely upon how he will act in particular circumstances.

This sociological ability on the part of the people whom he observes has been something of an embarrassment to the sociologist. He lives with it in his own private life. But since scientific knowledge must be public knowledge and this other kind of knowledge seems to be derived from unverified intro- spection, it seems necessary to reject it.

The great central contribution of Max Weber, and that which makes his sociology so distinctive, was that he held that we could understand social relations in terms of the subjective intention of an actor, without having to resort to some kind of sympathetic introspection (Weber, 1968, Vol. I, Chap. 1). What we had to do was to construct models of social relations which started with the assumption of an actor who has goals and who structures his world in terms of its subjective meaning. Since such assumptions have consequences for how people behave towards one another, there is no reason why we should not empirically verify models constructed in these terms.

Sociology, then, is the study of social relations. But social relations are not themselves directly observable phenomena. They are relatively complex theoretical constructs which enable us to predict and explain human behaviour. And they presuppose a more elementary and fundamental construct still, namely that of a hypothetical actor, who has goals, who gives his world meaning in terms of those goals and who has expectations of the behaviour of others.

Parsons (1937) coined the term 'the action frame of reference' for sociological theory which was stated in these terms and it is convenient to classify his own work, together with that of Weber and that of most economic theorists, under this heading. None- theless there are distinctive features of Weber's use of the action frame of reference which mark him off sharply from Parsons, and it is on these that I wish to dwell.

I have said that the Durkheimian tradition led eventually to the construction of analogical models for social facts based upon the analogy with animal organisms. Explanations in terms of these models came to be called functional explanations and they seemed to be quite different from the kind of explanations of social relations which would be given in terms of the action frame of reference. In functionalist explanation, something is explained in terms of the contribution which it makes to maintaining the life of the social system or organism. In explanations in terms of the action frame of reference, something is explained by the place it is shown to occupy in the orientation to action, the purposes and the meaning of a hypothetical actor. Yet the extraordinary thing about the work of Talcott Parsons is that, having declared himself for the action frame of reference, he goes on to call himself a functionalist.

He does this, of course, without bringing in the organic analogy. His functionalism derives from a more general notion than that of the organism, namely that of a system.[1] But the notion of a system as Parsons uses it has the essential properties of an organism and demands similar types of explanation. If the concept of system is central, we say that something is explained if we can show that it is system-maintaining. How then does he get from the concept of a social relation to that of a system?

Parson's argument here is that we can only speak of social relations if we presuppose various supporting mechanisms which make it possible for one particular actor to rely upon the behaviour of another. There must, for example, be some sort of sanctions which force the other's compliance; the second actor must have come to want the first actor's approval; they must have some means of communicating their expectations to each other; they must have internalized common norms and so on.

Now all this is at least partially true. Social relations do, to some extent, presuppose social systems in this way. But we still have a further choice to make about the nature of our sociology. Either we shall say that there are as many different kinds of social system as there are possible goals, or we shall ignore the goals towards which the systems are directed, concentrate on the formal aspects of action, and show, in very general abstract terms, what supporting mechanisms are required for each of a limited number of forms of social relationship.

The latter course is the one chosen by Parsons. Thus he does not discuss, as Weber does, what social institutions are necessary,

[1] Talcott Parsons, *The Social System*, 1952. See also Parsons's (1964) Introduction in *The Theory of Social and Economic Organization* by Max Weber.

given the goals of a Calvinist, or given the profit motive. What he discusses is what social institutions are necessary, if the basic social relations, which are to be maintained, are affective, instead of affectively neutral; diffuse, rather than specific in the obligations which they impose, and so on. Thus Parsons's possible types of social system are very abstract indeed. They tell us what is necessary for the maintenance of affectively neutral, specific, universalistic, and achievement oriented patterns. But they do not tell us, for instance, what the difference is between a communist and a capitalist social system. Still less, do they help us to discriminate between the more subtle variants within each system.

This was not the alternative adopted by Max Weber. In his sociological studies, he begins with some purpose or some meaning with which particular actors approach their situation, and uses this as a guiding thread to unravel the total pattern of social relations. Thus, given that we have Calvinists, certain that God has predestined some men to work for the establishment of His kingdom on this earth, yet uncertain, at least secretly, of their own election, one expects certain patterns of social relations to follow. Or, given that one has a Chinese emperor intent on total control of his people as though they were all a part of his household, certain administrative arrangements follow.

The great point about Weber's work is the richness of historical content included in his sociological studies. This has certain important corollaries which I should like to emphasize.

The first is that, contrary to a widely and mistakenly held view, Weber does not reduce sociological to psychological factors. What he does say is that a model of a social system must have as its starting point the meanings and goals of a hypothetical individual. But these meanings and goals are by no means those which are determined solely by the personality systems of individuals. They are culturally given meanings and goals, and they have great, if not unlimited, variety.

The second corollary is that what may be necessary from the point of view of one set of goals and meanings is not necessary from another. Thus one has the possibility of conflict within the system and a total rejection of the conservative tradition of de Maistre, Comte, Durkheim and Parsons. We may say that certain institutional arrangements are necessary, given a particular goal of the system; but we may also go on to say that, given other goals, totally different institutional arrangements would be necessary. This line of sociological thinking has since been much more explicitly developed by Karl Mannheim (1960) and Gunnar Myrdal (1958).

Third, the Weberian approach involves the rejection of any sort of monistic determinism. It may be useful, as Weber (1949) saw as the editor of a journal of economic history, to ask what patterns of behaviour are necessary if economic organization is given primacy, and it certainly seemed to Weber to be the case that this assumption of economic determinism was useful in approaching his own times. But this is by no means to say that one cannot ask useful and important questions about the kind of economic and other institutions which the pursuit of purely political or purely religious goals would require.

Fourth, Weber was sensitive to the fact that the relationships which held between institutions were not merely causal relationships. You could not say that, given an institution A, you had to have an institution Y, because this would depend upon the relationships of meaning which were taken for granted in a particular culture. For instance, you only know what actions a man will take in pursuit of 'salvation' when you know something of the meaning of salvation, and the rules for attaining it, in that particular culture. It is true that Weber rejected the notion that these meanings could only be known by intuition and that he sought to outline procedures for discovering them. But he was as sensitive as his great antagonist Dilthey to the need for incorporating the study of relationships of meaning in sociology.

I believe that Weber's sociological method is the one that works, and that the real reason for the sterility of much of our sociological research lies in the fact that his achievement has been so little understood. I should like, by way of conclusion, to illustrate this by referring briefly to some empirical work which we have had in hand in Birmingham.

We studied a multi-racial community in a compact area which had come to public notice as a problem area. What we wanted to know was what sorts of social actions, interactions and social relations gave rise to these problems. One way of studying the problem would have been simply to classify the population by age, sex, place of origin, length of residence etc., and their homes, by their size and number of rooms and their available facilities. We did this, but it did not take us very far. What a functionalist would have urged us to do would have been to study the system as a whole and show how the various activities which we observed serve to maintain or change that system. There may be something in this, but the fact is that there is less obvious system about a ward in Birmingham, than there is in the Trobriand Islands. We could have administered tests of racial attitudes and scored people as more or less prejudiced. We could have categorized relationships in formal terms as Parsons does, but we rejected all of these approaches in favour of a more Weberian one.

What we did propose to do was to try to understand the meaning of immigration for a Pakistani, a West Indian or an Irishman in as rich a detail as possible. We then had to go on, having understood these meanings, to ask what they implied in terms of housing, of primary group formation and of relations with other groups. We did not assume that there was necessarily a community of purpose between these different groups or between them and the native residents or the public authorities. Rather we studied the organizations in which they segregated themselves or integrated with members of other groups, and the ways in which intergroup conflict was pursued or mediated.

We proposed to give a meaningful account of the action, interaction, conflict and co-operation in our area in the tradition of Max Weber. When we did this we had always been aware of the general factors affecting the situation and been prepared to see repeated there processes whose general form is to be found anywhere. But we should have missed the point if we had not realized that the Labour Club was a little bit of old Ireland, that the dear old lady who lived next to a Pakistani lodging house remembered the middle-class glory of the area as it used to be, or that the man who got off the No 8 bus was a Pathan preacher visiting Birmingham to hold his countrymen to the true faith.

5   Types of sociological theory in Britain

Despite the proliferation of departments in British universities which have the word 'social' in their titles, the subject of sociology has not hitherto played a large part in academic teaching and research. My aim in this chapter is to analyse why this is so by contrasting the academic situation in this country with that in France and Germany, and to suggest that we need sociology, precisely defined as a subject, as one of the basic disciplines underlying social research.

The characteristic British social science in the nineteenth century was political economy, and, even though its founder, Adam Smith, had regarded the subject as part of a larger science of government, the classical economists came to see it as giving a total account of the laws of society. Such a view implied a political philosophy and a political theory—this was supplied by Utilitarianism—which saw hedonistic individualism, either as a model to explain human behaviour, or as an ideal towards which society must tend.

Only one of the great economists and Utilitarians rejected these assumptions, namely John Stuart Mill, but he, having considered Comte's plan for a science of sociology, rejected it in favour of a science of individual character, which he proposed to call ethology.

In these circumstances there were three intellectual sources from which sociology as a distinct subject from economics might emerge. One was evolutionism; a second, social work among, and concern for, the 'submerged tenth' to whom an individualistic society did not appear to bring 'the greatest happiness'; and the third was the study of genetics and the question of population.

Evolutionism led Herbert Spencer, still perhaps the most important British sociologist, to a study of pre-industrial social

44

form. Being an evolutionist, he could not accept that individualistic society, and the rational man it presupposed, had existed from the beginning of time. He therefore posited earlier stages of social organization, leading up to a variety of forms of authoritarianism which he lumped together under the title 'militant societies'. But all of these were contrasted with industrial society, which worked essentially according to the laws of economics. Sociology was the discipline in terms of which we studied the past; economics, the present and the future.

Of some interest, too, is Spencer's scientific materialism. Societies are seen as more or less complex combinations of matter. They are to be explained in terms of natural science, in terms of laws, in terms of cause and effect. And, if some recognition has to be given to human agency and choice in the study of industrial society, nonetheless rational man is seen as choosing, for the attainment of his ends, those means which science declares to be appropriate. Thus, both in terms of its subject matter and its method, Spencer does not go very far in his conception of a special science of sociology.

The other great founding father of British sociology is always said to be Charles Booth (1902). How does he stand in relation to the tradition of economic thought and utilitarian philosophy? I think that the situation is something like this: if one started with Utilitarian assumptions, i.e. by believing that the sum total of human happiness was increased if each followed his own self-interest, or sought to maximize his own utility, then the poor were a problem. It was necessary, in order to complete one's explanation of human society, to discover the causes of poverty, i.e. to discover what other social mechanisms caused this exception to the generally optimistic picture which economics and philosophical Utilitarianism provided.

Implicit in Booth's studies was a concern to discover what new social structures could be introduced to alter the conditions of the poor. Booth was inevitably the founder of the study called social administration. From his time onward, this became a major concern of British social science, even though all those who felt it did not share Sidney Webb's total rejection of individualism in favour of totalitarian socialism (see Webb, 1962). Social administration, the servicing of the poor, became the complementary study to economics.

Closely related to this was what I might call the Malthusian tradition in British thought. It was dominated by the belief that the lower classes were having too many children and that they were physically and intellectually inferior. Following on from Sir Francis Galton's concern with the inheritance of genius and mental defect, this movement became concerned with improving the racial stock. It became interested in what was called eugenics.

But the eugenics movement was not simply a reactionary movement, blaming the workers for their poverty and stopping them from breeding. It had its left as well as its right, and its left urged the study of the environmental limitations on the life-chances of the poor and the disadvantaged. The poor, it was argued, are not poor because they are stupid or wicked, but because they receive too little money and because they do not have the same educational opportunities as the rich. Thus, on one wing of the eugenics movement, there emerged a kind of demographic study which fits in very well with the tradition of social reform and social administration initiated by Booth.

It was from these traditions that sociology was likely to draw its material when it finally became established as a university teaching subject at the London School of Economics. But at first the main emphasis was Spencerian. Like Spencer, Hobhouse[1] was concerned with the evolution of societies, and, though his philosophic position was neo-Hegelian and his concept of the good society to which we were tending much more influenced by a new conception of social welfare, one finds that same contrast drawn between rational man on the one hand, and the customs of the primitive on the other, which we find in Spencer. This tradition of comparative evolutionary sociology with a moral concern dominated English sociology throughout Hobhouse's long period of teaching and during that of his pupil Ginsberg.

The Booth tradition followed its own independent course and eventually led to the establishment of an independent Department of Social Administration. Richard Titmuss, questioning whether the Welfare State has in fact led to any substantial redistribution of income, and Peter Townsend, investigating the material conditions and social life of old people, are the out-

[1] See especially L. T. Hobhouse, *Morals in Evolution*, 1952.

standing modern successors of Booth.[1] Demography, however, still remains with the sociologists and the study of differential educational opportunity, a subject of immense topicality, plays a central role in the study of the sociology of modern Britain.

But sociology at the London School of Economics found itself outflanked on at least two sides. In so far as it was concerned with the poor, its role has been largely assumed by the Department of Social Administration. And, in so far as it was concerned with evolution and the past, it had to compete with social anthropology, brilliantly taught by Malinowski to a whole generation of colonial administrators and researchers in the field. There was precious little left if these fields were surrendered, and, if the sociologists showed any concern about the subjective aspect of social relations, they found departments of social psychology already in the field.

Of course we do not entirely sum up the situation which existed in Britain prior to 1939, by referring only to Britain's one sociology department. There were other points at which sociological concerns developed. One was in the departments of social studies, where social workers were trained, and in which the Freudian mystery of case-work was beginning to make its appearance. The other was amongst Marxist historians whose use of the materialist conception of history led them to formulate some kind of models of societies as institutional systems, however crude. But the thought of Freud and Marx had appeared rather feebly in British social science. It was vulgarized, and it failed to produce the stimulating intellectual encounter which it had produced in Karl Mannheim's Frankfurt.

The result of all this has been a subject lacking the courage of its convictions, unsure of whether it has a subject matter of its own, and meddling here and there with matters administrative, economic and psychological, to prove that it has something to contribute. At worst, it turns to producing men skilled in techniques of questionnaire design, administration and analysis, with no special knowledge of any subject at all.

How different was the situation in France and Germany where the Manchester doctrines of free trade had not gained so strong a

[1] See R. Titmuss, *Income Distribution and Social Change*, 1962 and P. Townsend, *The Family Life of Old People*, 1963.

foothold. Each produced its own intellectual tradition in the social sciences and we may set about understanding these by focusing on the work of their two greatest representatives, Emile Durkheim and Max Weber.

Sociology in France is born out of the reaction to the French Revolution. The naïve belief in progress through the increasing rationality of man had been systematically questioned by the great reactionaries of the times, above all by de Maistre and de Bonald. Thus any statement about the kind of social system which was coming to be, and which should come to be, was bound to be different from its equivalent in Spencer. And, when St-Simon and Comte began to formulate their ideal of industrial society, it was one in which 'order and progress' were duly combined. Men were exhorted to think scientifically and positively, not rationalistically; thinking scientifically meant discovering the natural social limitations on what was possible.

St-Simon and Comte are still very much caught up in ideological argument. Their heir, Durkheim, is far less so (see Durkheim, 1933). Yet his whole life's work is explicitly directed to showing that Spencer was terribly and disastrously wrong. In part his attack is metaphysical, centring upon the fundamental difference between natural and social facts. But, in part, it is also theoretical and sociological, arguing that Spencer's model just does not adequately explain the facts which we see about us in industrial society.

Durkheim's case is that Spencer reduces social to individual facts. This is what he means when he accuses him of treating the social division of labour as a matter of mere expediency. In making this accusation, Durkheim suggests that even the individualistic society which Spencer has in mind, must, if it is to be a society at all, rest upon controls which are outside the individual's will. The social for Durkheim is a reality *sui generis*.

On the most obvious level, Durkheim means by this that an industrial contractual society presupposes certain norms outlawing fraud and force. But, much more than this, he sees that acts of mutual service which take place in social and economic exchange have a lasting effect on the social personalities of those who participate. 'The image of the one who completes me', says Durkheim (1933, p. 61), 'becomes inseparable from mine.' Or, in other words, we cannot explain human behaviour if we work solely with a model of an isolated self-interested individual such as Spencer, for example, posits. The focus of sociological study becomes, not the individual and his characteristics, but the social relations binding one individual to another; or as Durkheim likes to say, the forms of social solidarity.

Nor is Durkheim satisfied with statistical studies of the recurrence of attributes in a population of individuals. Such studies provide only the starting point. If the sociologist is confronted with regularities in statistical indices, e.g. the marriage or the suicide rate, his real task is to discover the kind of social solidarity of which these indices are indicative. Thus in his *Suicide* (1952) he shows that there is a difference between the suicide rate amongst Catholics and Protestants, but from there he goes on to discuss what differences in Catholic and Protestant social structure could lead to these differential rates.

We need not go on to discuss Durkheim's ideas about the politics of industrial society, about education and about religion, in which he also applies these fundamental insights. What we do need to notice is that he does not see the study of the individual, or a statistical population of individuals, as of particular social interest. Nor is he concerned with those causes of individual behaviour which arise from within the individual or from the physical environment. What he asks us to look at are those causes of human behaviour which emanate from the social system, in which the individual plays a role, and which the individual experiences subjectively, as demands made upon him by other people, themselves acting in roles.

What Durkheim would perhaps have emphasized above all is that, in so far as industrial society lasts, it cannot simply be a non-society. It may be a very special type of social system arising from market relations; but it is a social system nonetheless, with its own presuppositions, its own norms, and its own roles. Thus economics by itself is lacking in depth of insight as a social science because it fails to look at the social presuppositions of market behaviour, and it also fails to recognize that other social presuppositions are possible. And, equally, philosophic utilitarianism offers a prescription for society which cannot work, but which can only lead to that kind of individual and social disorganization which Durkheim calls 'anomie'.

Max Weber approached very similar problems from another

direction. One of his first research concerns was with the conditions of immigrant labour in East Prussia.[1] As he saw it, what was happening was the product of a clash of social systems. On the one hand, there was the old semi-feudal social system of the Junkers, on the other, the new social system being generated by the forces of the market. His problem was precisely the same as that of Durkheim. What sort of society was possible as market forces came into operation? What presuppositions had to be made if the market was not to turn into Hobbes's war of all against all?

This led Weber first to an analysis of the role of religious ethics in capitalist societies. He was greatly helped in this by the pioneer work of Troeltsch (1931) and went on to argue that occidental capitalism, far from being merely the product of greed, which was universal, was the product of a quite peculiar dedicated religious attitude inspired by Calvinism. You could explain readily enough the behaviour of those entrepreneurs the world over who systematically made money in order to spend it on wine, women and Cadillacs. What was more difficult to explain was the behaviour of a man who made profits to plough back into his business to make more profits and so *ad infinitum*.

In order to prove this thesis Weber embarked upon a series of comparative studies.[2] No doubt his assumption was a Millian one, viz. that if you could find a civilization which differed from that of capitalist Europe and America in one crucial circumstance, namely the presence or absence of a Calvinist type religion, and did not have capitalism, the relationship between capitalism and Calvinism would be established.

Of course this was nonsense. There are too many variables in such comparative-historical studies to make a Millian proof possible. But it was precisely in locating these variables that Weber made his most lasting contribution to sociology.

What he showed was this, that civilizations differ in terms of a number of different structural continua. They differ in the kind of relationship which exists between the ruler and his administrative agents; they differ in the relationship which exists between kin-groups, guilds and cities, they differ in their religious ideas, in the structure of their religious organizations and in the relation-

[1] See Reinhard Bendix, *Max Weber: An Intellectual Portrait*, 1960.
[2] See especially Weber's works, *The Religion of China*, *The Religion of India* and *Ancient Judaism*.

ship holding between priests, prophets and administrators, they differ in the systems whereby individuals are allowed to exploit natural resources and the labour of others. And these are only a few of the variables which Weber placed at the centre of his work.

But Weber did more than this. He realized that in each of his ideal models he was positing a different kind of actor from the *homo economicus* assumed in economic thought, and he therefore went on to try to deduce each of his structural models from more elementary models of typical actors, to whom he imputed different patterns of action-orientation, from that which is attributed to economic man (Weber, 1968).

The consequence was that Weber gave us a whole battery of concepts for analysing our civilization. Many of the institutional forms which he had earlier taken for granted in his analysis of capitalism now appeared highly problematic. They were not just part of a natural order, but particular forms chosen from a range of possibilities. Why had the particular choice been made and what supports were necessary to sustain a particular institutional form? For example, how had rational-legal authority and its accompanying bureaucratic form of administration developed in the West, rather than the far more usual form of patrimonial administration which was found in Ancient Egypt or China? Would such bureaucratic forms last, and what would they give way to, if they did give way? These are surely very relevant questions for us, as we face a period of dramatic technological, economic and political change.

I have focused this chapter, for illustrative purposes, on the inadequacies of economics as the sole social science. This is not of course to underestimate its importance, because there are many issues that are settled, and many needs that are met, in our society, through the operation of market mechanisms. But there are other mechanisms, other forms of social interaction also, and for these we need a wider framework of possible types of human action and interaction.

English social science in the nineteenth century had three modes of explanation of human behaviour. One was to assume that it was rational in the sense that, given the actor's goal, he obtained a full scientific view of the means available to him and chose those means to achieve his goal which a scientist would deem appropriate. A second was to explain any deviance from this rational pattern in terms of lack of information or error on the part of the actor. And a third was to see his behaviour simply as caused, in a natural-science sense, either by internal biological and psychological factors or by the physical environment. What such explanations left out was non-rational action which is not irrational; action in which the end chosen and the means used were governed by rules.[1] I think this notion of rule-governed behaviour is at the core of sociology. We are always in the position of a man who, not having seen chess before, comes upon two chess-players, and, watching them play, asks himself, 'What are the rules of this game?'

People are playing a lot of different games in England. We have only the crudest idea of what the rules are. Our job, as sociologists, is to discover what these rules are in order to be able to predict people's behaviour; to know how they will respond to economic changes, to know what services they need and how they will respond if these services are provided.

I think that social anthropologists will understand what I am saying better than almost anyone else. For the anthropologist, studying a primitive tribe, is always quite explicitly in the position I have in mind. Here we have the Trobriand Islanders exchanging armlets and necklaces and giving yams to their sisters. How do we explain it? It took Malinowski many years of investigation and much personal yam-eating to find out. But as a result we now have four or five volumes which tell us the rules of the Trobriand game.[2]

The trouble is that when we turn to England we think we know what the game is. We know what they are up to in Sunderland.[3] Basically, we believe that it is the market game, but we do surveys to find out what is happening to the old, and any other groups who fall within Booth's submerged tenth, or devote lots of resources to studying the various social service agencies.

I wouldn't want to underrate this work which is being carried on in the fields of social economics and social administration, but

[1] See Talcott Parsons, *The Structure of Social Action*, 1937, p. 76.
[2] See especially, Malinowski's *Coral Gardens and Their Magic*, 1966.
[3] The references which follow are to research projects undertaken in Durham County.

it leaves many questions unanswered. In conclusion, I want to list what some of these questions are; I want to talk about what the sociologist can contribute to the study of towns, to the study of the young and the old, to the study of social class, to the study of deviance and to the study of industrial relations.

One of the features of urban development is the growth of suburbs, of suburban society and suburban culture. The people who are moving to suburbia, whether on a council or a private estate, have once participated in a game called being working class, a game whose rules have been spelt out on the domestic side by writers like Richard Hoggart and Michael Young and Peter Willmott and on the industrial side by a host of different writers. But what kind of social system does suburbia imply? What are the rules of the suburban game? Very few of us have any idea, ready though we may be to condemn the suburbanite. I suggest that this kind of question, rather than such questions as whether people want a lavatory downstairs, is the kind of question to which sociologists should be addressing themselves. And there are many other questions about the different styles of social life in different urban zones which crowd in upon us waiting for an answer.

On the question of age-groupings, and what I might call age-cultures, it is now almost platitudinous to remark that most of us have lost touch completely with the springs of youth culture. Young people organized in cultural sects fight on our beaches and, their parents, of whatever class, are puzzled. What is the logic of the situation as it presents itself to a Mod or a Rocker? We have little idea as to the answer.

Far less spectacular a subject for investigation is that of the social world of the old. In the past we have dealt with them purely by concerning ourselves with whether they have enough money, enough food, enough medical care, adequate housing. But do we know what it means for a man to be old, to be declared no longer to have an industrial role, when his industrial role has provided the meaning of existence for forty years, to be socially dead before he dies physically? Or is it the case, or could it be, that old people can be born again into a new society which has a role for the elderly? I want to know what the rules of the game called old age are in our society.

The question of social class is a peculiarly interesting one in the North East of England, for this is the most solid centre of Labour voting in England and Durham is the home of the greatest ritual of the English working class, the Durham Miners' Gala. But what implications does this predominance of working-class culture have for the style of local government, for the development of industry or the arts? And what changes are going on before our eyes in the game of being working class? We are, perhaps, particularly well placed to study these changes here because they have not yet gone as far as they have in other places.

We are asked by the Home Office to work out the relationship between unemployment and crime and we try as best we can, with the statistics available, to trace correlations. But what we lack, and what the Home Office lacks, is any knowledge of the rules of the unemployment game or the crime game. So we have little idea as to which statistics are really relevant. I do not believe myself that there can be an effective criminology until we have more understanding of these sociological questions.

And finally I turn to industrial sociology. We have in the North East, or so it seems to me, a veritable laboratory for industrial sociology. We can see what happens to men when they transfer from the special world of the mines, and the communities which they sustain, to other industries and to new towns. We can contrast an old industrial social system, such as that of the steelworks, with that of the newer chemical industry which is so sharply juxtaposed to it. And we have a variety of government-owned, government-sponsored and private enterprise firms in which we can make comparisons of the effect of ownership on industrial social systems.[1]

And, above and beyond all of these questions, there is a larger one, the one which any sociologist worth his salt would want to face. What kind of over-all social system are we living in? The models which our politicians use in practice are too often derived from the past, and sociologists since Marx and Weber have done

[1] The areas of research referred to here were areas of interest in Durham during my stay there. Amongst those who aroused my interest in their research were Peter Kaim-Caudle, Roger Hood, Tony Rees, Laurie Moseley, Peter Hollowell, Norman Dennis, Ann Edwards, Mark Beeson, Richard Brown, Peter Brannen, Martin Bulmer, Ellis Thorpe, Stan Cohen and Ken Patton.

too little to give them new ones. It is our concern with this question which will, I hope, inform and inspire all of our special studies, and I hope that the students we shall attract will be precisely those who care about answering it.

6

The main types of sociological theory

A remarkable thing has happened in English academic life in the past ten years. Sociology, which ten years ago was a pariah subject, existing on the margins of the academic curriculum, has now become fashionable. More than twenty new departments have been founded and every day the man-in-the-street is bombarded with information, instruction and advice, purporting to come from sociologists. It seems only right in these circumstances that anyone aiming to introduce sociology into the curriculum should give his colleagues some idea of what exactly he is about. What I hope to do, therefore, in this chapter, is to say something about the main traditions of sociological thought, to present some of the difficulties inherent in the subject and to dissociate myself from the popular sociology which is now so much in vogue. I can best do this by saying what I believe the nature of sociological enquiry to be and to show how its main problems have been dealt with in three intellectual traditions—those of England, France and Germany.

Sociological enquiry is concerned with those determinants of human behaviour which derive from the involvement of human beings in systems of social relations. Or, to put this in another way, it is concerned with describing such systems of social relations. To say this, is not to say that all human behaviour is determined, or that it may not be determined in part, by biological, psychological and physical environmental factors. But it does mean that sociology has a special subject matter of its own and that historical, biological and psychological studies, and studies emphasizing causes in the physical environment, are not themselves sociological.

In nineteenth-century England, a theory of social systems of this kind was worked out by the economists and by the utilitarian philosophers. According to them, the most advanced society and the most desirable society was one in which the only important social relations would be those which individuals had freely contracted to enter in the course of maximizing their own utility. Society was seen as a market system operated by rational, self-interested individuals. The view that a society run on these lines was not only possible, but desirable, was shared by Adam Smith, Jeremy Bentham and Herbert Spencer.

But, although this was in fact a sociology, sociology was pre-empted by economics. Economics appeared to give a full account of the social order which was necessary for free and rational man. Hence, if sociology was to exist at all, it could exist only as a subsidiary science which explained deviations from the pure rational type, or suggested remedies where the market system failed to provide minimally acceptable standards of welfare. Inevitably, English sociology came to consist of a number of qualifications of the economists' and the utilitarians' assumptions.

The first of these qualifications concerned the limits placed on the flexibility of human behaviour by biological and psychological factors. Thus the anxieties of Malthus led to the development of a science of population. Galton's concern with biologically inherited characteristics led to the idea of eugenics, an idea which loomed large in the meetings of the first British Sociological Association. Graham Wallas, alone amongst his fellow Fabians, drew attention to the non-rational motivation of human beings in politics and in due course Trotter and McDougall were to codify these in terms of a theory of individual instincts. None of these, however, recognized any constraint on the individual which arose from any source other than that of the biological and psychological constitution of the individual. To recognize any such constraints was a conservative heresy. Biological and psychological restraints on human choice there may be, but English social thought remained, even with this qualification, profoundly individualistic.

The second main qualification of the economists' model derived from a concern with the condition of the poor. The assumption of utilitarian thought about the cure of poverty had been that the only way out was self-help. The sanction of the workhouse would drive men back to industrious participation in an economic system in which, and only in which, their wants could be satisfied. But such an assumption could not withstand the research findings of Booth and of Rowntree. Clearly, there were those in England for whom the free market did not provide the minimum of subsistence, however industrious they might be, and for these it was recognized that some other provision must be made.

But neither in their diagnosis, nor in the cure which was proposed for the evils they disclosed, was there any new approach to the analysis of social systems. They had been concerned to locate the poor so that separate provision could be made for them. They were therefore concerned with the characteristics of individuals and not with the characteristics of their society. Of course, they discovered much of the kinds of family life and the types of employment which were associated with poverty, but it was not their aim to analyse the total system of social inter- action of which these were a part. What they produced was a kind of social book-keeping, in which individual hardship could be disclosed, and appropriate measures of reform taken. These measures would be taken by voluntary agencies and state bureaucracies, whose own structure was thought to be too self- evident to require any far-reaching analysis.

The third qualification of the economists' picture arose from the study of the past and from the study of Britain's imperial subjects who had not yet reached an advanced industrial state. It was never wholly clear whether the utilitarians and the economists claimed to be advancing natural laws of human society or making recommendations regarding a social ideal. The ambiguity had to be cleared up by a theory of social evolution in which men were seen as struggling throughout history to attain the rational, scientific and individualistic standards of behaviour of civilized Englishmen. Thus Spencer contrasted his own industrial society with pre-existing 'militant societies'; Frazer dis- cussed the emergence of scientific out of magical thinking; Westermarck and Hobhouse traced the principles underlying the evolution of morality. In the course of so doing, all made lasting contributions to comparative sociology, but none went further in the analysis of their own society than the models of the market and an administratively provided welfare system suggested.

The three outstanding limitations of English sociology are its empiricism, in a special sense, its positivism and its individualism. By empiricism I mean its concentration on facts at the expense of any sort of explanatory theory. This has meant in practice an unwillingness to go beyond statements about the observable characteristics of individuals to statements about social relations. By positivism I mean the assimilation of the problem of the causes of human behaviour to that of causation in natural sciences. This again has meant an unwillingness to differentiate between normative restraints on human behaviour and natural causes. Both empiricism and positivism in this sense inhibit English sociologists from writing about social relations and social systems. But, in so far as English social thought in a wider sense is concerned with social systems and social relations, it reduces these to the product of the interaction of rational self-seeking individuals.

There may be a great sophistication about English sociology today, but it still bears the marks of its origins. If eugenics is no longer a major preoccupation, demographic research remains central and many studies of social structure turn out to be nothing more than a mass of statistical classifications. If sociology is no longer simply concerned with the study of the poor, the tradition of social book-keeping persists in the study of inequalities of income and educational opportunity. And the study of social evolution as progress towards a rational social order dies hard in some of our schools. The result has been the neglect of social interaction, social relations and social systems in favour of the study of the quantitative characteristics of individuals.

Quite different emphases, indeed, even contradictory emphases, are to be found in French sociology. It is born, not in a situation in which men are exhilarated by the progress of individual freedom and industrialism, but in a mood of sober caution as the optimistic expectations of the French Revolution fail to be realized. It views the new order of industrial society with the gravest suspicion and hankers after a new priesthood which can fulfil the functions of the church in a similar society. And even when the debate continues into the twentieth century, the greatest exponent of French sociology makes the rejection of rational individualism and utilitarianism the main thread of all his major studies.

This may seem surprising to many of those who have been taught to see Auguste Comte, the father of sociology, as the heir of the French Enlightenment. And it is true that his Law of the Three Stages, a theological, a metaphysical and a positive stage, appears at first to be nothing more than a rehash of eighteenth-century accounts of the progress of human reason. But, in fact, there is a crucial difference. What Comte asks for and what he sees as inevitable is not the liberation of individual reason, but a social order in which men accept the restraints on individual freedom which science shows to be necessary. It is because he asks us to see society as a reality *sui generis*, and not merely as the product of individual action, that he calls himself a sociologist.[1]

Durkheim takes up the same battle with Herbert Spencer. A society based purely upon contract appears to him impossible. There must be some underlying pre-contractual agreement to order before contracts begin. And to find out what this order is we have to have a scientific study of social, as distinct from individual, facts. His problem is this: 'What are the constraints which are placed upon human conduct, not by individual, biological or psychological factors, nor yet by the physical environment, but by the fact of living in a system of social interaction, a society?'

The study of facts about individuals is not of itself relevant to this question, and Durkheim indicts much English sociology when he says:

> The designation social is used with little precision. It is currently employed for practically all phenomena generally diffused within a society. But, on that basis, there are, as it were, no human events which cannot be called social. Each individual drinks, sleeps, eats, reasons and it is to society's interest that these functions are exercised in an orderly manner. If all these facts counted as social facts, sociology would have no subject matter exclusively its own, and its domain would be confused with that of biology and psychology.
>
> (Durkheim, 1938, Chap. 1)

Thus Durkheim proposes, and I think he is quite correct in this, that sociology should bring within its purview only those facts which are external to the individual and exercise constraint over him. This is not, of course, to suggest that psychology,

[1] See Auguste Comte, *The Positive Philosophy*, I, Chaps 1 and 2 and II, Chaps 1–6.

biology and other disciplines are not necessary, and that all human behaviour is explicable in terms of such external constraints. What it does suggest is that there is a special discipline whose interest lies in these particular constraints, and that it is irreducible to any other. A couple of examples may serve to illustrate this.

In the study of racial prejudice and discrimination, a great deal of work has been done to show that a small percentage of our population is governed in its behaviour towards outgroups by prejudice which arises from personality disturbance. The implication of this is that, in any social context at all, these people are likely to behave in a prejudicial way because prejudice has a function for their personalities. No one would wish to deny that prejudice has such roots. But what are we to say when a group which in one social context does not exhibit prejudice, exhibits it in another? Mill's Method of Difference would suggest that here the roots are to be found in the social context: in the system. It is this kind of determinant with which sociology is concerned.

Or again, take the problem of illegitimacy. It might be argued that illegitimate motherhood, which, although it may often be due to accident, occurs more frequently to the accident prone, is due to disorganization of the personality. But if it is shown that this phenomenon occurs more frequently among groups with one religious or, say, class affiliation than the other, it might at least be asked whether there is anything about such group membership which is conducive to illegitimate motherhood, with or without personality disturbance.

The distinction which we make here is between those causes which arise from within the observed individual and those which, from his point of view, appear as external. To make this distinction at all we must posit an actor with goals who attributes a certain meaning to his or her own acts and situations. We do not see this actor. We only see the behaviour and characteristics of individuals. But we interpret them in terms of a theoretical actor caught up in a social system; in a network of relations and norms, of expectations and sanctions.

Now unfortunately Durkheim grossly over-simplified the methodological and theoretical problems involved here. He decided that if sociology was to be objective it must treat social facts not as existing in the minds of observed individuals, but as things independent of the individual consciousness. They must not only be external from the point of view of the observed actor. They must be independent of all consciousness, having an existence of their own, outside of the individual.

The simplest example which Durkheim offers us, though it is in fact by no means simple, is law. Law exists independently of the individuals who obey it or administer it. It is therefore an external fact and one way to study society is to study law. But when there is nothing to be studied on paper or parchment or stone, there may still be vaguer forces which influence individual conduct from outside. These Durkheim calls 'collective currents'.

Now one cannot see or touch collective currents. One cannot get at them except through the subjective viewpoint of a participant actor in the situation. Durkheim, however, argues that in these circumstances the sociologist might manufacture an external thing which he can look at in the form of a statistical rate. Thus, suicide is seen as having social causes in the same sense as we suggested illegitimate motherhood does. Durkheim suggests that it is due to collective currents and that the indicators of these are to be found in differential suicide rates.

This presents us, if we follow Durkheim, with a curious dilemma. Either sociology becomes a purely statistical exercise and we are back with the kind of empiricism which he has rejected; or the statistical rates are indicators of vague and shadowy collective currents: things in themselves which we are incapable of observing or describing. The second alternative appears to lead to a highly unscientific sort of social spiritualism. Having rejected the individual mind as inaccessible to observation, Durkheim presents us with a much less defensible concept of a collective mind.

For myself, I accept Durkheim's insistence on the distinction between individual and social facts and causes. But I cannot follow him in his methodological advice as to how such facts are to be conceived. I think that we must arrive at the social, not by a simple act of observing things, but by making theoretical constructs of action and relationships in terms of which behaviour can be explained. To try to short-cut this process of theoretical construction, to suggest that the social may be distinguished by some ostensive definition, leads only to woolliness.

It should be noted, however, that Durkheim's practice is far more sophisticated than his methodological theory. He *does* talk about the action and relation systems lying behind the statistics, and it is here that he has contributed most sensitively to the development of sociology. In seeking to explain the higher suicide rate amongst Protestants as compared with that of Catholics and Jews, he does not simply suggest that some Protestants are struck by an ill-defined collective suicidal current. He sensitively discusses the meaning of the Protestant's situation in order to show how suicide may fit within that pattern of meaning. And, throughout his work, Durkheim is exploring and comparing the different ways in which individuals may be related to one another and to their society. Thus, for example, in one particularly sensitive passage he discussed the other polar extreme to the sort of contractual relationship which Spencer saw as normal in industrial society. He writes:

> The image of the one who completes us becomes inseparable from us. It thus becomes a permanent and integral part of our conscience to such a point that we can no longer separate ourselves from it and seek to increase its force.
>
> (Durkheim, 1933, p. 61)

It is clear from these examples, as it is from his discussion of the relation between the individual and the realm of the sacred in his *Elementary Forms of the Religious Life*, that Durkheim was engaged in a complicated business of theoretical construction in which his starting point was the subjective viewpoint of the observed actor. Unfortunately, he never analysed the logic of this procedure and his own formulations of the methodology of sociology point in another, and quite misleading, direction.

In practice, the tradition of Emile Durkheim has taken us far further in the understanding of human society than the English tradition ever did. It is always clear in his work that the sociologist has a special subject matter of his own, and is not engaged simply in the business of gathering statistical fact. For this reason his *Rules of Sociological Method* remains as a basic book in the sociological curriculum. Yet because of his own failure to articulate the methodology which he used, what has become recognized as the Durkheimian method remains subject to severe limitations.

The first of these is the lack of clarity in what has come to be known as 'methodological collectivism'. Social facts which exist in the air and have no relation to the individual conscious-ness seem incapable of any sort of operational definition, and many who claim to be disciples of Durkheim have eventually abandoned trying to talk about them, and have simply fallen back on a kind of statistical empiricism. Or, in so far as they have sought to describe the realm of the social, they have done so in terms of an analogy. In this case, what is described is a kind of social organism with functional subsystems which are said to control the activities which we actually observe. Such analogies usually leave us more confused than ever about the nature of social processes, especially when they are wrapped in sociological jargon.

The second defect of the Durkheimian method arises from its positivism. Durkheim was attempting, as much as any English sociologist, to assimilate social to natural causation. This is what he means when he says in his *Division of Labour* that he aims to give a positive account of the facts of the moral life. But moral norms, in fact, affect behaviour in ways quite different from natural causes. Durkheim eventually saw this in his last and greatest work, but died before he could revise his position. Thus he gives us no satisfactory analysis of the notion of social causation.

Third, and perhaps most important of all, the Durkheimian tradition leads to a kind of sociologistic fatalism. The external social facts of which Durkheim speaks become extrahuman facts unalterable by human agency. Rational control of his social situation appears as impossible for man, and it is difficult to see how social change can occur at all. If this is not simply to lead to a conservative ideology, recognition must be given to the extent to which men do control their own social situations. For the paradox of sociology lies precisely in this, that though we are compelled by forces external to ourselves, those forces are nonetheless made by men and can be changed by men. The French positivist tradition is never able to recognize this and this, if anything, is its major defect. While it does try to differentiate between social and other sorts of determinants of human behaviour in a way which English sociology does not, it seems inherently incapable of understanding the theoretical problems involved in studying the social.

Thus it is no accident that to find an appreciation of the nature of social relations and social systems, we have to look at another tradition, within which positivism was regarded as suspect. That tradition existed in Germany, where, because of the heritage of Hegelian and Kantian philosophy, a radical distinction had always been made between the social and the natural sciences. The problem here was that no kind of scientific method seemed applicable at all. Too often, historical and sociological writing was devoted to the alleged discovery of the *Geist* which gave meaning to a particular historical period or culture, and, in so far as it had a method at all, it was based on some kind of sympathetic introspection of other people and their cultures.

But the debate which broke out at the end of the nineteenth century did not turn simply upon a negative assertion of the impossibility of applying natural science methods to human affairs. The problem for Simmel, Dilthey and their contemporaries was how to define the method of the human studies with the same sort of rigour as was applied in defining natural science methods. Their starting point was an attempt to describe the process whereby we obtained knowledge of other minds and, arising from this, how we interpreted the behaviour of others as social.

Simmel gave a kind of Kantian answer.[1] If we start by assuming that we are capable of talking about social facts after observing human behaviour, he tells us, it must be because in the act of perception we impose social forms on what we see. What is required therefore is a sociology *a priori*, which, from an analysis of the contents of our own consciousness, discovers the main forms of social life. In fact, this sort of conceptual analysis has been very fruitful in sociology, but it fails to give us the means of interpreting concrete and particular situations.

What Dilthey proposed was somewhat different. Given that the object of the human studies was the understanding of the meaning of human behaviour, his problem was to describe how

[1] See Georg Simmel, 'How is Society Possible?' in Kurt Wolff (ed.), *Georg Simmel 1858–1918*, Ohio State University Press, 1959.

we were capable of understanding the meaning of the behaviour of those whom we observed. Dilthey[1] thought that this was only possible if we could create a cultural psychology which analysed the contents of human consciousness as such. This cultural psychology would then be the 'mathematics', the basic and elementary human science, which would provide us with the key to the meaning of all the concrete and particular situations we encountered.

What Max Weber sought to show when he joined in this argument was that, while *Verstehen* might be the object of the social sciences, and that, therefore, their method could not be totally assimilated to the natural sciences, it was nonetheless possible to show that the process of understanding conformed to the general canons of scientific procedure. He sought to show this first in the case of the understanding of the action of an individual actor and then in the much more complex case of the understanding of social relations and structures.

The key to Weber's interpretation of the understanding of action is that he suggests that what is involved is the testing of hypotheses. He does not claim that the meaning of action is grasped by an unexplained act of sympathetic introspection. Rather, confronted with phenomena of human behaviour, we hypothesize that such behaviour has meaning for a hypothetical actor. The hypothesis is subjectively formulated. It posits an actor who may, or may not, have goals but who in any case imputes meaning to the objects in his situation. But on the other hand, these meanings are explicitly formulated and therefore open to test. In this respect, Weber's conception of understanding is quite different from that of his predecessors, who suggest no such explicit technique of hypothesis formulation and testing (see Weber, 1968, Chap. 1).

Merely to make such a hypothesis explicit, however, is inadequate. We may simply be putting forward a plausible story or, as Weber says, giving an explanation which is adequate on the level of meaning. What we have yet to do is to show that the meaningful hypothesis, in terms of which we have explained the action, does actually apply. This we must do by showing that other consequences of our hypothesis do, as a matter of fact,

---

[1] See H. A. Hodges, *The Philosophy of Wilhelm Dilthey*, 1952.

occur. This is what I believe Weber means when he speaks of a causally adequate explanation.

An example may serve to illustrate the point. We are confronted with the behaviour of a man suddenly going out into his back yard and chopping wood. The positivist would seek to explain this by correlating the behaviour of wood-chopping men with their other behaviour and characteristics. The school of *Verstehen* as a whole would say that this misses the point, which is to grasp the subjective meaning of the behaviour for the wood-chopper. Weber suggests that this can be done by the testing of alternative hypotheses. Two alternative stories about our man would be (*i*) that he feels cold and is about to make a fire, (*ii*) that he has had a row with his wife. Both of these are plausible stories; both make sense. But on investigation we may find that whereas he makes no effort to return to his house to build a fire, but does avoid his wife or snap back angrily at her in conversation, it would seem that it is our second hypothesis which holds.

It should be noted that explanations of action of this sort are not, in the ordinary sense, psychological explanations. They make no immediate reference to the drives and instincts of individuals. They explain action in terms of the subjectively understood meaning of the situation for the actor. Such explanations in terms of the situation's meaning bring us towards sociology, or at least are explanations in terms of a theory of action.

We become more explicitly sociological in our explanation, however, when the meaning of the situation given in our hypothesis involves reference to other actors. As Weber puts it, 'action is social in so far as, by virtue of the subjective meaning attached to it by the acting individuals, it takes account of the behaviour of others and is thereby oriented in its course.'[1] There is reference here to external social factors as in Durkheim. And, as in Durkheim, the social is not regarded as irreducible to the psychological.

The notion of 'taking account of the behaviour of others' is, however, ambiguous and according to which meaning we attribute to the phrase, we get sociological explanations of varying difficulty. On the one hand, we may mean simply that the actor adjusts to the expected behaviour of others, in which case

[1] Max Weber, *Economy and Society*, 1968, I, p. 4.

the other's behaviour is simply a brute fact of the external environment. Or, on the other hand, we may mean that our actor makes demands on other individuals. In this case it is not only his own behaviour which is explained in terms of the meaning of his situation but also that of all the others whom he brings in as allies.

It is here that we approach the Weberian notion of social relations. Given a hypothetical actor imputing meaning to his situation, the behaviour of whole chains of individuals may be explained. If I expect that other individuals will abstain from interfering with my property and that policemen will prevent people from doing so, the behaviour of the policemen may be explained by reference to the meaning of my situation. It may, of course, be explained in other ways too, but the specifically sociological type of explanation lies in the reference to the meaning of the situation for the actor whose action is the starting point of our model.

We see here an alternative to Durkheim's 'methodological collectivism' which Popper has called 'methodological individualism'.[1] It cannot be too strongly maintained that this does not involve any sort of psychological reductionism. The individual is still seen as subject to restraints external to himself and distinct from the restraints of his own psychological and biological make-up. But these external restraints cease to be mysterious supra-individual entities and are explained, in the model, in terms of the interaction of individuals.

A further important corollary of Weber's position is this. The system of social relations which affects our behaviour is shown to be a human thing, and it is therefore subject to human control and manipulation. While it is of the first importance for the sociologist to show that human beings are, as a matter of fact, affected by, and responsive to, the expectations implicit in a meaning system, it is also the case that they may reject these demands. Hence a sociological explanation always takes the form, 'In so far as a system is to be maintained in which a specific kind of action can be pursued, behaviour b, c, d, etc. will be required of second and third parties. But there is always the possibility that

[1] Karl Popper, *The Poverty of Historicism*, 1957. Popper understood Weber's type of methodological individualism. Unfortunately, very few of Popper's disciples or his critics have done so.

such a system will be rejected and overthrown by second and third parties.'

This approach to sociology, which retains Durkheim's distinction between the sociological and the psychological and yet does justice to human freedom, was, for Weber, not merely a matter of methodological theory. It was an approach which he applied and validated in the course of comparative studies of civilizations, and of institutions within civilizations, which is without parallel in sociological literature.

In the first place he used it to make sense of Western capitalist society. Instead of starting with the meaning of the individual's situation described by Marx, in which primacy is accorded to the individual's involvement in economic production, Weber starts with the meaning of the situation for the typical Protestant Calvinist, who knows that God has predestined some to work for his inscrutable purposes. Weber shows that such a set of attitudes might lead to a personal self-discipline and rationality, which would have institutional consequences for business enterprise, for technology, for bureaucratic organization and many other aspects of life. And his predictions here appear to be at least loosely validated by the observed differences in institutional development in capitalist and non-capitalist countries.

Like Marx, Weber was not afraid to attempt a general model for our society as a whole. It may well be that this model, like Marx's, is imperfect and relative. Weber would not have denied this. But he was sufficiently aware of the chains of institutional interconnection not to limit sociology to simple causal relations between one institution and another. The idea that we should confine sociological analysis to these is one which has been propagated by Karl Popper. He never justifies it, however, and it seems to derive from his ideological view that only piecemeal social reform is desirable, rather than from the nature of social facts. What Weber has shown is that there is some use, albeit a limited one, in trying to establish a general model in order to obtain an over-all understanding of our civilization.

At the same time, Weber did not stop there. He was not simply concerned to establish some sort of philosophy of history. Much more important to him was the detached work of analysing basic institutional structures and their immediate interrelations in a variety of civilizations. To give only one example, he produced an account of bureaucratic structures of administration, by contrasting them with other administrative forms. Here he started with the notion that the object of bureaucratic administration is that the will of one individual may be carried out rationally and reliably by many agents. Given this assumption, a variety of consequences follow for the pattern of social relations, which are incumbent upon bureaucrats, inside and outside the organization. In similar fashion, he went on to explore the different possibilities which might exist in labour markets, in cities, in religious thought and organization, in the relation between religious and administrative functionaries, in social class and status systems and in many other areas. Always his approach is faithful to the method of *Verstehen* which he originally proposed. He starts with the meaning of the action situation for a typical participant and, having clarified this, goes on to draw out the patterns of social relations which it implies.

This style of sociology, as distinct from that of either the English or the French tradition, has been subjected to two opposite criticisms. On the one hand, positivists have maintained that its hypotheses and ideal types cannot in their nature be tested, and hence cannot be accorded scientific status. On the other, anti-positivists have argued that because Weber failed to close the gap between *Verstehen* and causal proof, the goal of a science of sociology must be abandoned.

My own sympathies probably lie with the latter critics, for if science cannot grasp social action and social relations as meaningful, so much the worse for science. Yet I do believe that Weber did point the way to a relatively rigorous and relatively scientific way of analysing social structures. It may be that experimental circumstances rarely arise in which his hypotheses and types may be fully tested, but there is something to be said for logical rigour in defining social structures, so that the pure types may act as yardsticks against which actual cases may be measured. I believe that we need such a method for the analysis and understanding of our own and other societies today.

What I suggest we should be doing as sociologists today is this. We must avoid all those short cuts which appear to give us respectability, because they involve quantification, even at the expense of failing to refer to social facts. Thus we should not substitute the statistical categorization of the population for studies of the structure of social action. And we should not think that when we have cross-tabulated and correlated hundreds of variables on a computer, that we have said anything sociologically significant. We should be concerned, as Marx and Weber were, to try to understand the dynamics of our own and other societies. Is there a social system which may be called the welfare state or welfare capitalism? If so, what pattern of institutional interrelations does it imply? Can the structure of social interaction in one-party states only be understood emotionally as a pattern of butchery and imprisonment without trial, or has this kind of society an understandable and meaningful pattern? Is there perhaps a convergence between all industrial societies of a certain level of development, whether they call themselves communist or capitalist or democratic? We badly need a Marx or Weber to answer questions on this scale.

And at a more immediate level, we need to establish working models, in terms of which we may analyse the structure and dynamics of our class system, of urban life in our expanding and declining urban centres, of the social relations involved in setting up planning machinery in a market economy, of the relations between immigrant groups and their hosts, of different types of industrial and administrative organizations, of occupational cultures and of communal sub-cultures.

In understanding these tasks we should seek to distinguish our work from that of mere journalists by the logical rigour of our concepts, and by the precision of our description. And we should take all possible advantage of modern techniques of mathematical analysis and data processing. But if there is one thing that is more essential than all these it is the exercise of the sociological imagination, and the ability to grasp the social processes which lie behind the facts of human behaviour. It is this that we can learn from the classic sociological tradition which I have been trying to describe. And it is this which gives sociology its place in the university curriculum, above all, as one of the humanities.

I do not think that this view of sociology is one which will command immediate assent in Britain. Our individualistic, empiricist and positivist traditions are all inhospitable to it: the present fashionableness of sociology will mean that many who call themselves sociologists will set themselves lesser objectives.

But I am convinced, nonetheless, that the tradition which I have described can do much to illuminate the present human condition, and that the vocation of the sociologist is one to which it is well worth while trying to recruit our students.

7

Institutions and men

Professor C. Wright Mills caricatured the views of his great contemporary Talcott Parsons on the question of social change as follows:

> One point does puzzle me a little: given this social equilibrium and all the socialisation and control that man it, how is it possible that anyone should ever get out of line? This I cannot explain very well, that is in terms of my Systematic and General theory. And there is another point that is not as clear as I should like it to be: how should I account for social change, that is for history? About these two problems I recommend that whenever you come upon them you conduct empirical investigations.
>
> (Mills, 1959)

This *is*, of course, a caricature of what Talcott Parsons says, but it is a relevant caricature for, like most sociological theorists, Parsons, having built up his theoretical account of society as a system of social action, and having shown why all social roles and institutions are as they are, has the greatest difficulty in offering any reason as to why they should change. And since this sort of theoretical attitude has practical consequences, it is worth while asking whether some sort of alternative sociology is not called for. I want, in this chapter, to suggest some of the main lines of such a sociology, and to indicate what I believe to be its consequences in terms of the attitudes which we adopt towards existing institutions.

The reason why the approach to the study of society typified by that of Professor Parsons has such wide currency is easy to understand. The nineteenth century, in which the main lines of the sociological tradition were laid down, was a century of rapid change, and hence a century in which men frequently projected utopias for their own future. When such utopias proved impossible of realization, it was natural that the more profound thinkers of the time should have injected into social thought a strong dose of political realism. The burden of their argument was that all spheres of human activity, all social institutions, were so interconnected that it was not possible to bring about social change at will within any one sphere without making change in other spheres as well. Comte went on from this to draw conservative conclusions, devoting many pages of his *Positive Philosophy* to deriding wild-eyed idealists who, although they could accomplish little in the long run, might, as he put it, 'make terrible devastation in the interval'. Marx, on the other hand, drew the conclusion that scientific socialism demanded revolution in the economic base, as the prerequisite of all other forms of revolution.

More recently, a similar argument has been put forward by social anthropologists engaged in advising colonial administrators. They would protest at the ham-handedness of these administrators in trying to reform the customs of the tribes entrusted to their care, without really understanding the meaning of these customs. They went on then to argue that a culture or a social system must be understood as an interconnected whole, in which change in any one sphere must be accompanied by change in all the others.

One result of this static approach by sociologists to their subject matter has been a radical split between the historians and the sociologists. The historians have been inclined to present history as a mere chronological sequence of events without looking for general underlying causal factors. And the sociologists have concentrated entirely on a quest for these general factors to the exclusion of any interest in historical change. This split, however, could be overcome if sociologists would take another look at their theory of social institutions, to see whether it should not be restated in such a way as to account for change and development.

The social anthropologists who have contributed so much to our understanding of the nature of social systems were themselves always aware of an important difficulty in their theory. In answering the question, 'What determines the nature of an institution?', they saw that a distinction had to be made between its declared purpose and what they came to call its 'function' or sometimes its latent function. But having made this distinction they concentrated solely on the latent function, which was seen either as the contribution which the institution made to satisfying the biological needs of the population, or as its contribution to maintaining the social structures of the *status quo*. In either case this meant that the form of the institution was tied down to, and determined by, an unchanging factor. Thus, despite its insights gained from switching attention to the unintended consequences of human action, the theory offered no explanation of historical development.

Now I should like to draw attention to three major points at which this theory of institutions might be revised and would suggest that, if it is revised in this way, not only would it be better able to account for historical development, but it would also profoundly affect our attitude to the institutions with which we have to deal.

First, I should like to raise the question of the role of the creative individual in social progress. Second, I should like to deal with the problem of the inherent conflict of purposes which affects most institutions, and third, I want to talk about the role of the ordinary individual, the layman, in shaping the institutions in which he participates.

A particularly useful contribution to sociological understanding has, I believe, recently been made by Raymond Williams (1961b) in his book *The Long Revolution*. It arises out of his attempt to reconcile the different usages of the term 'culture' by sociologists and critics. Unlike many of his colleagues, Williams accepts the sociologists' usage of the term to refer to the whole way of life of a people, not just its books and pictures, but its methods of production, its form of education, its way of forming trade unions and so on. The problem then is to show how the creators of culture in the other sense participate in this way of life.

Williams draws attention, as many of the critics of sociology have drawn attention, to the lifelessness of most sociological and historical studies of past epochs and cultures, and suggests that what is missing is any understanding of what he calls 'the structure of feeling' of the period as it appeared to its more sensitive participants. In so doing, he suggests the one important factor in the institutional complex which most sociologists leave out. This factor is the work done by the artists and intellectuals of a period in articulating the meanings and purposes of the cultural system and in positing new meanings and purposes which will shape the culture in the future.

I would not wish, in opposition to anthropologists like Malinowski, to suggest that the satisfaction of biological needs is irrelevant to this system of meanings, or, in opposition to Marxists, that they are not intimately bound up with an understanding of the form of the social relations of production. But by tying social institutions down to biological needs we leave many problems unresolved. Whose needs are to be satisfied and at what level? Surely this is a matter of the values implicit in the culture. And as to the Marxist interpretation of institutions, Marx himself was always at pains to point out that the social relations of production were not simply imposed on us by nature, but were themselves the product of human agency. Thus, much fruitful thinking is now going on within the framework of revisionist Marxism about the kind of relation which exists between basis and superstructure.

Hence, it is quite compatible with the sociologist's picture of an institutional system to argue that the determination of institutional forms depends in part on the meanings and purposes which a people sets for itself, that these may change, and that the articulation of new meanings is always the work of a creative minority in a society.

A similar point to this, in fact, emerges very strongly in the course of Max Weber's historical and comparative studies of religion and social structure in China, India and Palestine. One of the major distinguishing features of the ideological situation in Ancient Palestine (Weber, 1952), as Weber saw it, lay in the existence of a class of freelance prophets, who were not merely state employed literati, or a group of royal chaplains, but visionaries who attempted to re-orient the religious thinking of the masses in accordance with what they saw as the needs of the time.

The second point about the sociological theory of institutions which I should like to criticize is the apparent assumption that those who participate in them consciously share common purposes. This, it seems to me, is only rarely the case in history.

Far more usually, the situation is one in which the officers of an institution impose rules of conduct on the laity and the laity more or less willingly, or more or less sullenly, acquiesces. At one extreme we might, it is true, have total agreement on, and internalized commitment to, the values pursued. But at the other extreme there might be total opposition to the officers so that they rule, in effect, by force. And the usual situation is one in which the activities of the officers are consented to, not because they are those which the laity desire, or because they fulfil purposes internalized by the laity, but simply because the officers are believed to hold some kind of legitimate authority. Again, it was Max Weber who saw that the concept of legitimate authority was the central one in the analysis of institutions.

Such a concept, too, is at the core of Professor Dahrendorf's recent attempt to revise the Marxist notion of class conflict in his book *Class and Class Conflict in Industrial Society*. According to Dahrendorf there is always, in every institutional situation, a conflict between those who possess authority and those who do not. And it is when conflicts in one such situation overlap with or mesh with those in another that we get the sort of over-all conflict of social purposes which the Marxist model of revolutionary development suggests.

Now if this view is correct, our theory of institutional interconnections must be considerably modified. Institutions might be looked on as imposed by a ruling élite, contrary to the aims of those who are compelled to work within their framework. Or it may be held that, while in the first place they arose to meet a commonly felt need, in the long run the officers ran counter to the purposes of the laity, who would then work out techniques of resistance, or even seek to develop their own counter-institutions to work against those of the officer élite. In either case one would expect to find within the institution, not a clearly defined purpose, but a latent conflict of purposes, which would provide the dynamic for institutional change.

This brings us to the third point. Because institutions are imposed they can never be really static; for the ordinary men and women on whom they are imposed will continually be groping for new forms which give more adequate expression to their needs. Hence it is to these ordinary men and women and their needs that we must look, in part at least, for the creative element in social institutions. This was a fact noted by both Max Weber and Ernst Troeltsch in their work on the sociology of religion. Weber always couples his studies of the creative religious ideas of intellectuals with an account of the economic and religious interests of ordinary people and he seeks to show why particular religious formulations have always appealed to certain classes. Troeltsch goes even further, stressing not merely the fact that the religious response of the masses is related to their economic interests, but that by their very naïveté, their innocence of the doctrines of the schools, they are equipped to play a genuinely creative part in religious history. As he puts it,

> It is the lower classes who do the really creative work, forming communities on a genuinely religious basis. They alone unite imagination and simplicity of feeling with a non-reflective habit of mind, a primitive energy and an urgent sense of need.
>
> (Troeltsch, 1931)

Intellectuals and prophets, as we have said, have their part to play. But it is only because of this substratum of unsatisfied and incoherent aspirations which underlies the institutional super-structure, that they have the power to influence history.

Now the three points which I have made are not really distinct. The creative minorities and the masses unite to form new movements. And the new movements often develop in an atmosphere of revolt against the authority of an institutional élite. What is certain, however, is that no objective study of institutions is complete unless it includes an account of the movements and incipient movements which arise within them. A study which fails to take them into account can have little but ideological significance.

The issue here, however, is not merely a theoretical one. Our way of studying and analysing institutions profoundly affects our attitude towards them. If all that our sociology shows is that institutions, as they are, are 'necessary' then there is nothing for it but to submit. But if we recognize that most institutions have, within them, an inherent conflict of purposes, we are bound to take sides. As Karl Mannheim (1960) pointed out in his greatest work *Ideology and Utopia*, the conception of a purely objective sociology is naïve. Sociology is concerned with showing the necessity of social facts. But what is necessary from the point of view of those who wish to preserve the *status quo*, is by no means necessary from the point of view of those who wish to change it.

Nonetheless, there is a warning here both for those who set up institutions and for those who organize men to change the existing order. For it is easy to see how any organization which fails to take account of the changing purposes of men will ossify, how its offices will cease to have meaning except for their incumbents, and how those incumbents may come to be merely a privileged élite intent on preserving the perquisites of office. In such circumstances there is less and less possibility of an appeal to common purpose, less and less acceptance of the legitimacy of the office holder's authority, and more and more reliance on authoritarian methods of rule. This is as true in the history of churches as it is in the history of political parties, and as true in those parties and sects concerned with promoting change as it is in those intent on maintaining stability. The point is well made again by Raymond Williams when he protests against what he calls the 'refusal to accept the creative capacities of life, a habit of thinking that the future has now to be determined by some ordinance of our own mind', and then goes on to say that, 'We do this as conservatives trying to prolong old forms, we do this as socialists trying to prescribe the new man' (Williams, 1961a).

Of course the advantages of bureaucratic organization are obvious. Max Weber saw it as the perfect mechanism whereby a single will could be made effective through many separate agents. The communist method of political organization known as democratic centralism has harnessed the same principles in the service of social change. But the benefits of such organizational methods are bought at a price. Ultimately, effective and lasting organizations depend not merely upon the clarity of their organizational principles, but on their capacity to give expression to newly felt needs, on the freedom of the laity to express itself and on the freedom of the creative minority to articulate the new meanings and purposes which appear. Once an institution, or a society, closes the channels of communication to ordinary men and renders its intellectuals harmless by putting them to work justifying the *status quo*, the life has gone out of it and it is ultimately doomed to extinction. The test of life in an institution will be the extent to which its intellectuals are able to talk directly and listen directly, not just to the office holders, but to the ordinary men and women whose needs it purports to serve.

I have spoken primarily about the life-cycle of individual institutions. But the same problem exists if we look at total societies. There is a tendency in every society for the way of life of a privileged stratum to masquerade as the culture of the society, for its educational system to become more and more concerned with perpetuating that way of life, for techniques to be worked out to exclude the cultural participation of the masses, and for the intellectuals to concentrate on the learning of ritualistic academic formulas. For myself, I believe that all these things are in large measure true of contemporary British society. Our educational system is still riddled with class privilege, it fails to adapt its curricula to the needs of a new age, and the only channels of communication open are those of the mass media, usually better fitted to the purposes of manipulation than to any genuine interchange of feeling and meaning and ideas. If I am right about this, we are living with a dying culture whose life can be saved only in so far as its intellectuals are willing to look beyond the walls of their closed academies, and to relate their thinking to the aspirations of ordinary men and women.

8

The likely future of British sociology

In trying to say what the discipline of sociology will look like in the 1970s, one is torn between writing about what one hopes and what is likely to be. Two factors may lead to a divergence between these two. One is the technological revolution in data-processing and computation which means, among other things, that technicians may take over the discipline, leaving little scope for a discussion of its fundamental theoretical problems. The other is that with headlong university expansion there will be dilution in the teaching profession. Many barbarities are therefore likely to be committed in the name of sociology and much depends upon the capacity of those who stand for the classic tradition to make themselves heard.

Yet there are, at present, reasons why hope may be realistic. For the challenge of the computer has itself provoked a fierce debate about the nature of the discipline and an anti-positivist voice has been heard more strongly than it had been for many years. In the United States, despite a systematic attempt to denigrate and devalue the work of the late C. Wright Mills, the methodological tradition for which he stood lives on, and not only among writers of the left. Peter Berger's *Invitation to Sociology* (1966), aptly subtitled *A Humanistic Perspective*, is a good example of the kind of work which a good philosophic training can produce. And a book such as Aaron Cicourel's *Method and Measurement in Sociology* (1964) shows that the argument may be carried to the point of detailed analysis of the inadequacies of the sacred methods of survey research. What may emerge from all this is a much more sophisticated research strategy than is usually evident as interview schedules are ground through the computer.

The same argument is likely to be carried on in Britain. Here, Winch's little book *The Idea of a Social Science and its*

Relation to Philosophy (1958), arguing that relationships of meaning are not capable of being handled by natural-science methods, remains as an embarrassment to those sociologists who have understood its critical argument. Hans Rickman's *Understanding and the Human Studies* (1967) may serve to revive interest in the work of Wilhelm Dilthey and the notion of *Verstehen* (the understanding of cultural meanings) in social science. And recently some important papers have been published by W. G. Baldamus[1] of Birmingham, questioning the idea that social science proceeds by making crucial discoveries which confirm, falsify or generate theories and arguing for the importance of the activity of 'theorizing' in its own right.

These arguments are the most important because, at least in America, they have led to a degree of fight-back from those interested in the development of mathematical sociology. Whereas previously quantitative methods were developed largely in the context of market research for which the concept of interaction was not central, much recent work has been derived from conflict research, which though it may take a mathematical form does take the 'double contingency' of interaction situations seriously. This sort of mathematical theory cannot proceed very far without some sort of engagement with the classic tradition. Hence it is not surprising that, among those who welcome the revolution in research technique which has taken place, there are those who are insisting that the questions which are fed into the computer should be sociologically significant.

Theoretical debate may in these circumstances assume a new importance. And at the centre of this will be the growing convergence of functionalist and conflict theory. No one today seriously holds to the theory of the perfectly integrated social system; equally no one believes that Hobbes's war of all against all provides an adequate sociological model. The functionalist gives growing emphasis to the mechanisms whereby conflict is adapted to, and managed, and the conflict theorist investigates the details of conflict resolution. And it is increasingly clear here that what matters is not the attempt to state a formal theory of integration or conflict, but the alerting of the researcher

[1] W. G. Baldamus, University of Birmingham, Faculty of Commerce, Discussion Papers Series E, Nos 1, 2, 5, 12, 13, 16. See bibliography for full references.

to important problems, whether in the field of international, interracial, industrial or intergenerational relations.

If this remains our goal, then the tradition of conceptual analysis applied to the forms of social interaction, passed on to us by Parsons from Simmel, becomes extremely important. It is true that the conceptual fecundity of the later work of Parsons has led to a kind of scholasticism in sociology, and there seem to be an increasing number of sociologists in Britain, as in other countries, who spend too much of their time in sterile conceptual controversy. But the debate about formal concepts has left a useful legacy and one would hope that students of the next generations will use it well. The hope is not that they should become 'role-theorists' or 'reference-group theorists' but that they will become familiar with the forms of social relations in order to apply these concepts in the course of empirical research.

At a time when sociology threatens to break down into a series of sub-disciplines (organizational theory, or industrial, political, educational or urban sociology) this set of formal concepts, more precisely spelled out than in the past, may help to provide one focus of unity. But at this as at any other time, there will also be other reasons of a more practical kind for maintaining a community of interest. It is certain that the driving force behind the work of many workers in many different fields will be a desire to make sense of their times, just as it was the driving force behind the work of Comte, Marx, Spencer, Durkheim or Weber. It is therefore convenient to survey the various special fields of investigation which are opening up in the light of certain general questions about the nature of advanced industrial societies, of underdeveloped societies, and of the international social system.

As far as the first of these is concerned, the following questions are raised in recent sociology. Is it the case that advanced capitalist societies have solved their major problems of economic and political stability? Is it the case that the working class has now been successfully 'incorporated' into the value-system; that there is a consensus about the degree of public and private ownership and about appropriate measures of welfare; and that ideological politics must be explained as deviance? Is there a common level of mobility which is achieved by all societies at a certain level of industrial advancement? In what ways are the motivations of owners, managers and workers tied into the organization of the modern corporation? What is the effect of welfare provisions and housing on the family? Is there a universal trend towards the isolated conjugal family, and if so what are the implications of this for the system as a whole? Does the typical pattern of suburban life mean that democratically controlled middle-level organizations have been weakened; or are there still opinion leaders who play a mediating role between the big bureaucracies and the family? What is the long-term significance of mass protest movements in the modern state?

American sociologists have produced a number of important and well-documented books which give optimistic answers to these questions,[1] and respectable Sunday-paper sociology in Britain has largely echoed what they have to say. Their ideas are, however, being subjected to critical scrutiny by the best graduate students in both countries and this may lead to some of the most significant work of the 1970s. Although such work may have considerable ideological significance, it will at least raise basic structural questions. One of its implications may be a move away from the social book-keeping tradition of British sociology which arose in a generation whose main preoccupation was with poverty and inequality. It is impossible, here, to go on to specify in great detail the kind of study to which this may lead, but something may be said of likely shifts of interest in the fields of political, industrial and urban sociology.

Political sociology in Britain in the past has tended to centre on a sort of political market research, and somewhat journalistic accounts of the structure of political parties. Assumed in this is the permanence of the basic framework of British politics. What may now begin to happen is that questions will be posed in political sociology about the changing nature of political activity itself. We shall, of course, still derive much important information from the older sort of study about the class composition of party membership and about élites and oligarchies in political parties; but these will be placed within a wider framework, which includes the study of mass society, of the mass media, and of protest movements which challenge the consensus or are directed

[1] See, for the optimistic and conservative answers to these questions: S. M. Lipset, *Political Man*, 1959; Daniel Bell, *The End of Ideology*, 1960; and William Kornhauser, *The Politics of Mass Society*, 1960.

to issues (like nuclear warfare, race or the Common Market) where the consensus breaks down or has nothing to say.

In the industrial field we may pass beyond the kind of study of informal work groups which courses in management serve to foster, and produce an industrial sociology which draws on the tradition of Weber and Marx as well as of Mayo. Sociologists may refuse to be simply technicians and may attempt to produce a typology of industrial enterprises which does justice to the complexity of the conflicting motivations among managers and workers that are built into them. At the moment it must be admitted there is a confusion of voices in this field, but a debate has taken root among sociologists which should be fruitful. Equally, the industrial sociologist may find himself liberated from his purely technical role by the application of objectively formulated theories of conflict resolution to industrial disputes, and the study of occupational sub-cultures may do much to refine crude models of working-class behaviour.

In urban sociology the outlook may, at first, seem rather more bleak. The sociologist may find himself called upon either to provide data for the planner or to make vague recommendations about the good life in new terms. But studies are going on, especially in the sphere of family sociology and race relations, which raise far more fundamental questions about the nature of the city. Does the city inevitably consign its unacceptable and deviant population to ghettos? Is the suburban trend, and its extension into commuter villages, inevitable? What effect does working-class political power have on the structure, and what differences are there in this respect as between America, Britain and Europe? These are, in a sense, old questions, which were raised by writers like Park and Wirth a generation ago. But they may be raised again as pragmatic planning begins to present us with new problems.

Underlying the problems of all these fields is the problem of social stratification. The popular view is that, in Harold Macmillan's words, 'the class struggle is obsolete'. Maybe, in the simplest forms in which vulgar Marxism envisages it, it is. But, as Goldthorpe and Lockwood (1969) have shown, the crude thesis of the *embourgeoisement* of the affluent working class does not stand up to empirical examination. There are still important cultural differences between classes in our society. There is still a degree of corporate class consciousness. And there are, if not class conflicts in the simple old-fashioned revolutionary sense, at least built-in group conflicts which it is the job of the sociologist to understand. Maybe, as Coser (1956) and others have suggested, these conflicts are diverse in nature and cancel each other out, thereby ensuring the stability of the society. But even if this were true, the mapping of these conflicts would be important in any adequate model of our society; and if it were not true, it would be even more important for any real understanding of our likely social future.

All these developments, however, assume a certain insularity. They exclude not merely the study of the underdeveloped countries, but also of advanced industrial countries in the communist world. But already a fierce argument has broken out about the degree of similarity or convergence between capitalist and communist society. Goldthorpe (1964), for instance, has questioned the ideologically comforting thesis that all industrial societies at a certain level of advancement must, because of technological factors, have similar patterns and rates of mobility, and directed attention to the sorts of empirical evidence necessary to answer such questions. Issues of this kind will be resolved the more readily, now that the Iron Curtain has to some extent been lifted between western sociologists and their colleagues in Russia and eastern Europe. One thing which we should surely be able to look forward to is a widening of our theories of industrial society to include both the capitalist and the communist varieties.

A central argument which arises in this context concerns the implications of industrialization for presently underdeveloped countries. Is there a complex of institutions which necessarily goes along with industrialization, or are some at least of those which we take for granted optional for newly industrializing countries? Much patient comparative work of the kind to be found in William Goode's *World Revolution and Family Patterns* (1963), will have to be undertaken to answer this question. But, as Goode realizes, industrialization may not always be the crucial variable. It may be political independence itself or urbanization or the modernizing effect of education and contact with the advanced societies.

A great deal has been accomplished in the past ten years by way of empirical studies of the political systems of the ex-colonial territories. We are now at a stage where we might perhaps begin to establish some sort of typology of the single-party state. Weber's analysis of the main types of political authority will be helpful here, as writers like David Apter (1965) have shown, but these concepts need to be supplemented by others to take account of all the nuances of modern political systems.

Urbanization has again been extensively documented and it may soon be possible to classify some of the major phenomena to which it leads, and to produce some significant generalizations, at least for the major cultural regions. One thing which is certain is that the African or Asian town will show marked differences from the European and North American variety. But perhaps more interesting than an analysis of rural-urban differences will be the theme of what Lerner (1967) has called the passing of traditional society; the continuous erosion of traditional patterns of culture and social organization even at village level, in the face of schooling, the mass media, wage labour and the political socialization of the population. In studying this phenomenon we may even learn something about ourselves.

Finally, if it is to be the characteristic of sociology in the future, as in the past, that it engages with the major political problems of its time, sociologists will increasingly be concerned with the study of the international social order which has been produced by the nuclear stalemate. It would be foolish here, as in most areas of social organization, to suppose that sociologists can discover laws which will determine human behaviour. The sociologist, with his handbook of conflict resolution, may be blown up with the rest of us if a politician miscalculates. But it is nonetheless true that sociological analyses of the development of crisis situations has already found an answer in governmental interest in the sociological theory of the international power game. The fact that a major session of the World Congress of Sociology at Evian was devoted to the sociology of international relations suggests that sociologists have this topic high on their agenda for the future.

It must be emphasized that the development of sociology will not proceed through some sudden new discovery on the empirical level. Nor are we to expect the emergence of a sociological Newton. What we may expect is that, because of new ways of looking at things, because of hard slogging empirical research, and because new social and political factors become problematic, sociology may look considerably different in ten years' time. We should remember that the theory of the classics was focused particularly on understanding the new social order brought into being by the early Industrial Revolution and the French Revolution. Today, as we embark on a new industrial revolution in the advanced countries, as we face the problems involved in the relation between these countries and the developing ones, and as we confront the world order of the nuclear age, we need a sociological theory far less insular in outlook. It could be that in these circumstances we will find a new Comte or Marx or Weber or Durkheim.

At the moment this is just what sociology has not produced. It seems to be caught, as C. Wright Mills suggested, between grand theory and abstracted empiricism. The most popular form of grand theory offered to us by Talcott Parsons turns out to be simply a searching conceptual analysis which, useful though it is in suggesting ways of formulating problems, does not tackle these problems themselves. And on the other hand the journals report article after weary article in which yet another correlation is tested and established or discarded, leading to little cumulative knowledge about social systems. But here and there the kind of argument which Comte started continues. It is to its continuance rather than to the revolution in research technology that one must look for the emergence of a new and more illuminating sociology in the 1970s.

The grand masters of sociology

Part II

9   The sociological tradition and its ideological context

The object of this chapter is to try to understand the reasons why problems of sociological theory and method emerge in the form in which they do at the present time, by showing the way in which the classical tradition of sociological theory emerged from the ideological context of its time, by contrasting some of the developments and forms of contemporary sociology with those of the great tradition, and then by asking why it is that contemporary theory should be taking the special form which it does. Naturally no such exercise would be undertaken unless one were convinced that it was possible, at least partially, to transcend one's times and to draw out of the great tradition as well as out of more recent theories the way towards a less timebound and insular sociology.

The notion of a science of society was a late development of the European enlightenment and developed differently in England, France and Germany in terms of the particular version of the enlightenment doctrine which prevailed in the three different countries, in the light of their own experience of political and industrial revolution. The first significant figures who could be counted as sociologists, who arose from these traditions, were Spencer in England, Comte in France and Marx in Germany, or, perhaps one should say in the German tradition. It is only possible to understand their positions, however, if one sees Spencer against the background provided by Adam Smith and Jeremy Bentham, Comte against that provided by de Maistre and St-Simon, and Marx against that of Hegel and the young Hegelians. Moreover, it is only possible to understand fully the implications of their work in so far as one recognizes how complex was the dialectic between them, so that the full extent of the difference between Comte and Spencer becomes apparent in Durkheim's critique of the utilitarian tradition, and the long-term implications of Marxism are only understandable in terms of his engagement with the thought of St-Simon on the one hand, and the English economists on the other, and his consequent break with his Hegelian past. Finally an alternative sociological method and an alternative conception of human nature to that of Marx and of Durkheim, emerges in the neo-Kantian movement and above all in the work of Max Weber. The result of this complex interplay of intellectual traditions is that the sociological heritage of the nineteenth century is eventually embodied in the work of Marx, Durkheim and Weber.

The central notion of the enlightenment is that of human progress and on the face of it the notion of progress towards greater human happiness and rationality would seem to be a unitary one (see Bury, 1932; Becker and Barnes, 1961). Yet as soon as one looks at the way in which this notion is developed in different contexts, it becomes evident that it is capable of a variety of different interpretations. In England, the idea which takes hold is that of greater and greater individual rationality and the liberation of market forces which that implies. In France, what appeals is the growth of science and technology and the application of scientific principles of investigation to discovering what the future social order must be like. In Germany, on a peculiarly abstract level, the question is whether mind or spirit can assert itself over matter, and over sheer historical accident, so that the shape of human history can be creatively controlled and determined.

These different emphases are clearly not simply a matter of intellectual preference. The choices made are those which seemed to commend themselves because of specific economic and political circumstances. Thus, in England, where the forces of capitalism made most rapid headway, it seemed natural to assert that if individual self-seeking were given its head the surest way to progress would be found. In France a new bourgeoisie, reacting against both the *ancien régime* and the threat of proletarian insurrection, posited a new social order in which all the useful classes (i.e. both workers and their capitalist employers) exercised political power guided by social science. And, finally, in Germany, the growth of Prussian absolutism, led both to the acceptance of the absolute state as the means of controlling the historical future, and the diversion of libertarian tendencies into purely intellectual activity.

Spencer was the first English thinker to apply the characteristic English forms of thought to the task of creating a sociology. He had, early in his career as writer, been an editor of *The Economist* and was therefore schooled in the ideas of classical economics and utilitarianism, and it was this body of ideas which in the long run asserted itself in his sociology, despite the fact that the philosophic and scientific researches which he undertook in preparation for his sociological work seemed to lead in a very different direction.

The first principles on which Spencer tried to base his work were derived from the study of evolution, and the first principle of all which seemed to prevail in the development of matter up to its more complex organic forms turned on one ultimate principle; namely that of progress from incoherent homogeneity to coherent heterogeneity (Spencer, 1915). Thus the higher forms of life could be expected to take an organic form, involving differentiation of function and co-ordination of effort. The question, then, was whether supra-individual entities like human societies were to be thought of as organisms. Oddly, although Spencer is often treated as an organicist theorist, his own work makes it clear that in any literal sense of the term he was not. For him, when it came to discussing societies, the principles of evolutionary organicism had to be reconciled with utilitarian thought, or, if they could not, they had to be abandoned. Thus one is told that the social organism has curiously unorganic characteristics; that there is no *social censorium* and that, in opposition to the general law of organisms, here the whole exists for the good of its parts (Spencer, 1896, Vol. 1, pp. 435–590).

When it comes to sketching the main historical social types one finds that Spencer's contrast is not between 'incoherent homogeneity' and higher, more organic forms, but between hierarchical societies highly organized for warfare (the 'militant' type) and individualistic societies organized for industry (the industrial type) (Spencer, 1896, Vol. 2, p. 2). Moreover, when it was pointed out to him by the English Marxist, Hyndman, that industry might better be promoted in a planned economy (Hyndman, 1890), Spencer specifically stated that what he meant by an industrial society was really an individualist one (Spencer, 1896, Vol. 2, p. 2).

Spencer's sociology shares with much nineteenth-century liberal social thought a somewhat hypocritical claim to be positing a society based upon freedom of contract. It was clear enough, however, by the time Spencer wrote his *Principles of Sociology*, that this was, at best, a very partial description of the social order of capitalist England. Freedom of contract there may have been for capitalist entrepreneurs, but the contract signed by workers in the shadow of a penal workhouse was a mockery of a contract only, and it is hard to imagine how British industry could have developed had it not begun to apply the hierarchical principles of bureaucracy to industrial management. Such criticisms suggest themselves immediately when Spencer's sociology is confronted with that of Marx and Weber. Apart from this, a more honest and consistent liberalism eventually asserted itself in the writings of Spencer's successors who saw that freedom of contract can become a universal principle in industrial society only when the right of a worker to a job and to free collective bargaining is recognized (see especially Hobhouse, 1952; Beveridge, 1945).

The immediate reply to Spencer, within the sociological tradition, however, came from the positivism of Comte. This posited a collectivist, if unequal, social order and saw it as the task of the sociologist to outline its general principles (Comte, 1853 and 1966).

One of the most fascinating aspects of Comte's work is the way in which virtually the same body of ideas as those of St-Simon, which were to become the basis of European socialism, were pushed in a conservative direction. Both shared the adulation of the scientist and the engineer and both posited a state ruled by the useful industrial classes. But there was a qualification in the work of St-Simon which became crucial for his successors. This was that political power must be exercised by a technocratic parliament in the interests of the most numerous class and the right to property is qualified by the assertion that the particular form taken by the institution of property might vary according to social needs (Rodrigues, 1832). This notion drops far into the background in Comte.

What is important for Comte is the notion that the basis of a new social order must be found through social science and this social science is seen as pointing in a quite different direction from the wild schemes of idealists and revolutionaries. These idealists cannot, of course, impose their kind of social order in the long run, because unless it is in accord with what is scientifically possible, it will fail. Nonetheless, such people, according to Comte 'make terrible devastation in the interval' and it is necessary to remind them of those limitations on individual freedom which may appear irrational from the standpoint of individual rationality, but, which, as de Maistre had pointed out, have always underlain any lasting social order. Thus even social science, if it is to have social effect, must take a religious form, even to the point of having its own priesthood; and of the need for political authority there can be no doubt (Comte, 1853, I, Chap. 1).

The result of this is that although Comte makes much play with his Law of the Three Stages and with the notion of social dynamics, the crucial chapter in the whole body of his work is the one on social statics (Comte, 1853, II, Chap. 6). Here the notion of individual freedom disappears entirely. With a degree of insight surprising for one writing so long before Freud or George Mead, Comte recognizes that the idea of a purely individual personality is psychologically untenable. The basic unit of society is the family, and the individual personality is formed, and operates, only in relation to other members of the family. Second, family heads are held together by the division of labour, which appears here, not as it does in Adam Smith or Herbert Spencer, as a means of increasing individual happiness, but as a principle of social unification. Finally, since there is always a possibility that the division of labour will not lead to the collaboration of the differentiated units, political and ideological control by the state is necessary to ensure that integration is achieved. Characteristically, Comte includes under the division of labour, the division between the property owners and the non-owners, but his main fear is not of class conflict between these two, but of a failure of integration between occupations.

This body of ideas, counterposed to those of Spencer and English utilitarianism, is the basis from which Comte's great successor, Emile Durkheim, starts. *The Division of Labour in Society* (Durkheim, 1933), simply takes Spencer's notion of the

transition from incoherent homogeneity to coherent heterogeneity seriously, and sees the latter goal as fulfilled in Comte's
sketch of the basic necessities of social order in his *Social
Statics*. The earliest form of social solidarity is that in which
all individuals are the same and have the same ideas and are
united by this fact. This is what Durkheim calls mechanical
solidarity, and it may be seen as the exact social equivalent of
Spencer's incoherent homogeneity. But as this social form breaks
down, it gives way to the organic social solidarity which is
based upon the division of labour. The division of labour is
described as 'a moral fact' (i.e. as a means of imposing supra-
individual obligations on the individual) and it becomes the main
goal of Durkheimian politics to achieve this kind of moral
community as against the possibility that modern society will
collapse into a state of disjunction between individuals for which
Durkheim coined the term 'anomie'.

When Durkheim was called upon by his students to give some
attention to the problem of socialism, he saw in the socialist
movement not a new doctrine relating to the ownership and control of property but 'a cry of pain' (Durkheim, 1959) of industrial
man faced with the prospect of anomie. Moreover, he did not
see the way out of, or away from, anomie as lying in greater state
control. Rather it was to be found in the institutionalization of
moral regulation in occupational groups themselves. To this
extent he took a 'liberal' stand with Spencer against the extension
of state control (Durkheim, 1933), but his notion of the subordination of the individual to social control, taken together with
his relative lack of concern over the question of the justice of the
property system, left his politics sufficiently ambiguous for him
to be hailed as a founding father, equally by guild socialists, and
by fascists.

Apart from taking up the dialogue with Spencer and raising it
to a new level of sophistication, Durkheim also addressed himself to the problem of the nature of the subject matter of sociology
and the nature of the science in terms of which it was to be
understood. In doing so he laid the foundations of one of the
main methodological traditions of sociology, although here,
once again, there were ambiguities in his formulations which
have made it possible for him to be hailed both as the founder
of statistical empiricism and of what is called methodological

collectivism, together with more sophisticated veins of thought which make a recognizable contribution to recent sociological humanism.

Comte's peculiar version of the enlightenment doctrine, as requiring that man use science to discover the restraints to which his conduct was subject, is reflected in Durkheim's insistence on the idea of social facts as 'things' (Durkheim, 1938, Chap. 2). It is an odd notion and does seem to suggest a certain fatalism about the human condition which is also evident in Durkheim's later discussion of anomie in which he seems to assert that unless man subjects himself to external restraints, he will find life itself insupportable (Durkheim, 1952, Chap. 5).

There is, however, an internal contradiction in Durkheim's approach to the scientific study of social facts. At all costs he wants to eliminate mental entities of any sort from his sociology; but defining social facts both as external to the individual and exercising constraint over him makes it clear that the socialness of these facts can only be experienced indirectly, by finding some means of discovering how they might look from the point of view of the observed actor. In order to get out of this difficulty Durkheim, therefore, offers a quite distinct second definition of social facts which has no logical connection with the first, but which he claims by a happy coincidence happens to refer to the same class of facts. Thus while the first definition refers to 'any ways of acting (*sic*) external to the individual and capable of exercising constraint over him', the second refers to 'any way of acting . . . which recurs in a given society while at the same time existing independent of its individual manifestations' (Durkheim, 1938, Chap. 1).

What Durkheim is seeking to accommodate here, of course, are social facts as represented in statistical rates. Manifestly, social statistics record events which are recurrent; but what does it mean to say that they exist independently of their individual manifestations? Durkheim's claim here is that *there are sometimes social trends, to which individuals are subject, of which they are unconscious and which indeed have no external form*. What the social statistician has to do therefore is to make these facts apparent and to give them external form.

One interpretation of what Durkheim is doing here is that he is bringing social statistics before the sociologist as a possible form of social data; that is as evidence of external constraining social facts. Indeed, he even argues that 'crime is a normal phenomenon', implying that even though a form of behaviour might be found in only a minority of the population, it is still not merely accidental but normative. The task of the sociologist, therefore, is to use social statistics to go beyond the more formal rules of behaviour, which are set out, for instance, in codes of law, and to find the more subtle and fleeting social pressures on the individual. Thus the use of averages and of the method of concomitant variations are made available as a means for raising sociological questions and for making possible sociological theorizing.

Durkheim, is, of course, often interpreted in a sense very different from this, as having given up the metaphysics of external social entities in favour of the hard facts of statistics, thereby making sociology finally scientific. This interpretation is hard to hold, however, if one reads the texts which lie between Durkheim's tables (Durkheim, 1952, pp. 156–60). What he posits as determining changes in statistical rates are the ways in which men relate to one another and the way in which they subjectively perceive their relations. But if this is true, it can be seen that Durkheim is far more a contributor to humanistic sociology than to statistical empiricism or methodological collectivism.

This tendency is, however, more implicit than explicit in Durkheim and the whole tone of his *Rules of Sociological Method* speaks against it. What does emerge far more strongly in his work is a change in his view of the nature of social facts. At the outset he posits an individual pushed hither and thither by external social entities. But gradually he attributes a changing meaning to this constraint, till finally the personality of the individual is seen as itself shaped by, and made the agent of, society; and in *The Elementary Forms of the Religious Life* we are told that society exists only in, and through, the individual (Durkheim, 1915, Chap. 7).

It is clear that the methodological and theoretical import of Durkheim's work, as well as his politics, are problematic, and that he himself underwent a radical process of change and development. But the change which he did undergo is very far from being that which Parsons attributes to him (Parsons, 1937, pp. 77–84, Chap. 10). He did not move towards 'voluntarism', though this is suggested by his humanistic interpretation of social statistics in *Suicide*. What he does in *The Elementary Forms of the Religious Life* is to posit the most complete determinism of all, in which not merely is the individual buffeted by collective currents, but the individual who is so buffeted is made entirely by society. Here, one might say, the last surviving hope of the enlightenment fell to the doctrines of de Maistre.

The third tradition of classical sociology, that of Marx, starts, as we have said, with the philosophy of Hegel and, the fact that Marx is regarded as the founder of a doctrine called dialectical and historical materialism notwithstanding, this places it firmly in the idealist tradition when compared, for instance, with the scientific work of Herbert Spencer. The essential notion with which it starts may be stated very simply in highly abstract form. It is that history is a process in which spirit creates a world by expressing its own attributes in external form, and then, seeing them as alien, attempts to regain control of them by understanding them and making them once again its own. Applying the same notion to politics, the institutions of civil society constitute spirit in an alien form. It is the task of the state to control these institutions and the state may be conceived here as spirit at work in history.

Obviously such ideas, although they were used for conservative purposes, could also be regarded as having revolutionary implications. Feuerbach began the process of radicalizing the doctrine by suggesting that man, instead of being conceived ambiguously as part spirit but partly as an alien form of God, might be conceived as the only subject of history; the individual who idealized his own essence and called it God. This opened the way not merely for a Feuerbachian and atheist re-reading of Hegel; it opened the way for a number of other re-readings, and for what became known as transformational criticism (Tucker, 1961). Money was seen by Hess and by Marx as having the properties of Feuerbach's God, as being a human creation which came to dominate men, and in the *Critique of the Hegelian Philosophy of the Right*, Marx reversed the roles of the state and civil society to posit a revolution in which civil society rose against the alien being which it had created in the state (Easton and Guddat, 1967, pp. 249–64). And, reading of the various elements involved in the French Revolution, Marx saw the proletariat as the agent of this social revolution. Moreover he was convinced by Hess that the state of affairs which would follow the overcoming of alienation could be called socialism, even though he departed from Hess in connecting that notion with the revolution of the proletariat (Berlin, 1963 and Tucker, 1961, p. 116).

The crux of Marx's development, however, was yet to come. It could only come after 1844 when he used the transformational criticism of Hegel to argue that what Hegel had been talking about in an inverted form in the *Phenomenology of Mind* was nothing other than the process of production described by Adam Smith (Marx, 1956). But whereas for Adam Smith the result of the division of labour was an increase in individual human happiness, and for Durkheim the division of labour was a moral fact, for Marx it was a form of alienation which underlay all other forms of alienation. Moreover, Marx distinguished, as Comte and Durkheim had not done, between the division between owners and non-owners and the division between functionally specialized workers, and, though remotely speaking the division of labour itself might prove to be the source of alienation, initially the objective of revolutionary change must be the overthrow of the capitalist class. Thus the theory of the overcoming of alienation and the theory of the revolution of the proletariat, now defined as the industrial working class, were united.

Perhaps of more fundamental theoretical importance, however, was the implication of the 1844 Manuscripts for the developing materialist conception of history. If the division of labour in capitalist industry was the basic form of alienation, whose elimination would mean the elimination of alienation in its other forms, this appeared to imply some kind of functional inter-dependence between one institution and another. True, in Marx's theory, such a system of interrelated institutions would involve the notion of a leading institution, and it would be characteristic of all institutions that they were in a state of conflict and change. This would seem to imply that the materialist conception of history was one version of what came to be called functionalism. Marx's vocabulary however was so different from that of modern anthropology and sociology that it is doubtful whether this interpretation is justifiable. Moreover, the various qualifications of the doctrine of basis and superstructure, which he and Engels were to make later, are such that the possibility of fundamental disjunction between one institutional sphere and another does not appear to be excluded, at least in the short term (Marx and Engels, 1964 and 1953, pp. 498–500).

During 1848, and in the immediate subsequent years, Marx developed his theories of class and revolution, and throughout the 1860s and 1870s he was forced to define and redefine his ideas on these matters as he struggled against counter-tendencies within the International and the German Social Democratic movement. In doing so he did something which was unique in sociology, namely he put forward a theory of the dynamics of capitalist society. Backed by profound research in economic theory and economic history, his theory, quite distinct from any of his contemporaries such as Lasalle, Blanqui, Proudhon or Bakunin, was that while capitalism would survive so long as it was able to go on developing production, a time would come when it was in a crisis and at this time a working class based upon a trade union movement, which had grown up to negotiate for improved wages and conditions, would create the political instruments necessary for the overthrow of capitalism (Cole, 1954, p. 2).

Marx was not simply, or primarily, a sociologist. Some Marxists and anti-Marxists argue that he was not a sociologist at all. Nonetheless, there is one important issue relating to sociological conceptualization on which Marx is particularly interesting and which is of some relevance to our discussion of Durkheim, Weber and their heirs. This is the fundamental question of the nature of social facts. In his irritatingly ambiguous, but undeniably profound, theses on Feuerbach, Marx declares that the human essence is the ensemble of social relations (Marx and Engels, 1964, p. 645), that social relations are not, in the usual sense, material entities but rest upon 'sensuous human activity', and though men may be unable to alter the social order as they please, other parts of the social order rest upon 'the earthly family' of the social relations of production which could be understood in their contradictions and revolutionized in practice. This suggested a position not unlike that in the sentence which appears at the very front of this book, namely that although we are made by institutions they are themselves human creations and can be altered by human beings; that is to say that Marxism seemed to support a methodological and theoretical humanism in sociology.

This view, which held a lot of influence in the immediate aftermath of the publication in English of the 1844 Manuscripts, has recently come in for severe criticism. For one thing, as early as 1845, Marx had declared in a letter that the social relations of production which men had could not be changed at will.[1] This much was always recognized, but it was argued that this still left a limited role for human agency in times of crisis at least. What has recently been suggested, however, is that there was a radical rupture in Marx's thought after 1845 and that in 1857 he produced certain basic manuscripts known as the *Grundrisse* (Marx, 1939–41) which rejected this kind of humanism and focused upon a structural analysis of social formations which required no reference to relations between men or on the action and mutual expectation which such relations implied. Thus the Marxist tradition, like the Durkheimian, seems to offer support to either a tradition which involves the use of humanized concepts in sociology or one which uses dehumanized ones. This is crucial in any discussion of the relation between Marxist and Weberian sociology.

In Germany the intellectual aftermath of Marxism was more evident in political than in academic circles. The debates around the Gotha programme, in which Marx joined critically (Marx and Engels, 1962a, 2, pp. 13–37), and that about the Erfurt programme in which Engels joined sympathetically (Lichtheim, 1961, pp. 259–64), went on and Marxism divided between a number of different views on whether capitalism was capable of reforming itself and producing a kind of welfare state or not. But though this left a legacy of writing in the works of Kautsky, Luxemburg and Bernstein, its impact on academic life, in any immediate sense, was small. Amongst sociologists there was some stirring of conscience amongst academics about the social question and the so-called Socialists of the Chair, headed by Schmoller, formed the *Verein für Sozialpolitik* (Roth, 1968) to discuss some of the issues posed for bourgeois, capitalist and more traditional forms of German society by Marxism. But intellectually more significant was the fact that, in the seclusion of academic life, a number of social scientists began to address themselves

[1] Marx to Annekov, *Selected Correspondence*, 1953, p. 39.

critically to the question of the nature of social science and this meant going back beyond Hegel to some of the issues posed by Kant. This was not simply to get away from the challenge of Marxism. Right-wing as well as left-wing Hegelianism had left its mark on German historiography and it was, as much as anything, dissatisfaction with the intellectual sloppiness of much that was written about various *Zeitgeister* that produced the neo-Kantian revival. This is probably the best point at which one can begin to understand the work of Max Weber, although the resultant sociology is one which produces intellectual confrontations with the traditions of Marx and Durkheim at nearly every point (Parsons, 1937, Chap. 13).

The problem raised by neo-Kantian thought in the social sciences was this: if the world of nature, as perceived by natural science, was a purely phenomenal one, and law-like because of categories imposed by the human mind, how far were these, or any other categories, applicable to human life, and consequently how far was that life understandable in terms of laws and generalizations? One answer which appealed to many historians, who saw their role as a creative one quite different from that of the scientist, was that the *Geistwissenschaften* were totally distinct from the *Naturwissenschaften* and that, hence, there could be no codified methodology in the former case as there could in the latter. This, together with vague Hegelian intuitions about the *Zeitgeist*, led to much work which was undisciplined and much which was frankly propagandist. Such historical writing still passes muster in academic circles today, although without even a loose Kantian kind of justification.

Three major alternatives were pursued as a means of bringing intellectual discipline to bear in the wake of the neo-Kantian movement. One was that of Georg Simmel (1959) who did at least suggest the idea of *a priori* social categories in terms of which it was possible to observe the manifoldness of human behaviour and interpret it as social, even though in practice the categories which he discussed seemed to have been arrived at by way of a peculiarly urbane introspection rather than by any other method. A second alternative was that of Dilthey (Hodges, 1952) who attempted to formulate a distinctive method for human studies called *Verstehen* and left behind him a historic legacy which went far beyond Max Weber's particular synthesis to have a profound influence on the Frankfurt school, on the Marxism of Georg Lukács (Lichtheim, 1970) and on the phenomenological movement in sociology through Schutz (1967). Finally, there was a different type of distinction drawn by Rickert (1962) between the nomothetic and the ideographic disciplines. While admitting the possibility of the application of scientific method to human affairs, Rickert still sought to show that there were distinct methods which characterized the work of the historian. The basis of his distinction was that, whereas the natural scientist selected from his experience that which was recurrent, the social scientist started from what was relevant from the point of view of various value standpoints which provided starting points for historical analysis.

Weber's definition of his own position is somewhat difficult to understand because it seemed to change as he entered into argument with each of these positions. The result is that there are a hundred and one interpretations of Weber's method. In the present author's own view, Weber moved through at least four stages in his methodological writings, and these have been systematically discussed in another essay as well as in a later chapter of the present volume.[1] Briefly we may recapitulate here that at an early stage his method was more like that of Rickert, although the values to which social studies must be relevant, according to Weber's view, have no absolute validity and are a matter of research convenience. At this stage, moreover, Weber explicitly rejects both the Simmelian notion of pure social forms and the notion of sociological laws, whether theoretical or empirical, in favour of ideal types which were thought of as yardsticks with which reality could be compared.[2] Second, Weber sought to define his own position, as against Dilthey's, on the question of *Verstehen* and seemed to use, as his basic building brick for sociological theory, patterns of motivation imputed to the observed actor which could be thought of as 'ideal types' which would serve to interpret behaviour as action (Weber, 1968, I, Chap. 1). Such a process of the imputation of motivation

[1] See my chapter 'The Four Methods of Max Weber', in Arun Sahay (ed.), *Max Weber and Modern Sociology*, Routledge & Kegan Paul, 1971, and Chap. 17 of this volume.

[2] See Max Weber, 'Objectivity in Social Science' in *The Methodology of the Social Sciences*, 1949.

could have no scientific validity, however, unless the explanations which were adequate on the level of meaning, were turned into, or supplemented by, explanations which were causally adequate. There is much disputation as to what Weber meant by this but, if he still wished to retain the notion of ideal types in this context, he had clearly transformed it. These ideal types, unlike those of his early essay, were clearly subject to empirical test.

The problem of *Verstehen*, in so far as it involved individual human action, however, did not exhaust Weber's sociology. What he came to be concerned with was to establish an adequate language of the social forms, which was not *a priori* like Simmel's, nor yet gathered from the language and action of everyday life, as a latter-day phenomenology was to suggest, but which was a language that could be agreed on amongst the community of sociologists and which proved useful in historical analysis.

Much confusion has arisen from the reading of Weber's *Economy and Society* because it is not commonly recognized, and Weber himself did not recognize, that in his first chapter he was doing three things. First, he was showing how the business of interpreting human behaviour as motivationally meaningful could be put upon a systematic and more disciplined basis. Second, he sought to show that group concepts in sociology need not be dehumanized and reified. They could be understood by the scientist in terms of more elementary concepts referring to the subjectively formulated motivation patterns and mutual expectations of a hypothetical actor. Nonetheless, third, since no sociologist could ever claim to know a pattern of motivation or expectation as it really was in the subjective experience of an empirically observed actor, the validity of Weber's group concepts lay, not in the fact that they reflected the actor's own real view of his situation, but in the fact that they had multiple empirical referents so that it was possible for the social scientist to point to these as possible falsifiers of what he said about the presence and operation of social relations and processes.

It should be recognized that this outcome is a somewhat disappointing one for those who wish to claim Weber for a soft, humanistic and phenomenological sociology. For ultimately, though his concepts can be broken down into action terms, they have one 'thing-like' quality, namely that they suggest externally observable events, albeit of a complex kind, to which the theoretical group concepts refer. They are not intuitive accounts of what is actually going on in actors' heads.

It should be noted here that the tension between the analysis of social structure in terms of subjectively interpreted motivation, and its analysis in terms of social 'things' is present in Durkheim, Marx and Weber. In Durkheim the commitment is much more to 'thingness' and in Weber much more to subjective motivation, it is true, while Marx moves from an early subjectivist, to a later structuralist and possibly scientistic position. In the last analysis, all of them would be bound to agree that the data of sociology consist of historical facts and of social statistics, but that their interpretation must be in terms of a sociological language of action and social relations. Durkheim, as a result of his work on suicide, came to lay emphasis upon statistical comparison; Marx and Weber much more upon the structural comparisons made available by a sociologically informed history.

It remains to be pointed out that although Weber made little acknowledgment of the fact, his sociology eventually took on much of the formal quality which Simmel had been searching for, and that he must have owed many of his concepts on the micro-sociological level, as much to Simmel, as to his comparative researches. The result is that Weberian theory, if it can be called theory, is strictly about social forms and has relatively little to say overtly about the cultural uses to which forms of social organization might be put, or about the interconnections, of a systematic kind, between one institution and another. True, much of his work on the sociology of law, of politics, of religion or economic action does explore specific relations of meaning between one institutional area and another,[1] but he does not see societies as systems, nor is he unwilling to recognize that social forms repeat themselves in history. What Weber may be said to have done is to have finally abandoned the notion of sociology as a kind of universal and encyclopaedic history, and to have brought to bear upon history the specifically sociological insights which derived from an understanding of the forms of social interaction.

One further point may be made about the relationship of the

[1] It is arguable that Parsons's notions of the imports and exports between one functional subsystem and another owes much to Weber's insights. See Parsons and Smelser, 1956, and Parsons 1965.

work of Weber to that of Marx and Durkheim. This is that whereas Durkheim's theory is ultimately completely deterministic, resting on the claim that the individual personality and individual patterns of motivations themselves are ultimately social creations which fit the functional needs of society, Weber's overall conception of the more advanced societies, at least, is that they are held together by power and authority. This authority is not seen as deriving from any commitment to ultimate values, but, at most, to a 'subjective feeling that authority is legitimate'. In Weber's sociology, actors have the capacity to disobey (Rex, 1961, Chap. 7). Equally, in the theses on Feuerbach at least, Marx posits actors who are not socialized out of existence by the heavenly family but live in an earthly family which can be understood in its contradictions and revolutionized in practice.

So far as questions of politics and, more generally, of subject matter were concerned there were differences of some importance between Marx and Weber as to what was, and what was not, problematic in history. Thus Weber was interested in the ideological presuppositions of capitalist behaviour and did not see these as mere epiphenomena arising from the material base; and he was greatly pre-occupied, not simply with class relations, which he did attempt to discuss systematically in a way which was complementary to rather than incompatible with, Marx (see Weber, 1968, Vol. 1, Chap. 4), but with structures of authority and their administrative staff (Weber, ibid.). It is possible, of course, to attribute the first preoccupation to an intellectual and ideological opposition to the materialist conception of history, and it is possible to see, in the second, the lingering ghost of the state bureaucracy as a universal class displacing the proletariat in historical importance. But if it is possible, it is because it was hardly likely that someone cut off in terms of class and occupation from the working class, and living in an academic atmosphere, should not have shared ideas which had common currency amongst his colleagues. But what this assertion misses is that, in spelling out the relationship between religion and economic behaviour or the relation of the bureaucrat to the means of administration, Weber was very far from being an academic mystifier. He brought to the analysis of these problems a hard grasp of structural reality not surpassed by Marx himself. It is not without point that he has been called the Marx of the bourgeoisie. It might be fair to add that he might also have been called the politicized Durkheim of the working classes.

On one point, of course, Weber and Marx do part company. Not merely did Weber stand opposed to a centrally planned socialist society because he believed it to be technically impossible (Weber, 1968, Vol. 1, Chap. 2; Parsons, 1964); he also opposed socialism and gave some very low-level anti-socialist lectures towards the end of his life (Weber, 1971). Yet, even here, the conflict between traditions is not complete. Weber fully understood that his anti-socialist polemics were to be separated from his sociology[1] and, on the technical question of the administrative possibility of socialism, his statement of the problem in terms of a society of bureaucratically run industrial organization connected by a market being replaced by one single all-encompassing bureaucracy does state the problem with which successful socialist revolutionaries in the advanced industrial countries would have to deal. There is no place here for the mushy utopianism which mars so much post-Stalinist socialist thinking.

We have now given some idea of the roots of the classic sociological tradition and of the dialectic between its separate elements. Perhaps, there does emerge from it a common conception of what sociology is about, despite all its ambiguity. But that tradition is not static. We are no longer simply living in a world which has to understand the nature of post-feudal society as such. Nearly a hundred years have elapsed since the writers we have discussed began their work and the world has moved on considerably, facing new sociological problems and rendering irrelevant many of the plausible guesses as to the future which were interwoven with the sociology of the masters. What we now have to do, therefore, is to consider two separate things. One is the set of major political changes which have challenged the sociological tradition anew. The other is the influence on sociology of modern intellectual movements, particularly those whose foundation was laid in the 1930s and which are now producing their crop of sociological consequences. This is to say that we now have to look at the political and intellectual seeding beds of second generation sociology before going on to indicate the main schools and divisions which face us and their possible

[1] See Weber's essay 'Science as a vocation', in Gerth and Mills, 1948.

ideological import, not excluding the possibility that sociology itself might have been a historically limited phenomenon, which cannot cope with events or survive in the world of the late twentieth century.

Politically we can understand the historical shortfall of the classical sociological tradition when we realize that Simmel, Weber and Durkheim were all dead by 1920 and that, most significantly, Weber did not live to see the collapse of the new German experiment in democracy which followed the First World War. When modern sociology developed, it had to develop in the light of the rise of Nazism, the exile of many of Europe's finest sociologists to the United States, and the development in Russia of a new form of industrialized society claiming legitimation in the works of Marx. The new alignment of world forces which resulted from these processes led to the Second World War, and in the wake of that war the division of the world into two power blocs and the creation of two intellectual orthodoxies. Of these, one, the Russian, it is true, was far more disposed to substitute dogma for sociology than the other, which in its very nature fostered a kind of free enterprise in trivialization. On the other hand, what appeared as a somewhat vain attempt to challenge the new orthodoxies in the name of the surviving revolutionary ideas of the 1930s and in that of a somewhat narrow-minded and anti-American European social democracy continued in the United States and Europe. The geopolitics of the post-war world were based upon the assumption that war between the great powers had become unthinkable even though they might go on to lay plans for an automated defence system which could destroy the world overnight, and, with this, West European Marxism had to adjust itself to a situation of permanent opposition disguised by revolutionary slogans. But the real shift of emphasis was from struggles between the great powers to their encounter collectively with the Third World. First Mao, then the FLN in Algeria, then Castro's revolution in Cuba, showed that Marx's dismissal of the peasants as a class had been based upon too narrow an experience. The inhabitants of the former British and French empires fought their last guerrilla battles with the retiring European armies, and then addressed themselves to the twin tasks of dealing with their own poverty and fighting neo-colonialism. And in the advanced countries themselves, despite the declaration by the leading ideologists of sociology that the basis of divisive ideological politics had been destroyed with the growth of the welfare state, new tensions arose which were highlighted by the riots amongst the black population of the United States and by the alienation from, and their disloyalty to, their country's new imperial cause—especially by the American young, but also to some extent by the educated young of Europe. The latter combined a veneration of some of the Third World's revolutionary leaders, like Che Guevara, with their own struggle for control of their destiny in their institutions of higher education, and also, in some measure, in the world at large.

The intellectual seedbed of the new sociology was to be found in the last debates of Marxist and social democratic academics in Frankfurt before the light of reason went out in Europe in 1933, in Vienna which sustained an intellectual climate in which both the psycho-analytic movement and the new radical critical philosophy of logical empiricism could flourish, and more widely in Germany and Paris where phenomenology deriving from Husserl, existentialism, and new forms of Marxism, provided the crucial subject matter of debate. The diaspora of German refugee scholars to the United States was no less influential in its attempt to revise Marx in terms of Freud to explain the defection of the German working class and to warn the United States of the political dangers which it too faced. In the post-war world, American influence was dominant, and within the new American tradition the new grandmaster of sociology, Talcott Parsons, provided a new and highly systematic basis for sociological theory while the practical needs of market research produced new empirical techniques which were rationalized and made the basis for a new empirical methodology, first at Columbia, then at Chicago. The refugee challenge to this new twin orthodoxy seemed at first to have little effect, reaching its highest point in the work of the refugees' most brilliant convert, C. Wright Mills; but gradually it began to do so, after the McCarthy witch-hunt of intellectuals which characterized the Eisenhower period, if not in an overtly political form at least in the new support given to deviance by conflict theory and phenomenology. Finally, the orthodoxy began to be challenged anew by the emergence of new ideologies, such as those of Fanon and Debray, and of anti-sociologies like that of Frank, which cast contempt upon the interpretation of the Third World's situation as one of underdevelopment and called it by the name exploitation.

The most immediate and powerful influence on post-war sociology was that of logical empiricism in one or other of its forms. This movement had started with the attempt of a group of European scholars to systematize Wittgenstein's earlier insights (Wittgenstein, 1961) and to discover and agree on the one true language in terms of which the world could be discussed. Its central tenet was the verification principle which asserted that any statement was nonsense which was not capable, in principle at least, of being verified. The revision of this carelessly formulated doctrine to the assertion that all statements must be capable of empirical falsification (see Popper, 1959) was of minor importance compared with the continuing drive towards empiricism which the new philosophy engendered.

The key connecting figure between this movement and modern sociology was the now too-easily forgotten figure of George Lundberg (1939), who had himself been directly influenced by the movement to create an Encyclopaedia of the Unified Sciences with its notion of a common theoretical language, all of whose terms could be operationally defined. So for any humanly interpretable theory one had substituted a physicalist terminology based upon the notion of measurable social forces. Lundberg's theoretical entities, however, disappeared almost without trace, leaving behind only his belief in operationalism formulated in the rather oversimplified form, 'intelligence (or, for that matter any other attribute you care to name) is what intelligence tests measure'.

In England the most significant empiricist philosopher of social science was Karl Popper (1957). In his work again there was a turning away from any sort of theory, particularly of what he called the holist sort, which suggested that all social institutions and social behaviour were systematically interconnected so that it was impossible to conceive of any serious social change which was not revolutionary, to a simple methodological doctrine of a search for short-term causal sequences and a political one of advocating piecemeal social reform.

Neither Lundberg nor Popper, however, was to have a truly lasting influence on sociology. The man who was to have such an influence was Paul Lazarsfeld. Lazarsfeld came to the United States having been brought up in the most profound European theoretical tradition, but became convinced that the social survey, already an established element of American political and commercial life was the means whereby sociology could be rendered truly scientific. Durkheim's work on suicide and the work of English demographers had already laid the basis for the exploitation of statistical material for sociological purposes. What Lazarsfeld now envisaged, however, was the opening up of vast new fields of investigation through the specially designed survey which was committed to a quest for kinds of knowledge which no census could aspire to. The improvement of statistical techniques to take account of large numbers of variables, coupled with the technological revolution in data-processing equipment, made the prospects opened up by the new empiricism even more appealing.

Had this new empiricism confined itself to Durkheim's limited claim that statistical rates were a mere starting point for truly sociological theorizing about social structures and forms of social solidarity, its implications for sociology might indeed have been profound. Unfortunately, its usefulness in market research and the operation of those agents of the lowest common denominator in research planning, the executives of the Research Councils, were to ensure that this did not happen. Social statistics, instead of becoming the tool of sociology, came to displace it and sociology became a mere technical tool in the hands of the market researcher or political pollster. The sociological journals, not merely of the United States, but of Europe too, were to bear the marks of this development for many years to come.

British social science had, however, been faced with other problems. True, Fabianism and its intellectual successors had produced a preoccupation with the social book-keeping of equality of opportunity, and the use of demographic techniques in this cause chimed well with the new empiricism of Lazarsfeld. But the more lasting influence came from social anthropology and its two greatest teachers, Malinowski (1944) and Radcliffe-Brown (1952). This produced the doctrine, central to most orthodoxy to this day, known as functionalism.

Malinowski first elaborated the doctrine of functionalism in reaction to the speculative historic reconstructions of anthropologists like Morgan and the misuse of the comparative method by others like Frazer. For him primitive man did not act simply because he followed customs which were 'survivals'. His action had its own inherent logic, either in seeing to it that in the long term the needs of the group were satisfied, or in meeting his own biological needs.

Radcliffe-Brown revised this doctrine to eliminate any suggestion of a reduction to biology and, at the same time, revived the organic analogy to explain what could be meant by the function of a social institution. More than this he developed a concept of social structure, not clearly evident in Malinowski's work, which had focused on culture. Social structure was thought of as consisting of the whole network of social relations between actors and the function of any secondary activity, at least, was the maintenance of this structure.

There was, in Radcliffe-Brown's definition of structure, an implicit humanistic reference to human action, even though this was subordinated to the explanation of human action strictly in terms of its contribution to the maintenance of the whole society. Talcott Parsons was to start much more explicitly from the action frame of reference, but he too was to go on to subordinate this to functionalist explanation and, indeed, more than this, to a systems theory far too abstract to include human beings as elements at all.

To fully understand the structural-functionalism of Parsons, however, it is not sufficient to trace it back to anthropological functionalism. We have already referred to Parsons as one of the grandmasters of sociology and, for better or for worse, it must be admitted that his command of the sociological tradition has been more complete than any of his contemporaries. In *The Structure of Social Action* he virtually rewrote Marshall, Pareto, Durkheim and Weber to show that all of them, however diverse their starting points, were dealing with the theory of action, whether in terms of positivism, utilitarianism or idealism (Parsons, 1937, pp. 77–84). What Parsons himself claimed to be aiming at was a production out of the convergences of their theories of a 'voluntaristic' theory of action. This aim, however, appears to be abandoned in his critical introduction to the first four chapters of Weber's *Economy and Society* in which he explicitly criticizes Weber for not having recognized the need for psychology and for underplaying the systemic qualities of action (Parsons, 1964). Thus, in his post-war symposium with Shils and others (Parsons, 1951) the whole aim of the general theory of action is to produce a theory in which the actor is socialized as in Durkheim's *The Elementary Forms of the Religious Life* and in which roles are seen as forming an integrated whole, not merely with the drives and capacities of the personality system, but with the roles of other actors in the social system. The only redeeming feature of his own account of the specifically social system which followed, at least from the point of view of those who believe that deviance requires, if not support, then explanation, is that Parsons does introduce his own version of Freudian socialization theory to explain that the personality system (Parsons, 1952, Chaps 6, 7) is not infinitely malleable and that as a result of the operation of defence and other mechanisms the socialization process may generate deviance and that the social system must therefore provide its own defences and controls.

Up till this point, however, there is still some point in seeing Parsons as writing in the 'action frame of reference'. After his collaboration with Bales, however, this approach disappears.[1] Whatever the actor thinks he may be doing, from the sociologist's point of view he can only be thought of as contributing to the solution of one of the system problems for the solution of which the system operates through one of four subsystems. More than this, eventually Parsons passes to a higher level of abstraction altogether. He speaks not merely of social systems and their functional subsystems but of a set of phenomena which have systemic attributes. Thus even the unit act becomes the focus for systematic analysis and what its structural elements are come to bear little relation to the goals, means and conditions of his earlier formulations.[2]

Parsons has naturally been criticized in two separate ways, one political and one methodological and theoretical. So far as the first of these criticisms is concerned it can be argued that the criticism is unfair since Parsons may be understood as describing only an ideal type of an integrated social system, but there is as little

[1] See Parsons, Bales and Shils, 1953; Parsons and Bales, 1953; and Parsons and Smelser, 1956.
[2] See Introduction and Chap. 1 in McKinney and Tiryskian, 1970.

emphasis in his work as there is in Durkheim's of the looming possibility of anomie. (Anomie appears only 'as a limiting case' in *The Social System* (Parsons, 1952, pp. 18–29) and is apparently thought to be not worth discussing.) The political implications of Parsons's work must therefore be faced, the more so because he has been used to give theoretical support to other writings of a far more ideological kind.

In America the principal writers who have drawn on Parsonian consensualism are Lipset (1959), Bell (1960), Shils (1959) and Smelser (1962). All appear to subscribe to the doctrine that advanced capitalist societies have solved their major political problems through a consensus between employers and workers that the welfare state and full employment are to be maintained. In particular this means that, to repeat the words of Macmillan, 'the class struggle is obsolete'. Any non-consensual politics then can only be explained as due to strain on the personality level, a view shared with these writers by William Kornhauser (1960). In rather less politically involved terms, a similar case is argued by the British sociologist T. H. Marshall (1950) who sees the British working class as now having won social rights to set alongside their legal and political ones so that citizenship has become more important than class membership.

Reaction to this consensualism came from two separate quarters, one of which might be described as liberal or social democratic, the other as revolutionary and alienated. The liberal response was to assert boldly in the face of the McCarthy purge of the American universities that disagreement, far from threatening American society, might actually be its principal guarantee. Indeed, wherever Parsons's model is applied, it could not, according to these theorists apply to the United States, since there, sociologists from de Tocqueville onwards had seen pluralism as its principal characteristic (see Coser, 1956).

More significant, perhaps, was the criticism of the German sociologist Dahrendorf (1959, 1968) who was probably the most articulate representative of the conflict school in the late 1950s and early 1960s. Dahrendorf was not prepared to accept that conflict could be explained away as functional for the system. With Marx he saw it as inherent in all institutions and as the source of change in those institutions. But the source of conflict according to Dahrendorf lay, not in the distribution of property, but in the distribution of power. Moreover, such power was differentially distributed in all institutional hierarchies and in each of them independently. Whether, therefore, conflict would lead to revolution, would depend upon whether or not the line-up of forces in one hierarchy paralleled that in another. Like his contemporary in the London School of Economics, David Lockwood (1964), Dahrendorf sought to draw attention not merely to the conflict between individuals and roles but to the conflict and malintegration which might exist between one sphere and another.

This criticism of functionalism, however, was far from likely to satisfy Parsons's more Marxist critics, and very unsatisfactory from the point of view of the Frankfurt refugees, either in America or amongst those who had returned to Frankfurt after the defeat of Nazism. True they might not retain much hope of an impending revolution in the advanced capitalist countries, but they explained this as due to the establishment of forms of mass manipulation which capitalism had perfected rather than a whole-hearted commitment by working-class leaders to the Lipsettian consensus. The model of the society which binds down its members with silken chains was expressed in his own terms by Herbert Marcuse (1964), but it had been stated far more tellingly, and less encumbered by Hegelian language, by C. Wright Mills (1956) some years before. Rejecting the 'Victorian labour metaphysic' which posited a worker-based revolution, as well as any hope that the new white-collar people might become politically effective, Mills was finally driven to a position of despair, calling on his fellow intellectuals to reject the military-industrial complex, and the power élite which ruled it, and to speak out boldly in the hope that somehow, somewhere, and sometime its voice might be heard and the nuclear war which seemed inevitable, avoided (Mills, 1958).

Not surprisingly, Mills found himself allied with the early editions of the British *New Left Review*, which, after the events of Suez and Budapest, united a wide range of political radicals around some form of humanistic Marxism. Bell (1960) specifically singled this group out for attack in his *The End of Ideology* drawing attention to the impossibility of their position in a world in which their ideas no longer had a political vehicle in the form of working-class action and support. The *New Left Review* maintained its line for a few years, nonetheless, but then abandoned its humanistic Marxist heroes Marcuse, Gramsci and Lukács for the mechanistic doctrines of structuralism, particularly in their Marxist form as outlined by Louis Althusser (1970).

As Parsonianism developed, and as the attack upon it and its ideological offspring rumbled on, American sociology, other than that of a purely statistical sort, became codified in the wide-ranging eclecticism of Robert Merton (1957) of Columbia. The big issues of theory were to be avoided by concentrating on principles of the middle range; functionalism could be accepted if it was modified here and there to take account of a measure of conflict; Durkheim's notion of anomie could be reinterpreted as being a built-in feature of American society, producing an expected number of kinds of deviation; and a whole range of other hypotheses about such matters as relative deprivation could be mined out of the great research exercise which had been carried out during the war on the American GI. Along with this there went on operationalization of the concepts of anomie and alienation so that the degree of dissatisfaction of the American worker could be assessed and put right.

Along with the consensual interpretation of the United States itself, functionalism came to offer its own interpretations of the political and economic processes which were evident in the Third World. The charge that it was a static doctrine was angrily rejected as first Smelser (1959) and then Parsons (1966, 1971) put forward their own evolutionary models of the development of European and American society through differentiation and specialization, and then these models were applied to the analysis of social change in the post-colonial and neo-colonial world (Smelser, 1963). This kind of theorizing continues, despite the work of André Gundar Frank (n.d.) who has argued that the so-called underdeveloped countries have been and very often are being systematically misdeveloped and dedeveloped in the interests of the European powers and despite the medieval scale of horror of events in the Congo, in Nigeria and in Pakistan. The moral basis of much of this work on the sociology of development, however, was cut away by the exposure of the involvement of American sociologists in the counter-insurgency planning of Operation Camelot (see Sjoberg, 1969).

Of recent times, the relative decline in American power *vis-à-vis*

Europe has seen something of a transfer of the locus of sociological theorizing back to the European continent and particularly back to Frankfurt and Paris. In Frankfurt, sociology itself is subordinated to a Hegelianized version of Marxism known as critical theory[1] which lives on precariously in the face of the Americanization of much German sociology and the reduction of another part of it to the Dahrendorfian version of Merton's middle level. It is in Paris, however, that the more significant, sociologically disappointing, developments are taking place.

The major intellectual development has taken place in the sphere of social anthropology. It was clear enough except to the in-group of British functionalist anthropologists by the end of the 1939–45 war that their functionalism had only limited explanatory power. There were too many things about totemism, about gift-exchange, about symbolism and myth and about kinship in primitive society which functionalism simply could not explain and which, nonetheless, had a certain coherence which demanded a general and abstract explanation. Lévi-Strauss sought to offer this explanation in terms of what he called structuralism.[2]

French structuralism has to be sharply distinguished from the structuralism of Radcliffe-Brown with which it compares itself, and the structuralism of Simmel and Weber, of which it remains largely ignorant. The difference is that, whereas these theories mean by structure, the social relations which arise and are sustained amongst men in the course of their interaction, what Lévi-Strauss proposes is the consideration of structures of a more abstract sort, which may be discovered in linguistics as much as in anthropology. The key terms in such structural analysis will be those like opposition or inversion, in terms of which unrelated phenomena in primitive society are shown to be related.

Lévi-Strauss is a Parisian intellectual and, as such, very much in touch with Marxism, which he refers to humorously as one of his three mistresses; but the one form of Marxism for which he has little regard is that of the Marxist critic, Goldmann (1969). What is wrong with Goldmann's work is his attempt to explain literary forms and content in terms of class interests, albeit

---

[1] See for instance the work of Adorno, Habermass and Marcuse.
[2] For a general introduction to Lévi-Strauss see Leach, 1970.

widely interpreted. What structuralism demands is an abandonment of these concerns in favour of the study of inherent
structure.

The Marxism which does have the closest relationship to Lévi-
Strauss's structuralism is that of Althusser (1970). According to
Althusser, Marx's thought underwent a radical rupture after
1845 and should not be understood from then on as having any
relationship to Hegelian thought at all. It becomes the science
of social formations and each social formation may be analysed in
terms of three practices, the economic, the ideological and the
theoretical. There is no automatic relationship between the
'contradictions' in one practice and those in another, but, as in
Dahrendorf, it is suggested that there are historical moments at
which the contradictions in one sphere become superimposed
upon another, that is to say, in Althusser's chosen terminology,
become 'overdetermined'. His own work was devoted to a study
within one of the practices, namely the theoretical, and this had
to be understood in terms of its structural elements. Here, as in
Lévi-Strauss, the structural elements operate on a supra-human
level of abstraction, but not because, as in Lévi-Strauss, this is
alleged to give them more explanatory power. Rather, it is
because, in rejecting the Hegelian origins of Marx, Althusser
actually prefers to call himself anti-humanist.

The striking thing about all contemporary sociology might be
said to be the way in which, almost whatever its tradition, it
moves away from the Marxism of the theses on Feuerbach.
American consensual theory celebrates the alleged stability of
contemporary American society, while French Marxism explains
away the absence of a Marxist-led French Revolution scientifically, and the divisions amongst political intellectuals become as
abstract and unreal as those amongst the academics. Meanwhile,
in the Soviet Union, the installation of Marxism as an official
belief system makes the existence of sociology as an empirical
discipline, if not impossible, at least likely to incur official dis-
pleasure. Nor is there any immediate prospect of a sociology
of the Soviet Union growing up outside its borders. There are
works which deal with such important questions as the relation
between the party and the planning apparatus, the problem of
democratic centralism, or the existence of classes and strata, but
these are nearly always marred by an ideological stance on the

part of the authors which represents the Soviet leadership in purely conspiratorial terms.

But in what we have been saying, we have almost accepted the assumption underlying the modern sociological tradition that Western capitalist societies are stable. This is far from being the truth. Their characteristic activity since 1945 has been fighting colonial and neo-colonial wars, they have nearly all faced open rioting on their streets, and amongst their educated young there is a widespread rejection of nearly all that is fundamental to the values of the societies concerned. If there is no class-in-itself to conduct a revolution, then at least it must be said that the populations of these societies are far from being adequately socialized.

This state of affairs is reflected in another dimension of differentiation in American and European sociology which draws its strength from the traditions of phenomenology, existentialism and symbolic interactionism. Indeed it is not too much to say that this type of theorizing represents something of a tidal wave washing away the positivism of America's research schools.

From a strictly sociological point of view, the key figure in this development was Alfred Schutz (1964, 1967), a student of Husserl, who taught for a long period at the New School of Social Research in New York. Husserl's phenomenology of course had not originally had any sociological intent. It was concerned to bracket away both the everyday and the scientific view of the world and to try to understand the essences which were to be perceived in reality; but neither Schutz nor the European existentialists who were influenced by Husserl accepted the notion of the bracketing away of the everyday view of the world (Roche, 1973). Thus, although Schutz had set out to give what he called a philosophical underpinning to the work of Weber, he was far from confining himself to the highly formalized constructs represented by Weber's hypothetical and ideal-typical actor. What he went on to talk about was the world as understood from the standpoint of everyday life. This fitted well with one native American methodological notion, namely that of W. I. Thomas, that sociology should seek to understand social reality by understanding first the actor's definition of the situation.

The Schutzian perspective was developed in a moderate and sociological form by Peter Berger and his European collaborator

Thomas Luckmann (1967). They argued that the actor's view of the situation and all that might be thought of as passing for knowledge in everyday life had to be built into our sociological models of participating actors. Moreover, 'knowledge' involved elements other than purely cognitive ones and the self, which was understood as emerging (as George Mead suggested) in the course of symbolic interaction, was already caught up in a tightly organized role system. Nonetheless, Berger and Luckmann did not ask for the replacement of sociology by the sociology of knowledge. They merely argued that the former presupposed the latter.

A more deliberate phenomenological attack on positivism, however, was mounted by Cicourel (1964) and Garfinkel (1967). Cicourel questioned the distortion of so-called data, which was involved not merely in official statistics, but in the survey data which lay at the basis of Lazarsfeld-type empirical research. Thereafter they went on to look not merely at the social categorizations involved in language, but at the underlying assumptions of that language as it was used in practical contexts.

It is no surprise that, apart from their phenomenological heritage, both Cicourel and Garfinkel were indirectly students of the later Wittgenstein. For Wittgenstein came, as his teaching went on, to renounce the dogmatic metaphysics which had laid the foundations of the Vienna Circle and logical positivism (Roche, 1973). Instead of calling for one true language to talk about the world, Wittgenstein now spoke of an infinity of languages and was prepared to attribute equal validity to all of them, provided that one did not create metaphysical chaos by trying to talk two languages simultaneously and getting frames of reference mixed.

The new humility of linguistic philosophy was eagerly adopted by many sociologists. If philosophy was simply the study of different language games then surely philosophy was a sociological discipline. Against this, however, the philosophers argued that since the sociologist always substituted his own explanation of the actor's behaviour, whether as caused or otherwise, for that of the actor himself, it had to be rejected. The study of action in terms of the actor's reasons for his behaviour was a philosophic rather than a sociological matter (Bryant, 1970). Little wonder then that Garfinkel should have invented for his own research exercises the title 'ethnomethodology'.

The intellectually sophisticated background of Berger and Luckmann, of Cicourel and Garfinkel, was not, however, shared by a group of sociological specialists who now began to develop theories apparently similar in kind. These were the deviance theorists led by such men as Lemert (1951), Matza (1964) and Becker (1963). What was called labelling theory grew out of the important assertion as against orthodox criminology that criminality or deviance was not an observable attribute of an act. There was a man who acted and another who labelled his act as deviant. Thus the study of deviance was epistemologically complex.

Unfortunately, this epistemological complexity and an attempt to explicate it was not what caught on amongst the deviance theorists and their pupils in America and elsewhere. With little understanding of sociological theory as such, they went on to describe one form of deviance after another as primarily a matter of labelling and even went on to extend these simplistic notions to the study of such phenomena as mental ill-health and political violence. It is hard not to see the areas of activity and inactivity in the deviance schools, as being more determined by an ideological identification with the deviant rather than as a genuine attempt to understand sociological reality (see below, Chaps 18, 19).

It is this state of affairs which leads one to doubt whether sociology as such is likely to survive as a discipline. While it is true that sociologists' explanation of action, from Durkheim's *Suicide* onward, has often been highly dubious, the current acceptance of the actor's own definition without criticism, whether in deviance theory or in what is called humanistic psychiatry (Laing, 1965, 1967), does not seem capable of getting us to any sort of discipline other than a purely empiricist phenomenology. The position taken in this book is outlined in later chapters. It is that the sociologist as observer does have the capacity to make observations of social reality distinct from those of the participant actors, and for any serious analysis of historical social structures on a comparative and historical basis, such a separate, controlled and disciplined perspective is essential. We are in substantial agreement with those Marxists like Lucien Goldmann who accuse phenomenology of trafficking only in false consciousness, even though we might not agree with what they wish to put in its place.

What one is witnessing in the advanced industrial countries which gave birth to sociology, is the substitution for sociology of the cult of privatized meaning (Gouldner, 1970), which is all that can be accepted once the consensus, which Parsonian sociology seems to assert, is denied. But if sociology loses its grip on the problems of the advanced industrial countries viewed in isolation, new developments might well occur as the result of the revolution of the ex-colonial and poverty-stricken nations which it is common to call the Third World. There is no possibility of pretending that there is a unitary value consensus and the forms of authority, domination and exploitation are of the kind which Weber described in his comparative and historical work. Often they are the self-same structures; sometimes they are new. But clearly it is in the type of conceptualization suggested by Weber and sometimes by Marx that their structure and dynamics are to be understood. This is a topic which we have sought to explore elsewhere (Rex, 1972).

Max Weber was born in 1864. He was the son of a wealthy merchant family and his father was prominent in the National Liberal Party at the time of Bismarck. His original studies were in law but he quickly turned his attention to economics and economic history. His first important academic appointment was as professor of economics in the University of Freiburg in 1893. Three years later he moved to Heidelberg.

At Heidelberg he suffered from a serious mental illness and was unable to continue his academic work for four years. After his recovery he did not return to his teaching duties, but devoted himself to research and writing while also assuming the joint editorship of the *Archiv für Sozialwissenschaft und Sozialpolitik*. During the period which followed, Weber embarked upon his methodological studies and comparative studies of Chinese, Indian and Jewish civilization. He continued to be concerned with political affairs, and, while remaining a German patriot, was a critic of the Kaiser and those who surrounded him. In the Weimar Republic he served on the committee of experts which drafted the constitution and unsuccessfully sought nomination to the newly constituted assembly. In 1917 he was visiting professor in the University of Vienna. In 1919 he accepted a chair in Munich. He died at the age of 56 in June 1920.

The work of Max Weber has had very little influence in England, and in the age of the computer, shows little sign of having much influence in the future. This is not due to Weber's inadequacy: even those who show least understanding of his contribution to sociology usually pay him lip service. Of all the great teachers of sociology, Max Weber was the most sensitive to the philosophical, methodological and theoretical problems of the discipline. Moreover, his empirical contributions to sociology were on a scale which has not been paralleled before or since his time, and any one of them is worth more than thousands of the little articles which crowd our journals. Weber is ignored in England simply because we know that few of us are capable of making an effective contribution if the discipline is defined in his terms.

Many who have become acquainted with Weber through his slight work, 'The Protestant Ethic and the Spirit of Capitalism', his chapters on bureaucracy or through secondary discussion of his use of 'ideal types' will think these claims extravagant. But if they read some of the increasing number of translated chapters of Weber's *Wirtschaft und Gesellschaft* (Weber, 1968) they will find there a comprehension of the problems of the subject and an illumination of their research problems which they will find nowhere else.

Perhaps the first thing to be said about Weber is that he was passionately engaged in the affairs of his nation and deeply concerned about the internal tensions of Western capitalist society. Throughout his life as a scholar he remained a member of, and participated actively in, the work of the Association for Social Policy, which was concerned with practical social and political questions. And throughout his life he remained actively engaged in German politics, spending his last few years trying to understand Germany's defeat in the First World War and trying to see some basis, in the future, for a stable German society.

But to have such concerns was by no means incompatible with a scholarly and detached approach to social questions, and Weber was always concerned to argue that the social scientist could make his own special contribution to the solution of social questions only if he was prepared for a time to suspend his value judgments and to study what actually occurred. To understand his work, therefore, we must begin by considering his methodological ideas.

The first of these ideas concerns the use of 'ideal types' in sociology. Many seem to imagine that this means a turning away from the facts to a contemplation of 'pure forms'. But what is the alternative? Durkheim, who advocated a radical empiricism in *The Rules of Sociological Method*, was sophisticated enough to see that sociologists could not talk about all social phenomena simultaneously and hence must have some conception of a species type. But he argued, without ever explaining what he meant, that this type could be based upon some sort of statistical average.

This idea turns out to be absurd. For what after all is an average frog? Or, what is more important, what relationship would this average frog have to all the particular frogs which the biologist observes? The problem of the scientist is to construct a type against which existing cases can be compared and their deviation from the pure type measured. For this purpose the statistically average type has nothing especially to commend it. Weber saw this and urged that our first task in the study of society and culture must be to clarify the elements united in a particular structure, and to set these out in an ideal type so that when we approached the particular case we should know what features were especially worthy of exact observation and measurement.

Weber, however, had a good historical training and he was aware how misleading abstract conceptions like that of 'economic man' could be. He therefore urged that the sociologist should go beyond saying, 'this is how it would be, other things being equal' to saying, 'this is how the thing works in this case, given its peculiar historical setting.' He wanted his types to be illuminating in unique and specific historical circumstances. In practice his resolution to do this broke down, and happily so. For, while it is true that there is a task to be done in illuminating the unique instance, it is also true that the unique instance is greatly illuminated by comparison. So Weber went on from a penetrating analysis of the uniqueness of Western capitalism to see that uniqueness as a particular value given to variables of social structure, whose other values could be seen in other civilizations.

But what are the special phenomena which the sociologist seeks to illuminate through ideal types? Durkheim had seen these as reified supra-individual entities and his empirical orientation ends up in the mysticism of some kind of group mind concept. In fact there are no such supra-individual entities. They are simply constructs which we all, sociologists and non-sociologists alike, make up to help us predict what other people are going to do. The concept of 'group' refers to nothing else but a set of expectations which individuals have of each other's behaviour and which they take into account when they plan their own action. Thus Weber concluded that the most elementary concept of all in sociology was that of 'action' and that all group concepts had to be built up from a starting point which posited a hypothetical actor planning his action and taking account of the action of others.

This seems laborious and it implies a lot of hard theoretical work. But such theoretical work clarifies the question 'What data are relevant?' It is the empiricists, who pretend that there is a class of facts 'out there' labelled 'social' which simply have to be read off, who really mystify the process of social investigation. The greatness of Durkheim perhaps lay in the fact that he saw how difficult his own position was. But it was Weber who undertook the labour of deducing every important general sociological concept from the notion of 'action'.

One of his earliest investigations was concerned with the condition of agricultural workers in east Germany, Weber saw in the situation there the clash of two cultures and two kinds of social interaction. One was the residually feudal order presided over by the Junkers. The other was the new market economy. Weber had little respect for the Junkers, who in practice behaved like capitalists, yet still had the pretensions of a feudal nobility. Thus he came to ask the questions which perplexed him all his life: 'Is market behaviour natural, or is it itself the product of a particular ideological situation?' and, 'Does market behaviour imply a collapse of social order into some sort of economic war of all against all or is a society based upon market relations necessarily dependent for its continued existence upon a particular type of social ethic?'

Weber naturally became associated with Troeltsch at Heidelberg, who had already produced something of a sociology of Christian social teaching, and who had shown very clearly the connection between Calvinist theology and capitalist ethics. Weber gave this work a sounder sociological foundation by showing that there was a factual connection between these two phenomena. He demonstrated that it was precisely in those areas where Calvinism had gained a hold that capitalism flourished, and he spelled out clearly the ideal types of the Calvinist social ethic and expected capitalist behaviour in the West.

The method which Weber uses in this and subsequent studies is of some importance. For Weber does not rest content with telling, as he says, 'a plausible story' about the congruence of Calvinism and capitalism. Such a proof, which would have been acceptable to many German historians, seemed to him to be

'adequate in the level of meaning' only. It needed supplementa-
tion by a proof which was 'causally adequate'. On the other
hand, however, Weber would not have been content with a proof
which was only causally adequate. It was the special feature of
sociology that it was capable of showing, and had a duty to show,
the meaningful relations between phenomena which were known
to be empirically associated.

This sensitivity of Weber both to the need for 'understanding'
in the human studies and to the need for scientific rigour of proof
in accordance with the canons of science is what really makes his
sociology distinctive. Historians, and critics too, often seek 'insight' without ever showing that their plausible interpretative
models actually apply to the facts. Empirical sociologists, on the
other hand, demonstrate correlations *ad nauseam* without ever
showing why such connections exist. Weber does justice to both
traditions and is able to do so because the theoretical models in
terms of which he interprets social phenomena are, on the one
hand, set out as testable hypotheses, and on the other, stated in
terms of the meaning of the situation as it appears to a hypothetical actor.

Weber's embarkation upon his comparative-historical studies
may have followed from his desire further to underpin the causal
proof of the relation between Protestantism and Capitalism, for
he begins by showing that, although there were many factors
conducive to the development present in China, a crucial difference
lay in the totally different world outlook of Confucianism. But
Weber was not naïve enough to suppose that European and
Chinese civilizations differed only in a single factor. In any case
he had already suggested in a study of the Western city that the
dissociation of the city from kinship and village ties and its
emergence as a confessional association was another factor
peculiar to the West and one which, along with Protestantism,
played an important part in the emergence of Western capitalism.
What he now set about was a study of the particular institutional
complexes of China, India and Ancient Palestine.

It is not possible here to review all the contributions to general
sociology which flowed from Weber's comparative studies. We
shall discuss only two. These are his types of legitimate authority
and administration and his systematic typology of religious doctrines and religious functionaries. It should be remembered,

however, that along with these went discussions of guilds, kinship, cities, social classes and status groups, types of law, and systems of what Marx called the 'social relations of production'.

No one can study China without being struck by the distinctiveness of its administrative system. To the Westerner it appears to have important bureaucratic elements and yet not to be a bureaucracy as we understand it. Weber described the situation in his *The Religion of China*, but returned to its analysis in his later systematic work where it is comprehended in a frame of reference which throws light upon European feudalism, religious leadership and modern European politics and administration and politics. Typically, here, Weber starts from a particular historical case but goes on to illuminate it by comparison.

The key notion which Weber starts with is 'authority'. There are many reasons why one man should be able to ensure the compliance of another. But the most important of these is a subjective feeling on the part of the other that the authority is legitimate. Once kinship and community collapse as bases of social organization, organizations based upon this feeling of legitimate authority are the most important in the analysis of social systems (apart perhaps from market structures).

Systems of authority are classified by the reasons which men give for thinking the authority legitimate. The first distinction is between traditional authority where the compulsion to obey a person in a certain position is justified on the ground that 'it has always been so', and charismatic authority where the leader or ruler is obeyed for an opposite reason that he has 'unusual qualities'. Both these forms of authority, however, are relatively arbitrary compared with the rational-legal form where the ruler is obeyed because he is thought to be acting in accordance with general principles or laws.

Each of these types has its own dynamics or tends to produce a characteristic type of struggle for power, and each has its own type of 'administrative' staff. Charismatic leaders initially rule with the aid of a 'band of disciples', the leader interferes with the administration at all levels, and there is considerably uncertainty about the succession. Traditional rule takes two forms, the patrimonial, in which the administrators approximate to the position of palace servants under the total power of the ruler, and the feudal, in which authority is decentralized and the vassals are bound to their lord by a voluntary contract of obedience. Rational-legal authority rules through bureaucrats, whose spheres of competence are precisely laid down, who are responsible to their superiors in a hierarchy, whose official life is clearly demarcated from their private life and who can never become indispensable.

Weber saw religious ideologies and organizations more clearly as a result of his Chinese studies. Confucianism represented a minimal type of religion, for it preached a doctrine of acceptance of the world, and its officials became secular officials. The great interest of religion as an element in history, however, really arose only in those cases where there was some kind of religious rejection of the world and where religious leaders stood outside the administration. But there were a number of different cases of this kind. The religious rejection of the world as it was might lead to an attempt to master it (the ascetic alternative) or it might lead to an attempt to escape from it (the mystical alternative).

The above paragraphs sketch only the essentials of what Weber had to say, even in the fields with which they deal. But it is now perhaps possible to consider their contemporary relevance.

The less insular our sociology becomes, the more we may need to turn to Weber's comparative historical approach. This is more and more forced upon us, as we recognize that our Western institutions are not readily transferable to the underdeveloped countries. We see the really problematic nature of rational-legal politics and bureaucratic administration, when an attempt is made to fit them into a charismatic or traditional setting. And we see how important some functional equivalent to the Calvinist world outlook is for economic development, when we witness the failure to achieve an economic take-off in those countries where Cadillac capitalism flourishes.

But Weber's importance is by no means confined to extra-European contexts. It is of the greatest importance for the achievement of any sensitive understanding of the problems of administration and stratification in our own society. One of the most absurd criticisms of Weber is that his theory of bureaucracy is wrong because it does not exactly describe systems of political and industrial administration as they are to be observed in our society. For the greatness of Weber lies precisely in the fact that he never merely described what he saw but, in setting up a pure type, also indicated the principle directions in which actual cases might deviate from it. Thus his theory of bureaucracy, taken together with his analysis of traditional and charismatic structures, still provides the most illuminating framework for analysing administrative systems.

On the question of stratification, Weber faced all the central questions which Marx did, but saw these as only a part of the problem. With Marx he sees that the existence of a labour market may give rise to class conflict. But when he equates a man's class situation with his market situation Weber goes on to point out a whole range of possible market situations (for example the landlord-tenant situation) other than that in the labour market. He also distinguishes status situations sharply from market situations, seeing them as concerned with the differential distribution of prestige. But he does not, like other theorists of status, see status groups as passive. He sees them as developing a 'way of life' which they might preserve as against that of the wider society, or which they might seek to impose on that wider society. And, perhaps most interestingly of all, he sees the possibility that the incumbents of a role within a particular social subsystem (for example the administrators, the priests, the merchants, the artisans) might form a status group in this sense.

It was with these tools that Weber sought to understand the institutional roots of Western capitalist society. We still need them to achieve that understanding.[1]

[1] For a good bibliography of Weber's main works see Reinhard Bendix, *Max Weber: An Intellectual Portrait*, 1960, and Guenther Roth, 'Introduction to Max Weber', in Max Weber, *Economy and Society*, 1968.

11 **Emile Durkheim**

Why should there be a special science called sociology? Why not simply a science of human behaviour in general? Is the behaviour of social groups not ultimately reducible to the behaviour of the groups' individual members? Questions such as these are bound to occur to anyone approaching sociological literature for the first time. But much of that literature fails to answer these questions. It is concerned with a rag-bag of problems, which might equally well be dealt with by a biologist, a psychologist, an economist, or a statistician. It looks for no special class of determinants, it asks no special questions, it brings no special insights to the facts under review.

The student who feels this way cannot do better than to pick up Emile Durkheim's *The Rules of Sociological Method*. For there, at last, he will find an author with a firm conviction of the distinctiveness of social facts and the importance of a special discipline to study them. And Durkheim clearly makes his case; for along with the purely individual, biological and psychological determinants of human behaviour, it is clear that there are others, which do not arise from the constitution of the individual. As Durkheim says:

> When I fulfil my obligations as brother, husband or citizen, when I execute my contracts, I perform duties which are defined externally to myself and my acts in law and custom. Even if they conform to my own sentiments and I feel their reality subjectively, such reality is still objective, for I did not create them.
>
> (Durkheim, 1938, p. 1)

Obligations, contracts, duties, laws and customs are thus isolated as a specific subject matter, and their distinguishing feature is (*a*) that they are 'exterior' to any individual and (*b*) that they exercise

132

constraint over him. If we confine ourself to facts of this kind we shall be studying 'society'.

Sometimes, however, individuals are constrained by external facts which are rather more vague and difficult to study. If one wishes to study the legal determinants of human behaviour one has data ready to hand in written legal codes. But if one seeks to study the effect of a crowd on its members, or vague social trends such as fashion, it is not quite so clear what kind of evidence one should seek. Durkheim believed that it was important that such social trends should be studied. Indeed he probably felt that they constituted the major part of the subject matter of sociology. He therefore argues that, if the social fact has no independent observable existence of its own, it is the sociologist's job to give it one. He should do this by discovering statistical rates which should be taken not merely as a counting of separate individual phenomena but as indices of social currents.

The empirical application of these ideas is to be found in two of Durkheim's most important works: *The Division of Labour in Society* and *Suicide*. In the first, his doctoral thesis, Durkheim argues that social order cannot be explained, as the English utilitarians sought to explain it, in terms of the enlightened self-interest of individuals. There must, as it were, be something there, apart from purely individual tendencies binding individuals together into social wholes. This 'something' is a form of social solidarity. In simple societies this form of social solidarity rests upon collectively held sentiments and ideas. In advanced societies it rests upon the division of labour which is not just an expedient device for increasing human happiness, but a moral and social fact whose purpose is to bind society together. Both forms of social solidarity, however, have this in common. They are expressed in legal codes and it is to the comparative study of these codes that Durkheim directs our attention.

In his study, *Suicide*, which still stands as a model of the specifically sociological use of statistics, Durkheim begins by showing that the available statistics do not seem to support any hypotheses which attribute suicide to individual causes. What matters is the rate of suicide and this, which varies only slowly, is indicative of a kind of society whose very structure compels a minority of people towards self-destruction. In a society having the first kind of social solidarity discussed in *The Division of*

Labour, the trend is towards 'altruistic suicide'. In a society of the second kind, suicide tends to be 'egoistic'. *Suicide* is a very complex book indeed, but what has to be noted here is the way in which it opens up the possibility of the sociological treatment of statistics. What Durkheim has done for suicide, could be done in relation, say, to patterns of marriage and divorce, delinquency or industrial unrest. By contrasting the statistical rates of these phenomena in different social groups we should be able to discover the strictly *social* concomitants of variations in the rate.

Because Durkheim inherited the tradition of nineteenth-century positivism, he did not confine himself to the empirical study of sociological data for its own sake. He was concerned to extract from empirical material a positive guide to action. And he believed that in showing what were the essentials of social order that he was also showing what were the conditions of human happiness.

The great enemy, as he saw it, to an adequate positive ethic was the tradition of English utilitarianism culminating in the sociology of Herbert Spencer. The utilitarians believed that human happiness could be increased by a continuous increase in the size and number of individual lots of pleasures. It seemed to Durkheim that, far from this being the case, human happiness could only be assured, if the pleasures of the individual were limited by socially imposed norms. In circumstances in which these norms collapsed, the individual found himself in the state of personal disorganization which Durkheim called 'anomie'.

The notion of anomie crops up both in *The Division of Labour* and in *Suicide*. In *The Division of Labour*, Durkheim recognizes that the division of labour does not in fact always produce social order. In many cases differentiation of function is actually accompanied not by reintegration but by conflict. This state Durkheim calls 'the anomic division of labour'.

He goes on to argue from this that what is needed, to overcome anomie and reintegrate our social order, is the organization of men into occupational groups, whose professional ethics will not merely integrate each group within itself, but also relate it to the other groups in the larger society.

The ambiguities of Durkheim's position here, together with his evasion of such problems as the economic basis of class conflict, have made it possible for him to be hailed as the prophet, both of guild socialism and fascist corporativism. But he does have the merit of having formulated what must be the central question of modern social organization, namely, 'when the old social order based upon kinship and the tribe breaks down, what will be the elements from which the new social order will be built?' In suggesting that the occupational group might be such an element, moreover, he offered an alternative to the individualistic and family-centred ideal which has played such a large part in English sociology.

In *Suicide* we again encounter the possibility of anomie; for along with the forms of suicide which are, as it were, inherent in forms of social order, there is another kind of suicide, anomie suicide, which follows from the collapse of social norms. And here Durkheim recognizes that the collapse of social order is accompanied by actual personality disorganization. The individual who commits anomie suicide is sick and he is sick because his society has collapsed.

The recognition of this fact in *Suicide* forces Durkheim to explore new ground; for while he maintains to the last his insistence on the distinctiveness of social facts, he finds it less and less possible to argue that such facts are solely and simply 'external' to the individual. That which is external is also a constitutive element of the social personality. It was to the problem of the intimacy of the relation between the social and the personality system that Durkheim addressed himself in his lectures on education and in his greatest work, *The Elementary Forms of the Religious Life* (1915).

This last is, like most of Durkheim's work, of complicated origin. As a Jew, brought up in a Catholic educational tradition and ending up as an agnostic, Durkheim had undoubtedly pondered long on the question of the validity of religious belief and he wished to defend publicly the shocking thesis of the equation God = Society. But, having devoted himself so long to the problem of the nature of social facts, he was equally interested in discovering why social norms should have the morally con-straining quality which they do. And finally, he was, as we have said, concerned with the relationship between the social system and the social personality of the individual.

What Durkheim purports to show under the first head is that on important social occasions amongst primitive people, when the whole clan or tribe has gathered, an atmosphere is generated, which is attributed to supernatural origins, but which, in fact, is simply due to the collective excitement of the crowd. This atmosphere carries over into the ordinary 'profane' life of the people, so that all the symbols of society's presence take on a sort of supernatural quality, which Durkheim calls 'mana'.

Now there is much in this, and anyone who has participated in great national rituals will recognize the similarity between our feelings about purely social, and religious, symbols. But it has often been asked whether this really proves Durkheim's point. Why do social symbols have the quality they do? Crowd excitement by itself seems a weak explanation. Would it not be equally true to say that the social has a divine origin as to say that the divine has a social origin?

What is much more important, however, is the effect of this argument on Durkheim's conception of the relation between society and the individual. The conception of social order as a mere expedient will not do; but nor will that of society as a purely external fact. As he says, society awakens in us not only 'the idea of a physical force to which we must give way of necessity' but 'that of a moral power such as religions adore'. Or again,

> When we obey somebody because of the moral authority
> which we recognize in him. . . . We do so . . . because a
> certain sort of physical energy is immanent in the idea we
> form of this person, which conquers over will and inclines
> it in the indicated direction.
>
> (Durkheim, 1915, p. 207)

For anyone who accepts these formulations, the nature of sociology is transformed. It ceases to be simply a matter of head counting. What we have to do, if we accept them, is to study man always as a member of a moral community. The first question which we have to ask of any society which we are studying is, 'what are the moral communities which compose it?' A question which leads on the one hand to the understanding of the dynamics of the society, and on the other hand to an understanding of the kind of man which the society produces.

The ideas of Emile Durkheim have, perhaps, had a more

widespread influence than those of any other sociologist. His insistence that social facts must have a sociological explanation has led to the development of the functionalist school of anthropology, which seeks to explain social customs in terms of the contribution which they make to the maintenance of the social structure. His use of statistical material has inspired many sociologists to carry out empirical studies, which do not fail to locate the specifically social determinants of human behaviour. His understanding of societies as moral entities has helped to give depth to the dynamic study of groups.

Yet there are points in Durkheim's thought which remain extremely arguable and which may, through overstatement, be extremely misleading. Two deserve special mention.

One is his emphasis on social consensus and integration. It may well be true that the utilitarian conception of a society, based solely on enlightened self-interest, is inadequate. But self-interest and class-interest are nonetheless factors which must be taken into account in any interpretation of actual historical events. It is surely not sufficient to dismiss a society, in which there is not a consensus but a conflict of norms, as not really a society at all, but a state of anomie. And, if such a society is to be reintegrated, we should say on the basis of which norms the integration is to take place.

The second point follows from the first. It is that, having said rightly that participation in a social and normative order is essential to human happiness, Durkheim seems to assume, wrongly, that any social and normative order, provided it is integrated, will guarantee this happiness. Here it is enlightening to compare Durkheim's philosophical standpoint with that of the early Marx. Marx too saw that, in his own words, 'the human essence is the ensemble of social relations'. But he also saw that while the system of social relations might liberate man and make him capable of 'self-activity', it might also become a thing alien to man, confronting him and constraining him from outside. We may say that Marx failed to describe exactly the kind of pattern of social relations in which self-activity would be possible. But he did at least see that there was a choice to be made, and that the mere fact of the involvement of man in an integrated system of social relations would not necessarily guarantee his self-fulfilment and happiness. It is his failure to see this which seems to make

Durkheim, among the great sociologists, the arch-apostle of the *status quo*.

Yet every sociologist's perspective is limited by the particular attitude which, for other reasons, he has towards social change. What we can say about Durkheim is that, given his standpoint, he was not afraid to pose the most important questions about the relation between the individual and society; and that when he turned to empirical studies, they were never sterile and meaningless, but helped to advance our understanding of the human condition. When more sociologists approach their chosen empirical fields in this way, the subject will become far more fruitful and illuminating than it is at present.

12 **Karl Marx, speaking for himself**

Marx's intellectual starting point was the idealistic, philosophic system of Hegel. Some fifty years later, Engels recalled what an impact Hegel had made on Marx and his contemporaries at the University of Berlin:

> One can imagine what a tremendous effect this Hegelian system must have produced in the philosophy-tinged atmosphere of Germany. It was a triumphal procession which lasted for decades and which by no means came to a standstill on the death of Hegel. On the contrary, it was precisely from 1830 to 1840 that Hegelianism reigned most exclusively and to a greater or lesser extent infected even its opponents. It was precisely in this period that Hegelian views, consciously or unconsciously, most extensively penetrated the most diversified sciences, and leavened even popular literature and the daily press from which the average educated consciousness derives its mental pabulum.
>
> (Marx and Engels, 1962a, 2, p. 365)

Marx's contemporaries, of course, claimed to be critics of Hegel. They called for a radical rejection of what they regarded as his false philosophical illusions. Marx himself described the position which they adopted:

> Hitherto, men have constantly made up for themselves false conceptions about themselves, about what they are and ought to be. They have arranged their relationships according to their ideas of God, of normal man, etc. The phantoms of their brains have got out of their hands. They, the creators, have bowed down before their creations.
>
> (Marx and Engels, 1964, pp. 23–4)

But all that the critics seemed to do was to substitute the rule of one set of ideas for another, instead of studying reality itself:

139

Once upon a time a valiant fellow had the idea that men were drowned in water only because they were possessed with the idea of gravity. If they were to knock this notion out of their heads, say, by stating it to be a superstition, a religious concept, they would be sublimely proof against any danger from water. His whole life long he fought against the illusion of gravity, of whose harmful results all statistics brought him new and manifold evidence.

(ibid.)

By contrast, Marx was prepared in 1846 to say:

The production of ideas, of conceptions, of consciousness, is directly interwoven with material activity and the material intercourse of man, the language of real life.

(op. cit., p. 37)

But it took Marx several years before he was willing to argue for so robust a materialism and it was always the mark of what he called 'dialectical materialism' that it continued to be preoccupied as Hegelianism was with the problem of alienation or self-estrangement.

The philosophy of Hegel, in fact, could be taken on many levels, but its intellectual heart lay in its metaphysics. In sharp opposition to contemporary thinking in France or to the evolutionary doctrines which were to come in England, the Hegelian view was that all which existed was to be understood as spirit rather than as the product of the interaction of particles of matter. Spirit expresses itself in created things in order, so this poetical and fanciful notion has it, that it may know its own nature. But confronted with its own attributes in this external form, it is estranged from its own self and must regain the external world for itself by knowing and understanding it. This is what absolute spirit or God is doing all the time in history. Spirit creates nature and then masters nature by a process of cognition. In this process man's position is ambiguous. He is in one sense a created object, that is spirit estranged from himself, but he is also spirit and it is through individual men and their acting and thinking that spirit regains possession of itself.

One of the young Hegelians, Ludwig Feuerbach, proposed a radical revision of this system by substituting man for God.

Far from God being estranged from himself in man, Feuerbach suggested that man failed to realize his ideal nature because he attributed what was best in himself to an alien being, God. As he put it:

> Religion is the disuniting of man from himself; he sets God before him as the antithesis of himself. God is not what man is, man is not what God is. God is perfect, man imperfect; God eternal, man temporal; God almighty, man weak; God holy, man sinful. To enrich God man must become poor, that God may be all man must become nothing.
>
> (Feuerbach, 1957, p. 33)

Marx remained interested in precisely this question. How could man overcome his estrangement from himself? How could he become free to make his own history? As he puts it in his *Critique of the Hegelian Philosophy of the Right*:[1]

> Man who sought a superman in the fantastic reality of heaven, but found there only a reflection of himself, will no longer wish to find merely an appearance of himself, only a non-man in the realm where he seeks and must seek his true reality.

If Marx therefore rejected Feuerbach, it was because Feuerbach attributed man's alienation to religion, not because he continued to discuss the question of alienation. Were there not other human creations which, once created, came to control him as it were from the outside, to impoverish him? The state, for instance, or money? Thus, in an essay on the Jewish Question he uses the language of Feuerbach to discuss man's subordination to money:[2]

> What is the worldly cult of the Jew? Huckstering. Who is his worldly God? Money. Money is the jealous One God of Israel, besides which no other God may stand. Money dethrones all the Gods of man and turns them into a commodity. Money is the universal independently constituted value of all things. It has therefore deprived the whole world, both the world of man and nature of its own

[1] Quoted by Robert C. Tucker in *Philosophy and Myth in Karl Marx*, 1961, p. 100.
[2] Quoted in Tucker, op. cit., p. 111.

value. Money is the alienated essence of man's work and being. This alien being rules over him and he worships it.

The real issue between Marx and Feuerbach is what form of alienation is primary? In 1845 Marx published his eleven enigmatic theses on Feuerbach:

> Feuerbach starts out from the fact of religious self-alienation, of the duplication of the world into a religious and imaginary world and a real one. His work consists in resolving the religious world into its secular basis. He overlooks the fact that after completing this work the chief thing still remains to be done. For the fact that the secular basis detaches itself from itself and establishes itself in the clouds as an independent realm can only be explained by the cleavage and self-contradiction in the secular basis. The latter must itself, therefore, be understood in its contradiction and then, by removal of the contradiction, revolutionized in practice. After the earthly family is discovered to be the secret of the holy family, the former must then itself be criticized in theory and revolutionized in practice.
>
> (Marx and Engels, 1962a, 2, p. 404)

Thus, Marx's so-called materialism does not simply take the form of saying that matter is prior to mind. What he appears to be saying is that the realization of human freedom has its primary inhibition in the economic sphere; in what he called 'the earthly family'. His whole life thereafter may be understood as criticizing this earthly family in theory and revolutionizing it in practice. That is why, above all, he came in 1867 to publish *Capital*. In his manuscripts of 1844, the centre of economic alienation is not, however, located simply in man's worship of money. There is a mass fundamental fact, namely, man's loss of control over his labour. He describes this precisely:

> In what does the alienation of labour consist? First, that the work is external to the worker, that it is not part of his nature, that consequently he does not fulfil himself in his work, but denies himself, has a feeling of misery not of well-being, does not develop freely a physical and mental

energy, but is physically exhausted and mentally debased. The worker therefore feels himself at home only during his leisure, whereas at work he feels homeless. His work is not voluntary but imposed forced labour. It is not a satisfaction of a need, but only a means for satisfying other needs. Its alien character is clearly shown by the fact that as soon as there is no physical or other compulsion it is avoided like the plague. Finally, the alienated character of work for the worker appears in the fact that it is not his work, but work for someone else, that in work he does not belong to himself but to another person.

(Marx, 1956, p. 72)

So by 1844 Marx had given his own answer to the central question which was being discussed by the young Hegelians, namely, the nature of man's self-estrangement and the way to freedom and self-fulfilment. But in the nine years since the beginning of his studies he had already lived through three careers.

He was the son of a free-thinking Rhineland lawyer who, born of a Jew and married to a Jewess, had himself and his whole family baptized when Karl was six. After a normal middle-class education, Karl Marx had started out as a student at Berlin and was introduced to Hegel by the professor of criminal law.

Marx spent some time trying to construct a rival system, but, after three weeks' almost ceaseless reading, announced his conversion to Hegelianism. As a result, he joined a graduates' club, a group of free-thinking intellectuals who argued about theology and politics in Hegelian terms.

One of Marx's closest associates at this time was Bruno Bauer, a lecturer in theology. Bauer, one of the founders of what was called the New Criticism, published a satirical pamphlet entitled 'The Trumpet of the Last Judgment over Hegel the atheist and antichrist'. Purporting to attack Hegel, it actually reinterpreted his philosophy in atheistic and humanistic terms. As a result, Bauer, who it is said would have sought a fellowship for Marx, was himself sacked, thus ending Marx's prospect of an academic career.

Fortunately, a group of liberal industrialists had recently founded a radical journal in Cologne and Marx was invited to contribute. Moses Hess, who was instrumental in founding the paper, describes him at this time:[1]

> He is the greatest, perhaps the one genuine philosopher now alive and will soon draw the eyes of all Germany. Dr. Marx—that is my idol's name—is still very young (about twenty-four at most) and will give mediaeval religion and politics their coup de grâce. He combines the deepest philosophical seriousness with the most biting wit. Imagine Rousseau, Voltaire, Holbach, Lessing, Herne and Hegel fused into one person—I say fused, not thrown together in a heap—and you have Dr. Marx.

By the end of 1842 Marx was editor of the journal, the *Rheinische Zeitung*, but it was not long before his leading articles brought him into conflict with the government and in April 1843 the paper was officially suppressed. He was not unduly distressed and wrote at the time of his career as a journalist:[2]

> It is bad to work for freedom in servitude and to fight with pens instead of clubs. I am sick of the hypocrisy, the stupidity, the brutal authority and of our cringing, complying tergiversation. And now the Government has given me back my freedom.

Before setting out for Paris, Marx was to marry Jenny von Westphalen. Jenny was the daughter of Baron von Westphalen, who was a Prussian official and who lived next door to the Marxes in Trier. Marx had played with Jenny as a child and although she was courted by many well-born or well-placed suitors, had waited seven years for Marx while he was at college. She remained devoted to him until her death in 1882.

In Paris, Marx joined Ruge in editing the *Deutsch-Französische Jahrbücher*, whose earliest contributors included Marx himself, Carlyle and Friedrich Engels. For two years he went to work studying the development of revolutionary movements in France and the theory of classical economics.

Moses Hess, who was a student of Proudhon, one of the founders of French socialism, had already convinced Marx that the way to man's liberation lay in communism. But as Marx saw

[1] Quoted in Isaiah Berlin, *Karl Marx*, 1939, p. 73.
[2] Quoted in Edmund Wilson, *To the Finland Station*, 1940.

it, Hess had no answer to the way in which communism was to
be achieved. In practice, the term 'communism' had come to be
attached to revolutionary groups of working men in the French
Revolution, but Hess specifically rejected the idea that communism would come about through the revolutionary action of the
urban working class. While he wrote:

> It is an error . . . diligently spread by reaction, that
> socialism develops only among the proletariat and among
> the proletariat only as a question of fulfilling the needs of
> the stomach.

> (Hook, 1962)

Marx replied:[1]

> Where, then, is the positive possibility of German
> emancipation? In the formation of a class with radical
> chains . . . a class which is the dissolution of all classes,
> a sphere of society which has a universal character because
> its sufferings are universal and which claims no particular
> right because the wrong committed against it is not a
> particular wrong, but wrong as such. When the proletariat
> declares the dissolution of the existing social order, it does
> no more than proclaim the secret of its own existence, for it
> constitutes the effective dissolution of this order.

Marx's study of economics brought him close to Engels, whom
he had known earlier as a Young Hegelian, but who now appeared
on the scene having gained some real experience of the new
capitalist order while working in his father's mill in Manchester.

Engels wrote about real flesh-and-blood working-class people
as he had seen them in their industrial hovels in Manchester.
But he also put his finger on what was to become, for Marx, the
central problem of all. Starting from Hegel, Marx had discussed
the self-estrangement or alienation of labour. Engels saw that in
capitalist economics, labour was regarded as a commodity. It was
essentially the same idea.

Twenty-three years later, *Das Kapital* began precisely with the
question of what it means to say that labour is a commodity.
Engels had made the point already in 1845: 'Adam Smith was

[1] *Critique of the Hegelian Philosophy of the Right*, quoted by George
Lichtheim, *Marxism*, 1960.

perfectly right in making the assertion, "that the demand for men like that for any other commodity necessarily regulates the production of men, quickens it when it goes too slowly and stops when it advances too fast", just as in the case of any other commodity.'

So Marx faced two problems. One of these was to work out what happened in a social system when man's labour was estranged from his self as a commodity, and the other was to show how the proletariat, by its revolutionary actions, might put an end to this self-estrangement. For the moment it was the second problem which occupied him. He set out to meet the proletariat. This was not so easy as it seemed. The sociology of the proletariat was more complicated than Marx allowed. It is easy to talk about 'a class with radical chains' but you cannot see and talk to such a sociological entity. In practice, the proletariat had meant the radical workmen's clubs of revolutionary days and it had come to mean little messianic sects of workmen organized by agitators. Such an agitator was Wilhelm Weitling, a German carpenter. The Russian journalist Annenkov has described Marx's meeting with him:[1]

> After we had been casually introduced to one another we sat down at a little green table at the head of which Marx took his place with his leonine head bent over a sheet of paper while his inseparable friend and companion in propaganda, the tall, correct Engels with his English distinction and gravity, opened the meeting with a speech. He talked about the necessity for labour reformers arriving at some sort of clarity out of the confusion of opposing views and formulating some common doctrine which would serve as a banner to rally around for all followers, who had neither the time nor the ability to occupy themselves with questions of theory. But before Engels had finished his speech Marx suddenly raised his head.
> 'Tell us, Weitling, you who have made so much stir in Germany with your communist propaganda and have won over so many workers so that they have thereby lost their work and their bread, with what arguments do you defend your social revolutionary activity and on what basis do you propose to ground them?'

[1] Quoted in Edmund Wilson, *To the Finland Station*, 1940, pp. 68–9.

Weitling began to explain that it was not his task to develop
new economic theories, but to make use of those which,
as was to be seen in France, were best adapted to open the
eyes of the workers to their terrible situation and to all the
wrongs committed against them. Marx broke in on him with
glowering brows.
'The awakening of fantastic hopes will never lead to the
salvation of those who suffer, but to their undoing.
To go to the workers in Germany without strictly scientific
ideas and concrete doctrine would mean an empty and un-
scrupulous playing with propaganda which would inevitably
involve on the one hand the setting up of an inspired
apostle and on the other simply asses who would listen with
open mouth.'

It is important to notice that at this point Marx begins to speak
of his approach to politics as 'strictly scientific'. It is a term which
he and Engels used in contrast to the term 'utopian'. His own
approach, though never as idealistic as that of Moses Hess and
the so-called True Socialists, had itself smacked of utopianism.
True, he had held that the social order could not be changed
without a revolution in the basic social relations of production,
but these he insisted were the product of human agency and
therefore subject to human alteration. As he said in his final
thesis on Feuerbach: 'Hitherto philosophers have only interpreted the world. The point is to change it.'
    But already in 1846 a more deterministic and pessimistic note
intrudes. The social relations of production are themselves the
product of the 'mode' of production, and one cannot choose the
mode of production. In 1846 he writes to Annenkov:

Are men free to choose this or that form of society? By no
means. Assume a particular state of development in the
production faculties of man and you will get a particular
form of commerce and consumption. Assume particular
stages of development in production, commerce and
consumption and you will have a corresponding social
constitution, a corresponding organization of the family, of
orders or of classes, in a word a corresponding society.
It is superfluous to add that men are not free to choose

their own productive forces—which are the basis of all
history.

(Marx and Engels, 1953, p. 40)

The implication of this is clear. Realistic politics depends upon
studying technological and economic development and understanding its mechanisms. Political proposals must be related to
the stage reached in the development of productive forces. Had
history allowed, Marx might well have sat down at that moment
and started writing *Capital*. But in France, the homeland of
revolution, the monarchy of Louis Philippe was breaking up and
all sorts of revolutionary options seemed open. What Marx and
Engels wrote was the *Communist Manifesto*, a document which,
although unsurpassed amongst political manifestos in its analytic
and theoretical brilliance, was concerned with immediate political
tactics.

The Manifesto was printed in London in 1848 and published
in German just before the February revolution in France, and the
first French edition appeared in Paris just before the proletarian
insurrection against the new bourgeois government in June. Yet
its effect was small. The Communist League which commissioned
Marx and Engels to write it was a small secret society. The
leaders of the proletariat at the barricades in Paris were hardly
influenced by it at all.

What was probably more important was Marx's attempt to
draw the necessary lessons from the events of 1848. They did not
lead him to any kind of revolutionary optimism. The fact was
that the revolution of February had been carried through with
the support of the bourgeoisie, and when the bourgeoisie chose,
it was quite capable of defeating its erstwhile proletarian allies.
As Marx puts it:[1]

> The February Republic was won by the workers with the
> passive support of the bourgeoisie. The proletarians rightly
> regarded themselves as the victors of February and they
> made the arrogant claims of victors. They had to be
> vanquished in the streets; they had to be shown that they
> were worsted as soon as they did not fight with the
> bourgeoisie but against the bourgeoisie.

[1] 'The Class Struggles in France 1848–50', in Marx and Engels,
Selected Works, 1962a, p. 139.

And eventually it was the peasants who revolted against the new republican government, but tragically by the installation of Louis Napoleon as Emperor!

> December 10th 1848 was the day of the peasant insurrection. The symbol that expressed their entry into the revolutionary movement, clumsily cunning, knavishly naive, doltishly sublime, a calculated superstition, a pathetic burlesque, a cleverly stupid anachronism, a world historic piece of buffoonery and an undecipherable hieroglyphic for the understanding of the civilized—this symbol bore the unmistakable physiognomy of the class that represents barbarism with civilization. The republic had announced itself to this class with the tax collector, it announced itself to the republic with the emperor. Napoleon was the only man who had exhaustively represented the interests and imagination of the peasant class newly created in 1789.
>
> (Marx and Engels, 1962a, p. 173)

The peasants' Caesar consolidated the rule of the big bourgeoisie against the petty bourgeoisie, proletarian and peasant alike and, ridiculous and unlikely a figure as Napoleon might appear, the new state flourished. Marx could not in these circumstances see much prospect of a renewal of the revolution:

> With this general prosperity, in which the productive forces of bourgeois society develop as luxuriantly as is at all possible within bourgeois relations, there can be no talk of a real revolution. Such a revolution is only possible in the period when both these factors, the modern productive forces and the bourgeois productive forces come in collision with each other.
>
> (Marx and Engels, 1962a, p. 231)

Back, then, it would seem to economics. But before Marx made this return he expounded for the benefit of his German comrades in the Communist League a theory of how the revolution should be conducted. The workers might conclude tactical alliances with the bourgeoisie, but they must maintain their independence and keep the revolution going under their own control:[1]

[1] 'Address to the Communist League', in Marx and Engels, *Selected Works*, 1962a, I, p. III.

As previously so in this struggle, the mass of the petty
bourgeois will as long as possible remain hesitant, undecided
and inactive and then, as soon as the issue has been decided
will seize the victory for themselves, will call upon the
workers to maintain tranquillity, and return to their work,
will guard against so-called excesses and bar the proletariat
from the fruits of victory. It is not in the power of the
workers to prevent the petty-bourgeois democrats from
doing this, but it is in their power to make it difficult for
them to gain the upper hand against the armed proletariat,
and to dictate such conditions to them that the rule of the
bourgeois democrats will from the outset bear within it the
seeds of their own downfall. Above all, the workers must
counteract as much as is at all possible during the conflict
and immediately after the struggle the bourgeois endeavours
to allay the storm and must compel the democrats to carry
out their present terrorist phrases.

Yet revolutionary excitement must not prevent scientific
detachment.

In general they must in every way restrain as far as possible
the intoxication of victory and the enthusiasm for the new
state of things, which make their appearance after every
victorious street battle, by a calm and dispassionate
estimation of the situation and by unconcealed mistrust for
the new government. Alongside the new official government
they must establish simultaneously their own revolutionary
workers' governments.
In a word from the first moment of victory mistrust must
be directed no longer against the conquered reactionary
party, but against the workers' previous allies, against the
party that wishes to exploit the common victory for itself
alone.

(Marx and Engels, 1962a, 1, p. 111)

These were words which were to guide Lenin in his dealings
with the Russian Duma in 1917. And they remain the core of
communist revolutionary theory, but the new prosperity of the
1850s meant that they were, for a scientific socialist like Marx,
theory only.

During the early phases of the revolution in France, Marx had gone back to Cologne to revive the *Rheinische Zeitung* and, with the aid of the Communist League, to prepare the German workers for their revolution. But the League was suppressed and Marx was expelled from the Rhineland. He went to France but was only permitted to stay there under conditions of rustication. His friends subscribed to pay his passage to London. Although he had intended to stay there only for a few months, in fact he stayed there uninterruptedly till his death in 1863.

His rooms were in Dean Street, Soho, then one of London's filthiest slums. A visitor has described conditions in the Marx home:[1]

He lives in one of the worst and cheapest neighbourhoods in London. He occupies two rooms. There is not one clean or decent piece of furniture in either room, everything is broken tattered and torn, with thick dust over everything . . . manuscripts, books and newspapers lie beside the children's toys, bits and pieces from his wife's sewing basket, cups with broken rims, dirty spoons, knives, forks, lamps, and inkpot, tumblers, pipes, tobacco ash—all piled on the same table. On entering the room smoke and tobacco fumes make your eyes water to such an extent that at first you seem to be groping about in a cavern—until you get used to it and manage to make out certain objects in the haze. Sitting down is a dangerous business. Here is a chair with only three legs, there another which happens to be whole on which the children are playing at cooking. That is the one that is offered to the visitor, but the children's cooking is not removed and if you sit down you risk a pair of trousers. But all these things do not in the least embarrass Marx or his wife. You are received in the most friendly way and are cordially offered pipes, tobacco and whatever else there may happen to be. Presently a clever and interesting conversation arises which repays for all the domestic deficiencies and this makes discomfort bearable.

In those years the Marxes were, in fact, kept alive only by sub-sidies from Engels and by what Marx could earn as correspondent

[1] Quoted in Isaiah Berlin, *Karl Marx*, 1939, p. 171.

for the *New York Daily Tribune*. Three of his children died, and in one case the Marxes had no money even to pay for the coffin. But he was in no way ashamed of this poverty which was the inevitable consequence of his devotion to a cause which brought no material reward. His reward lay in what he was able to accomplish both theoretically and practically for the working-class movement.

Practically, he was always busy. With the Communist League dead, the most important movement with which he had to deal was the General Union of German Workers founded by Lasalle. In fact, Lasalle's party was the most successful working-class party yet organized. His programme was to campaign against the restricted franchise and to ally himself with Bismarck against the bourgeoisie. As a reward for his support he expected social benefits for the working class and also the setting up, by the state, of workers' co-operation which would undermine German capitalism. He was entirely unconvinced about the potential achievements of trade unions and retained romantic nationalist ideas from his early Hegelian background.

Marx disagreed with him on nearly every point. His theory of revolution had led him to side with the bourgeois parties against Bismarck's autocracy, even though he coupled this with the notion of keeping the revolution under proletarian control. He was not opposed to producers' co-operatives but could not conceive of such co-operatives as being of any value if they were set up by the existing state, which in his view had to be smashed and replaced by a proletarian dictatorship. He was an internationalist and had no sympathy for Lasalle's romantic nationalism. And finally he was convinced that the trade unions could raise wages and were a valuable basis for working-class organization.

In 1863 Marx comments contemptuously on Lasalle's campaign for state co-operatives and for universal franchise in a letter to Engels:

Lasalle sent me the day before yesterday his open letter in reply to the Central Workers' Committee for the Leipzig Workers' Congress. He demeans himself—importantly bandying around phrases he borrowed from us—altogether like a future labour dictator. Settling the problem of wage labour is literally child's play for him. The workers simply

have to agitate in favour of universal suffrage and then send
people like him equipped 'with the unsheathed weapons of
science' to the chamber of deputies. Then they will form
workers' factories, the capital for which will be advanced
by the *state* and these establishments will by and by enhance
the entire land. This is at any rate surprisingly new.

(Marx and Engels, 1953, p. 171)

Later on, in a letter to Kugelmann, he attacks Lasalle for
'shaking hands with Bismarck on behalf of the proletariat' and
goes on:

For a theatrically vain character like Lasalle (who was
not, however, to be bribed by paltry trash like office,
a mayoralty, etc.) it was a most tempting thought, an act
directly on behalf of the proletariat, executed by Ferdinand
Lasalle. He was, in fact, too ignorant of the real economic
conditions required by such an act to be critical of himself.
The German workers on the other hand were too
demoralized . . . not to hail such a quack saviour who
promised to get them at once into the promised land.

(Marx and Engels, 1953, p. 204)

Curiously, however, Marx always retained some lingering regard
for Lasalle and when Engels wrote him a somewhat ghoulish
letter when Lasalle was killed in a duel in 1864, he himself
wrote:[1]

Dear Friedrich,
L's disaster has been damnably in my head all day. In
spite of everything he was still one of the old sort and the
enemy of our enemies. Besides the thing came so
unexpectedly that it's hard to believe that so bustling,
stirring and pushing an individual is now as dead as a
mouse and must forever hold his tongue . . . Even aside
from his abilities, I personally loved him. The unfortunate
thing is that we concealed it from each other as if we were
going to live for ever.

By 1864 the International Association of Working Men had
been formed and Marx had his own movement from which the

[1] Edmund Wilson, *To the Finland Station*, 1940, p. 234.

Lasalleans were excluded. He was to return to these questions later after the formation of the Social Democratic Party and his last important work *The Critique of the Gotha Programme* was devoted to an attack on Lasalle's continuing influence. The theoretical argument went on well after Marx's death and indeed might be said to be still alive today. In time it came to turn on the attitude of the working classes to democracy and the welfare state.

Politically, however, it was the International which pre-occupied Marx during the 1860s. It was by no means the move-ment which Marx would have liked it to be, but, as Engels explained:

> For the ultimate triumph of the ideas set forth in the
> Manifesto Marx relied solely and exclusively on the
> intellectual development of the working class as it
> necessarily had to ensue from united action and discussion.
> And Marx was right.
>
> (Marx and Engels, 1962a, p. 26)

What this meant was that much of the Marxist theory of revo-lution had to be played down, while emphasis was laid on the achievements of the co-operative and trade union movement. In his inaugural address to the new organization, Marx pointed to the Ten Hours Bill as an example of working-class achievement:

> After a thirty years' struggle fought with the most admirable
> perseverance, the English working-classes improving a
> momentous split between the landlords and money-lords
> succeeded in carrying the Ten Hours Bill. This was not
> only a great practical success; it was the victory of a new
> principle. It was the first time that in broad daylight the
> political economy of the middle-class succumbed to the
> political economy of the working-class.
>
> (Marx and Engels, 1962a, p. 382)

And he then goes on to comment on the growth of co-operatives:

> There was a still greater victory of the political economy
> of labour over the political economy of property. We speak
> of the co-operative movement, especially the co-operative
> factories raised by the unassisted efforts of a few bold

'hands'. The value of these great social experiments cannot be overrated. By deed instead of by argument they have shown that production on a large scale and in accord with the behests of modern science, may be carried on without the existence of a class of masters employing a class of hands; that to bear fruit the means of labour need not be monopolized as a means of dominion over and of extortion against the labouring man himself; and that like slave labour, like serf labour, hired labour is but a transitory and inferior form destined to disappear before associated labour plying its toil with a willing hand, a ready mind and a joyous heart.

(Marx and Engels, 1962a, p. 383)

Much of this was a concession both to the British delegates from the London Trades' Council and probably more importantly to the French followers of Proudhon who were very influential amongst the International's members.

In fact, however, Marx had always been appalled by the naïveté of Proudhon, a printer of peasant background whom he had met and talked to about Hegelianism in the early days. Apart from his woolly Hegelian rhetoric, Marx thought that his proposal for 'gratuitous credit' provided by a bank, set up by a state which having created the bank went out of existence, as misleading as Lasalle's proposal for state co-operatives. Even in his inaugural address, therefore, he goes on to say:

The experience of the period from 1848 to 1864 has proved beyond doubt that, however excellent in principle and however useful in practice, co-operative labour, if kept within the narrow circle of the casual efforts of private workmen, will never be able to arrest the growth in geometrical progression of monopoly, to free the masses nor even perceptibly to lighten the burden of their miseries. It is perhaps for this very reason that plausible noblemen, philanthropic middle-class spouters and even keen political economists have all at once turned nauseously complimentary to the very co-operative labour system they had vainly tried to nip in the bud by deriding it as the Utopia of the dreamer or stigmatizing it as the sacrilege of the Socialist. To save the industrious masses co-operative labour ought to be

developed to national dimensions and consequently to be
fostered by national means.

(Marx and Engels, 1962a, p. 383)

Apart from Proudhon, two other thinkers or leaders were
influential in the International, namely, Blanqui and Bakunin.
Blanqui had preached the concept of the capture of state power by
way of a *coup d'état* by secret groups of conspirators. Marx had
some sympathy with this, for it did take seriously the question of
political power. Indeed, in his pamphlet on 'The Class Struggles
in France of 1848' he had said:

> The proletariat rallies more and more around revolutionary
> Socialism, round Communism for which the bourgeoisie has
> itself invented the name of Blanqui.

(Marx and Engels, 1962a, p. 222)

But a *coup* which was not supported and controlled by the working class had little interest for Marx and, at least between the
two revolutions of 1848 and 1871, Marx moved sharply away
from Blanqui's position and concerned himself with open public
organization of the mass of the working class.

Bakunin was at the opposite extreme. He became associated
with the International only after he became dissatisfied with the
proceedings of the international anti-war organization, the League
of Peace and Freedom, and made Marx's life very difficult.
Bakunin believed that the state itself was the source of evil and,
far from wanting to see a new state in the form of the dictatorship
of the proletariat, wished to see it totally destroyed. As he wrote:[1]

> We revolutionary anarchists are the enemies of all forms
> of state and state organization. . . . We think that all state
> rule, all governments, being by their very nature placed
> outside the mass of the people must necessarily subject it to
> customs and purposes entirely foreign to it. We, therefore,
> declare ourselves to be foes . . . of all state organization as
> such.
> Intellectuals, positivists, doctrinaires, all those who put
> science before life . . . defend the idea of the state as being
> the only salvation of society—quite logically, since from
> their false premise that thought comes before life, that only

[1] Quoted in Isaiah Berlin, *Karl Marx*, 1939, p. 205.

abstract theory can form the starting point of social practices . . . they draw the inevitable conclusion that since such theoretical knowledge is at present possessed by very few, these few must be put in control of social life and that no sooner is the revolution over than a new social organization must at once be set up, not a free association of popular bodies . . . working in accordance with the needs and instincts of the people, but a centralized dictatorial power, concentrated in the hands of this academic minority. The difference between such revolutionary dictatorship and the modern state is only one of theoretical trappings. In substance both are a tyranny of the minority over the majority in the name of the people—in the name of the stupidity of the many and the superior wisdom of the few— and so they are equally reactionary, devising to secure political and economic privilege to the ruling minority and the enslavement of the masses, to destroy the present order only to erect their own rigid dictatorship on its ruins.

Such ideas were clearly directed, amongst other things, against the theory so clearly expounded by Marx in his address to the Communist League. And they appealed to the followers of Proudhon in the International. Eventually everything Marx stood for seemed threatened and he deliberately broke up the International by successfully proposing that its headquarters be moved to America.

Despite all these political involvements, Marx was able in London to pursue those theoretical studies on which political activity for such a man had to be based. Moreover, even politics was for him part of the superstructure of society. To be realistic it must be based upon an understanding of the 'earthly family'. By 1857 he had worked out his ideas on pre-capitalist society and produced a set of manuscripts which are only now being published in English. In 1859 he wrote a preface to 'A Critique of Political Economy', intended to be the first of a series of volumes, but having published it he began again and the outcome was *Capital*, of which the first volume appeared in 1867. *Capital* was not, and could not have been, simply a treatise on economics. It may be that it is that, amongst other things, but all the many strands of intellectual and political involvement from which the fabric of Marx's life had been woven are to be found within its pages.

In the first place, the problem of the alienation of man's labour is still there. Capital is, like Feuerbach's God, external to man yet drawing all that is best in man out of him. Thus, for instance, Marx writes:[1]

> Obviously throughout his working life the worker is to be nothing but labour power; all his available time is, by nature and by law, to be labour time, it is to be devoted to promoting the self-expansion of capital. In its blind unbridled passion, its werewolf hunger for surplus labour, capital is not content to overstep the moral restrictions upon the length of the working day. It oversteps the purely physical limitations as well. It usurps the time needed for the growth, development and the healthy maintenance of the body. . . . Capital does not enquire how long the embodiment of labour power is likely to live. Its only interest is in ensuring that a maximum amount of labour power shall be expended in one working day.

Second, *Capital* is clearly a moral tract, whatever protestations Marx may have made to the contrary. It shows how in pre-capitalist society labour produces commodities and how, when these commodities are turned into money, the money is used to purchase other commodities which represent stored-up labour. But in capitalist society, Marx argues, we start with money. Money is used to purchase a commodity, labour, which in turn yields more money. And when a man's labour is only a money-producing commodity he must cease to be fully a man. All too clearly this is a feature of capitalist society now as it was then and it was hardly possible for Marx to write *Capital* without hammering home the fact, again and again.

Third, *Capital is* a treatise on economics. Its terminology and language are those of Smith and Ricardo. Listen, for instance, to Engels expounding the doctrine of the labour theory of value for the benefit of the German workers:

> What is the value of labour power? The value of every commodity is measured by the labour required for its

[1] Karl Marx, *Capital*, quoted by Robert C. Tucker, *Philosophy and Myth in Karl Marx*, 1961, p. 210.

production. Labour power exists in the form of the living
worker who requires a definite amount of subsistence for his
existence, as well as for the maintenance of his family, which
ensures the continuance of labour power also after his death.
The labour time necessary for producing these means of
subsistence represents therefore the value of the labour
power. The capitalist pays this value weekly and purchases
for that the use of one week's labour of the worker. So far
messieurs the economists will be pretty well in agreement
with us. . . .

(Marx and Engels, 1962a, 1, p. 464)

It is true that Marx's economics now became distinctive, for
after 1857 his attention switched from labour as a commodity in
exchange relations to the exploitation of surplus-value from
labour in productive relations. But he had related his revolutionary theory to the tradition of classical economics.

Yet, and this is the fourth point, *Capital* was also a parody of
classical economic argument. Edmund Wilson quite rightly calls
Marx the greatest ironist since Swift. After each abstract
economic argument, and just as we begin to take delight in the
elegance of the concepts, Marx produces by way of illustration
some factory or court report which he had discovered in the
British Museum which tells us what the concepts used in the
analysis of market behaviour actually mean in terms of the
misery of the workers. Thus, after a painstaking exposition of
why capitalism will necessarily lead to attempts to lengthen the
working day, Marx introduces a historical section as follows:

After capital had taken centuries in extending the working
day to its normal maximum limit and then beyond this to
the limit of the natural day of 12 hours, there followed
on the birth of mechanism and modern industry a violent
encroachment like that of an avalanche in its intensity and
extent. All bounds of morals and nature, of age and sex,
day and night, were broken down. Even the ideas of day
and night, of rustic simplicity in the old statutes became so
confused than an English judge as late as 1860 needed a
quite Talmudic sagacity to explain what was day and what
was night. 'Capital' celebrated its orgies.

(Marx, 1961, 1, p. 278)

The length of the working day is itself a major theme in *Capital*. It was bound to be. Unlike the Lasalleans, Marx did not believe in any iron law of wages which would permanently hold wages at subsistence level. The trade unions, he believed, could shorten the working day and increase wages, just as the employers would try to lengthen the day and reduce wages. Intellectually, therefore, the political economy of the working class had to struggle against the political economy of the bourgeoisie. And practically, this meant that trade unionism was at the heart of the struggle to overthrow capitalism.

In fact, the very success of the trade unions was thirty years later to start a furious argument about whether revolution was necessary. And it is arguable that Marx was wrong in seeing them as a possible basis for revolutionary organization.

What is clear is that, unlike his predecessors amongst the classical economists, Marx is not concerned merely to expound the natural laws of the economy. He is concerned to show that this system contains within itself the seeds of its own destruction and that those it has exploited will overthrow it. Thus at the end of his long economic analysis he writes:

> While there is a progressive diminution in the number of capitalist magnates, there is, of course, a corresponding increase in the mass of poverty, enslavement, degeneration and exploitation, but at the same time there is a steady intensification of the role of the working class—a class which grows more numerous and is disciplined, and organized by the very mechanism of the capitalist method of production which has flourished with it and under it. The centralization of the means of production and the socialization of labour reach a point when they prove incompatible with their capitalist integument. This bursts asunder. The knell of private property sounds. The expropriators are expropriated.
>
> (Marx, 1961, 1, p. 763)

So Marx gave to the working class another fighting manifesto— one which declared their struggles to be concerned not merely to knock an hour off the day or to put a shilling on the wage—but to be part of a great historical process leading to a new age in which man would be truly free.

Has history proved him wrong? Inevitably in many respects it has. Capitalism has shown more staying power than Marx imagined and trade unionism has functioned successfully within its framework without seeking to overthrow it. Yet a hundred years after its publication *Capital*, and all that went to its making, remains a living part of our culture and civilization. For Marx was a moral and intellectual giant. It is right that we should celebrate him.

Later note

This chapter concentrates its attention particularly on the early Marx. Had it been written later more emphasis would have been placed on the change of Marx's concern with labour as a commodity in exchange relations to his concern with productive relations and the fact that under capitalism the relation between employer and worker was not a simple and equal market one. It was this fact which posed the basic problems of *Das Kapital*. The crucial development in Marx's thought on this matter occurred in 1857 and is outlined in M. Nicolaus, 'The Unknown Marx' in R. Blackburn (ed.), *Ideology in Social Science*, London: Fontana Books, 1972, pp. 306–33.

Marx and Malinowski

One of the difficulties which sociologists have with Marx is that, since the problems which conern him and his contemporaries were not primarily, or only, sociological, it is difficult to translate his ideas directly into sociological language and hence to say where Marxist sociology stands. In saying this, one knows that there are those who sincerely believe that such a translation should not be attempted, since it would miss what was essential and unique in Marxism. All that one can ask, therefore, is that such readers will suspend judgment on this point for the moment and see whether Marxism and sociology are not illuminated by the comparison. Others may agree that there is a central and simple ambiguity in Marx's formulation of the materialist conception of history, which more precise sociological formulations should clear up.

This central and simple ambiguity concerns the relation between basis and superstructure. What one finds is that Marx often writes, and it is understandable that he should so write, given his Hegelian upbringing, as though the distinction which he was making was between things on the one hand, and ideas on the other. In this respect, there is some parallel between his rejection of Hegel, and Durkheim's rejection of idealistic elements in Comte, even though Marx should be adjudged the clearer of the two in that his 'things' concern understandable productive activity, whereas Durkheim seems to reify 'collective currents' of thought and ideas.

On the other hand, any practical Marxist reading the foregoing paragraph would be bound to dissent from it, since, surely, it would be said, Marx, above all other writers, believed that theory was inseparable from practice. This much is certainly true, but the inseparability of theory from practice remains an uninterpreted slogan, unless it is given meaning within the context of the first of Marx's theses on Feuerbach which asserts, not merely the inseparability of thought from things, but also the inseparability of the thing-world or the object-world from 'sensuous human activity', which involves amongst other things 'thought', which is implicit in all human action and social relations.

Our argument here is that it is worth while to ask what these assertions mean when they are translated into a simple socio-logical language and, for this purpose, what we have chosen to do is to ask how Marxism looks when stated in the simple sociological language of Malinowski's *A Scientific Theory of Culture* (1944) and also how that scientific theory looks when illuminated by a Marxist perspective.

Malinowski's central concept is that of the institution. It is in terms of this concept that he proposes that the anthropologist should select from his observations of behaviour those elements which are central to the understanding of culture and society. This leads to the famous schematic diagram shown in Figure 1.

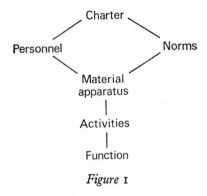

Figure 1

What has to be noted about this is that Malinowski includes amongst his categories and, amongst his observable elements, several different kinds. 'Ideas' appear as part of the 'charter' in their mere superstructural sense. That is to say they have little significance other than that of concealing 'function' which is a very 'material' category, namely the satisfaction of biological needs. On the other hand, given that it is this need-satisfaction which is central to any explanation, both material factors such as technological ones and ideal ones such as norms may appear as means functional to the attainment of these ends. On the level of ideas, 'charter' may be explained away as false consciousness, but personnel and norms remain as stubbornly ideal elements in real human action. On the other hand, on the level of the material, a material end (function) is contrasted with the material means, suggesting one interpretation at least of a Marxist distinction between the sensuous human activity which is at the heart of the material, and the mode of production which is a material element, which places restriction on that activity. One thing upon which Marx is absolutely insistent is the opposition between his materialism and any form of Owenite environmentalism.

It should also be noted, however, that Malinowski also includes another element, namely, 'activity'. This need not be taken very seriously as a theoretical category, for what it is above all, is a guide to the anthropological note-taker. Quite obviously, while it is possible to note down what the 'charter' of an activity is, who the personnel are, what norms govern their action, and what material apparatus they use, it is also possible and necessary to keep a record of what actually happens.

The category of 'activity', however, like that of 'function', has a more fundamental theoretical significance. Taken together they are the central *explanatory* concepts in an approach to social reality in terms of the 'action frame of reference'. The function of an activity is the end which it subserves in terms of a hypothetical action scheme, in terms of which some behaviour is explained. The notion of activity, itself, suggests simply that the whole sequence is to be understood, not causally and in terms of mere behaviour, but telologically in terms of rule-governed action. Thus Malinowski is not a behaviourist any more than Marx is a mechanical materialist.

There is another interesting relationship between Malinowski and Marx, however, which distinguishes them *both* from crude forms of behaviourism and materialism *and* from the more simplistic formulations of the action frame of reference. Malinowski chooses to emphasize both activity and the satisfaction of biological needs, while Marx has the interesting and deliberately chosen concept of *sensuous* human activity. Neither could therefore be satisfied either with the utilitarian notion that, as Parsons puts it, 'ends are random from the point of view of the system' or with Radcliffe-Brown's notion that the end of any particular activity is merely to keep other forms of social activity going. Parsons, it is true, comes closer to a dialectical materialist standpoint, for he recognizes that the incorporation of the desired object into self takes place at the outset, through that first sensuous contact with the material world, contact with the mother's breast. But this is solely in the phase of socialization. Once it has occurred the individual actor comes to develop 'need-dispositions' which society needs him to have and, at this point, Parsons's Freudian materialism gives way to functionalism.

What then are the main differences between the 'materialism' of Malinowski and that of Marx? They seem to be, on this level, two. First, the ultimate reference point of organized activity for Marx is 'production', while for Malinowski it is the satisfaction of biological needs. Second, it is assumed in Malinowski's scheme, though not explicitly, that the arrangement of personnel and of norms can be assumed as agreed amongst a plurality of actors. In Marx this is not so, because the social relations of production at the human level give rise, not to spontaneous organization, but to conflict. These two factors produce in Malinowski's scientific theory a static quality which is missing in Marxism.

Marx, of course, arrives at his conception of 'production' through the transformational criticism of Hegelian idealism. In his *Phenomenology of Mind*, Hegel posits Absolute Spirit which expresses its own attributes in created things and then, confronting its own self in an alien form, seeks to regain itself through knowledge of those things. The first humanistic criticism of Hegel, instead of treating man as occupying an ambiguous role in this process, part created thing, partly himself appearing as the creator of culture, treats man rather than Spirit or God as the sole subject of history. Marx's own eventual position involves beyond this a more literal, if inverted, interpretation of Hegel. Marx represents Hegel as describing the process of human industrial production. This is the process which classical economists discuss, and it is also the essential human activity which distinguishes man from the animals. Human history, therefore, is not to be reduced to a process of the functional satisfaction of biological needs. It involves a 'dialectical' interplay between human activity and the material world.

It is not surprising, given the origin of this body of thought, that the actual notion of production should appear 'metaphysical' and unclear. What is posited as the basic element in human history, however, is not something fixed and static, but one which has to change and develop with each successive challenge presented by the 'material apparatus', or by what Marx calls the mode of production. A difficulty with Malinowski's theory is that it is not easy to explain why, if the ultimate explanation of culture and society is to be found in the satisfaction of human needs, there should ever be any change in culture and social structure, other than what would follow from a continuously increasing level of need-satisfaction. This was, of course, assumed both by the English utilitarians and by Spencer as the main engine of history, and it was precisely on this point that Durkheim attacked Spencer in *The Division of Labour in Society*. A continually increasing level of need-satisfaction in the absence of collective order would, for Durkheim, have meant simply anomie.

The other difference between Marxism and Malinowski's functionalism, however, is even more fundamental. It might perhaps be pointed out that this would follow from a variant of Malinowski's theory which sought to explain change. This would be that a culture and social structure had the form which it did, not because the satisfaction of human needs in general required it, but because this followed from the attempt to maximize their own 'utility' or need-satisfaction by a ruling class. The satisfaction of the needs of those who were ruled would be necessary, only to the extent that it did not produce so high a death rate amongst them as to prevent their doing what the ruling class required.

Marx's whole critique of bourgeois economics was, of course, the logical conclusion of this point of view. Even, however, if we set aside 'need-satisfaction' and 'utility' as essential bourgeois social science categories, the business of production in Marx's view involves conflict. Clearly the worker who works for another man does not fulfil his need to produce. Nor, probably, does his employer, caught up in a world of competition and class conflict. What emerges, therefore, in the world of production are not the organizations of organization theory, but a state of conflict amongst men arising in the course of production.

We must now turn to the question of what, in vulgar Marxism, came to be loosely referred to as the 'superstructure'. In Malinowski what we have is a set of secondary institutions, which while they have the same elements as those of the basic institutions, have the function, not of satisfying basic needs, but of maintaining the basic institutions which satisfy these needs. What is valuable here as a corrective to Marxism is the recognition that what we have are not just ideas, floating as it were in a vacuum, but forms of human activity which are themselves subject to a structural analysis. There can be little doubt, surely, that if Marx had confronted this argument, he would have admitted that there were organizational forms on the superstructural level, and that it was possible to envisage a sociology of law, of politics, of education, of religion and so on, which was not simply a study in the history of ideas. On the other hand, two points of contrast need to be noted immediately. One is that Malinowski's schema, the renewal and maintenance of the material apparatus, is a function of one of the *secondary* institutions, while production for Marx is basic. The other is that, if Marxists tend to oversimplify the superstructure by representing it as consisting purely of ideas, Malinowski's suggestion that these institutions may be analysed in the same way as the basic ones, and that they have the same structural elements, appears a little mechanical. After all, there are relatively few cases, outside of the business of production itself, in which the material apparatus used in the conduct of an institutional activity are central. The judge's chair, the pulpit, the lecture-roon, the gallows, cooking pots and contraceptives, are less important to social change than is productive technology itself.

We should note, before we leave this comparison of Marx's and Malinowski's treatment of non-basic institutional forms, that Malinowski did also, albeit in a sketchy way, recognize a tertiary sector, rather more akin to Marx's superstructure. This was the sphere of pure values. Such values had to be cultivated since the performance of duties on the secondary level had no obvious and direct rationale. The participant in a culture, that is to say, could not see that many of the institutions of society were of any value in terms of need-satisfaction, and, if he was to be properly motivated, it was necessary that he should have another reason. Similarly, one finds Kingsley Davis (1948) in a chapter in *Human Society*, which is as profound as anything in the literature of structural functionalism, arguing that it is the existence of a sphere of pure values which makes possible certain kinds of action, which though non-rational from the point of view of individual rationality, are necessary from the point of view of society.

In fact, of course, Malinowski's discussion of this point was incomplete and it may be argued that it was uncertain whether he would have been led by the logic of his position to argue for a functional theory of values, or whether, *per contra*, he would have seen the sphere of values as the co-determining or perhaps primarily determining element in culture. There is an echo here of the problem of Durkheim who, having set out to prove that the divine was nothing but the social, ended by attributing divinity *to* the social.

We have not yet, however, drawn attention to the most fundamental differences between Marx's theory of institutional interrelations and that of Malinowski's, or any other kind, of functionalism. This is that what is supported and sustained in the basic institutional spheres by the secondary institutions is not order, but conflict. Thus Marxism requires not merely a theory of culture, but a theory of counter-culture. The productive order of the ruling class requires certain supporting institutions on a secondary level but the resistance of those who are ruled also has its secondary supports. That Marx had some such idea is clearly indicated, for example, by his reference to 'the political economy of the working class' (see page 160).

But at this point Marx's sociology involves a fundamental departure from functionalism. Its central structural concept becomes, not that of the institution, but the dynamic concept of class. Society and culture must be analysed not in terms of mutually supporting and integrated institutions, but in terms of classes fighting for their interests in the sphere of production and in all other spheres as well. Thus the prime question which the sociologist has to ask of any man or any action is not, what function does he or it have for society, but what function has it for a class in class-combat?

At the same time, of course, the concept of class is a dynamic one. At the outset the class arises merely in the productive system. It is simply a class-in-itself, or, at most is possessed of 'trade-union-consciousness'. But, in the course of a political struggle, this class not merely fights to defend its economic position, but carries the fight into all other areas, and, particularly into the political sphere, where it seeks hegemony, that is the establishment and enforcement of its social order against that of all other classes.

This Marxist goal, as has often been pointed out, has rarely, if ever, been realized in history. At most, classes have come into existence on a two-nations basis of the kind suggested by Disraeli, without the working class seeking to overthrow the existing order and establish its own hegemony. Moreover, even though it maintains its independent 'institutions', ideas and culture, these are essentially defensive in character. They co-exist with an extensive ruling-class authority and an extensive ruling-class penetration of working-class life and thought. Thus one cannot assume that, if working-class hegemony is attained, the defensive institutions and the culture of the days of struggle could become the basis of a new social order. That would depend upon the mode of production and the social relations of production which the victorious working class established.

But the fact that the Marxist perspective on the development of culture and society in terms of class conflict has rarely, if at all, been concretely realized by no means renders it valueless as an ideal type. It is only after the elaboration of such a type that the division of actual cultures and social structures from the functionalist model is fully explained. Moreover, this does not mean that what exists is a mere resultant of conflicting forces. It is rather something which has an inherent instability, and, within which, a balance of power and truce between the classes may quite suddenly give way to a situation in which both classes once again seek hegemony.

What is perhaps the most interesting set of problems opened up by this Marxist variant of functionalism is that, even in times of apparent stability, a struggle continues in the superstructure. This is why the most interesting areas of investigation in the advanced industrial societies, with their welfare-state and trade-union deal, and their truce in the class war, are those which deal with the attempt on the part of the ruling classes, when challenged, to impose their own definitions of reality, their own values and sentiments on those whom they rule and so to engineer their consent. What is least true of the present times in the advanced industrial society is that they have seen an end of ideology. Class-power in the basic institutions of production there may be, but ideological unity, which means in effect ideological ascendancy, is far from being fully established. Present developments in the mass media, in mass education and mass culture can be understood both in an evolutionary way, taking account of new possibilities opened up by media technology and skills, and even more interestingly, dialectically as a conflict between quite opposite tendencies. Of particular interest here is the widespread development in the advanced industrial societies of a drop-out movement with its attendant cultural institutions, not least of which is an underground press.

The necessary process of structural and ideological analysis which is suggested here must, of course, go along with the investigation of more basic power clashes in the sphere of production and of politics. It would, indeed be unfortunate for sociology if a failure to relate the perspectives of functionalism and Marxism were to prevent these investigations being carried out. Functionalism thus far has failed to appreciate that what is most interesting when looked at from a functionalist perspective is the interrelationship of conflict on different institutional levels,[1] while Marxism has failed to understand the structural complexity of the class struggle and of the transition from the objective fact of classes-in-themselves in the sphere of production to classes-for-themselves, class conscious and seeking hegemony, or perhaps accommodation with their adversaries.

[1]Dahrendorf in his *Class and Class Conflict in Industrial Society*, 1959, has put forward the rather surprising notion that whether or not these conflicts are related is a matter of accident.

There is probably nothing quite like the collaboration of Marx and Engels in the history of literature or politics. Many of their works were written jointly; and, in the case of those which were not, the actual author discussed the work with his partner, while it was in progress, and had his approval for its publication. Moreover, there developed between them a mutual trust and respect which is the more remarkable in that they disagreed with and distrusted almost everyone of their literary and political contemporaries.

It might seem that to attempt a separate exposition of the ideas of Engels is a waste of time, and it would be, if our interest were simply in the history of Marxism. In that case what mattered would be the body of Marxist ideas which took root in history. If, however, our concern is with those ideas in Marxism that might illuminate the problems of contemporary sociology, things are different. We then have to sort out some of the strands which were amalgamated, sometimes with loss of conceptual clarity, in the working political doctrine of Marxism. Even if Engels were not important in himself, it would be useful to assess his contribution, in order to arrive at a clearer picture of the original ideas of Marx.

Engels was born in the German town of Barmen in 1820 and was the son of a manufacturer of deep pietistic convictions. Such higher education as he received was acquired while working in an export office in Bremen, and during his year of military service in Berlin. In Bremen he became interested in the so-called Young Hegelians through reading Strauss's *Life of Jesus*, and, while in Berlin, met many of them. On completing his military service, he was sent by his father to work for his firm in Manchester, but stopped off in Cologne to meet the Hegelian editor of the *Rheinische Zeitung*, who, like himself, had been much impressed by the communist ideas of Moses Hess.

At this meeting, in 1842, it seems that Marx was not much impressed by Engels. He was himself a far more thoroughly trained philosopher and was at that stage wrestling with three separate philosophical conceptions: the Hegelian dialectic as mediated by Feuerbach, the theories of Hess, and the importance for world history of the new class, the proletariat, which had emerged in the French revolution. Engels probably appeared to him as little more than a romantic dilettante, not very different from other young 'critical theologians' he had met in Berlin.

Central to Marx's thinking at this stage was the work of Feuerbach whose ideas he was developing in a profoundly sociological direction. It is important to understand this development in order to grasp exactly the difference which his partnership with Engels was to make.

Feuerbach produced a naturalistic version of the Hegelian dialectic. Instead of seeking to understand history as a process in which Abstract Spirit expresses itself in material objects and then seeks to regain itself through human cognitive activity, Feuerbach suggested that man was the only subject of history and that ideas, including the idea of God, were simply human products. He further argued that, if man was to understand and realize himself, he must rid himself of the notion of an external and alien God.

Marx sought to develop these ideas further. If man was alienated in his idea of God, were there not other more important forms of human alienation? What about money or the state, both of which were really human creations but came to exercise an external control over man? Further, Marx felt that Feuerbach, like Hegel, placed too much emphasis upon thinking, whereas the important fact in history was not man's thought but his action. The real key to history was therefore to be found in the action rather than the thought of those historical actors who were trying to overcome their alienation through revolutions—i.e., the working class.

Marx's own thoughts on this matter were jotted down in his theses on Feuerbach. But by the time they had been written, Marx had already met Engels again (in 1844) and entered into a working partnership with him. Marx had moved to Paris and had joined Ruge in editing one edition of the *Deutsche-Französische Jahrbücher*. He contributed two articles himself and also reviewed

Carlyle. But, most important of all, he received from Engels a piece called 'A Critique of Political Economy'. He had already recognized that, if the social relations of production were all-important, it was vital that he should master and criticize the bourgeois theory of production. Engels now seemed to be pointing the way.

By this time, Engels was busy gathering the materials in Manchester for his great book *The Condition of the Working Class in England in 1844*. In doing so he met the real live proletariat in their industrial hovels, while Marx was still speaking of them as 'the instrument of philosophy'. It is difficult to imagine two discussions of the working class more distinct than those to be found in Marx's *Critique of the Hegelian Philosophy of the Right* and Engels's book.

But the greatness of *The Condition of the Working Class* (published in 1845) did not lie in its empirical description. Had Engels been merely an early Booth or Rowntree, Marx might have had little time for him. What interested Marx most was the theory which explained observable conditions. For Engels suggested that the misery of Manchester was to be explained by the simple fact of a system of class relations within which labour was sold as a commodity like any other. And he showed how this same system of class relations was leading to specific and successive stages of proletarian organization. This seemed to Marx to be the veritable 'secret of the earthly family', the key to understanding social development which he had thought about in theory but could now see exemplified in history. He immediately decided to adopt Engels as a pupil who would teach him about capitalism.

The ensuing important Marxist works are *The Holy Family* (1844) and *The German Ideology* (1846). The old Hegelian Karl Marx is still to be seen in *The Economic and Philosophic Manuscripts of 1844* and in his denunciation of Proudhon in *The Poverty of Philosophy* (1847), and these works remain helpful in understanding original Marxist sociology. But Marx was excited by the new prospect of his partnership with Engels and *The German Ideology* was intended to settle his accounts with Hegelianism and begin afresh.

What emerges in *The German Ideology*, is stated clearly in Marx's letters after 1846, and receives its fullest exposition in

Marx's preface to the 'Critique of Political Economy' (1859), which is a theory subtly but significantly different from that contained in the theses on Feuerbach. In the theses, production appears as a free human activity and the social relations of production, being a human creation, are subject to human alteration. The only nature to which they refer, as Lichtheim has pointed out, is human nature.

In the new statement of the materialist conception of history, social evolution becomes part of natural evolution. The social relations of production cease to be seen entirely as the product of human agency and become instead the inevitable consequence of a certain mode of production—i.e. the particular stage of technological development. Thus revolution can occur only when the existing social relations of production are incompatible with, or 'become a fetter on', production. The only choices left open to the theoreticians of the working class are tactical ones. The Marxist problem is to decide when technological and economic conditions are ripe for revolution.

This new doctrine of capitalist development and class struggle was worked out jointly by Marx and Engels and became the theory held by considerable sections of the working class after the publication of the *Communist Manifesto* of 1848. The *Manifesto* itself is a remarkable document, which we understand too little because we have read it too much. In fact it blends the theoretical and historical ideas of the two authors, and the traditions from which they came, in a quite remarkable way, and it contained enough ambiguity to provide a working basis for co-operation with Blanquists, Proudhonists, Lasalleans, British trade unionists and German social democrats in the years that lay ahead, even though Marx, in his political writings, might take occasion to denounce the political illusions of his allies.

In fact, the tactical compromises which Marx and Engels necessarily had to make in their political writings were not conducive to clear and consistent sociological thinking, and only the theologians of the socialist movement would wish today to take these writings as of first importance. Probably more important were those writings not concerned with immediate issues, and Marxists must be grateful that in the years of defeat and disillusion both Marx and Engels turned to theoretical questions.

Of greatest importance during these years was Marx's *Capital*.

Engels had first directed Marxism into the sphere of political economy; but it was now Marx, living partly on Engels's money, who sat in the British Museum ransacking government documents to bring up to date Engels's account of the condition of the proletariat, and tortuously working out an adequate economic theory which would justify the economic assumptions on which they had worked. The first volume of *Capital*—the only part published in Marx's lifetime, in 1867—was a formidable book, but it left a train of formidable economic problems. Its main problem was that it did not appear to explain actual price movements or why some firms prospered more than they should have done according to the theory of surplus value. In the end it was left to Engels to edit Marx's manuscript of the third volume in which he tried to solve some of these problems.

During this period Engels completely subordinated himself to Marx, even to the extent of writing some of Marx's pieces for the *New York Herald Tribune* for him while allowing Marx to claim authorship and the fee. But one finds in Engels's correspondence a wide-ranging interest in religious, political and military history and a growing interest in pre-history. Perhaps one of the most important outcomes of this was the Marxist recognition of a socio-historical type called the 'asiatic mode of production' which stood outside the general line of development from ancient, through feudal and capitalist, to socialist society. The recognition that oriental societies were not subject to the same laws of historical development as those of Europe was to be of great importance in twentieth-century Marxism.

Engels's interest in pre-history led him, after Marx's death, to incorporate the evolutionary ideas of the American anthropologist Morgan into Marxism. They certainly fitted well. For Morgan had apparently shown that both the family and the state were nothing other than means of defending property. It was a wonderful example of the superstructure being determined by the economic base, and Morgan's work was all the more acceptable because of his speculation that man would eventually have more than a mere 'property history'. Little wonder that Engels's rewrite of Morgan in *The Origins of the Family, Private Property and the State* should have become orthodox Marxist reading.

There is, too, Engels's *The Peasant War in Germany* (1850). Every sociologist of capitalist society must at some time have dealt with the Reformation, and Engels set out to assess the role of Luther and Thomas Munzer in the German Reformation. The work has none of Weber's subtlety, but perhaps that is its merit, because the political involvement of religious leaders is often pretty direct. This work supplements much else that has been written on the sociology of the Reformation, and is perhaps the one Marxist study in which religion appears both as 'the cry of the oppressed creature, the heart of a heartless world' and as 'the opium of the people'.

Marx died in 1883 and Engels was left as his intellectual and political legatee. Engels's speeches and newspaper articles gain in importance, and he remains politically active right up to his death in 1895, most notably in advising Kautsky on the 'Erfurt programme' on the basis of which the Social Democratic Party in Germany was to play a new parliamentary role. But of more central and long-term significance was the theoretical writing in which he attempted to sum up the method which he and Marx had been using. His *Anti-Duhring*, which had been published before Marx's death and approved by Marx, went into new editions. He also worked on a retrospective intellectual bio-graphical work, *Ludwig Feuerbach and the Outcome of the Classical German Philosophy*, and on some notes about scientific method, published after his death as *The Dialectics of Nature*. These works constitute a third Marxist philosophy and sociology which, for better or worse, has also become official Marxist doctrine (the first being Marx's own thinking, the second that of the Marx-Engels collaboration).

The new doctrine contrasts sharply with that of Marx's theses, despite the fact that these were published for the first time as an appendage to Engels's *Ludwig Feuerbach*. In the theses, Marx straddled the materialist-idealist distinction, and was explicitly anti-deterministic in the sociological ideas which he expounded. This is what Marx would have called 'dialectical materialism' in 1845.

The 'dialectic' which Engels now opposes to Duhring is nothing like this. The difference, as he sees it, between Duhring and the Hegel-Marx tradition lies solely in Hegel's and Marx's understanding of change and the laws of change in nature and society. This may separate Engels from Duhring, but it hardly separates Marxism from most modern science and philosophy. In its search for deterministic laws of progress, and in its belief in unilinear development, this later Marxism differs little from much nineteenth-century positivism.

Dialectics in this sense adds little to science or to sociology, and it is difficult to see why any such general philosophy is needed. It hardly helps to be told that a variety of things and processes—ranging from plant reproduction to the equation $-a \times -a = a^2$—are all examples of the negation of the negation. And when Engels replaces Marx's definition of materialism, in terms of its emphasis on 'sensuous human activity', with a Dr Johnson-like assertion that there are really things out there, we seem very far from a specifically Marxist philosophy of science.

A strong argument can be put that Engels had in fact assimilated Marxist sociology to a general materialistic evolutionary theory which was widespread in nineteenth-century England. Clearly he had not lived for so long in Manchester for nothing. But the sad thing about it all for sociologists is that Engels does not merely propose a revision of original Marxist sociology. He abolishes the need for sociology and for history altogether. The partial determinism of Marx's 1859 preface to 'A Critique of Political Economy' is now made complete. Man and his class struggles are all simply the continuation of nature's dialectical progression.

Such a doctrine is not of very much use in understanding either the social development of capitalism or of those forms of society which succeeded it. It could, however, provide an ideological superstructure for Marxist democrats in the West where no revolution happened, and for communist Russia where Stalin set about constructing a superstructure which would fit the process of industrialization on which Russia had embarked.

Yet to say that Engels was a poor systematic sociologist, or even that he sold out Marxist sociology to a kind of evolutionary positivism, is not entirely to deny his greatness. Marx was essentially a man of the study, the library and the committee room. Had he worked entirely on his own, had Engels not continually stimulated him by his writings and his arguments, even the rich sociological insights of Marx's early work—not to mention *Capital*—might have been lost to us; and we should not still be discussing Marxism today.

15

C. Wright Mills

C. Wright Mills is one of the few professional sociologists since the Second World War whose work has excited attention outside academic circles.[1] In a world increasingly dominated by, and resentful of, American power, his *Power Elite* was one of the very few sociological works with anything significant to say about the American power structure. And during Kennedy's eyeball-to-eyeball encounter with Khrushchev over the Cuban missiles, Mills's two latest works *The Causes of World War Three* and *Listen, Yankee* (later called *Castro's Cuba*) were almost startlingly to the point.

But precisely because his work is so relevant to the immediate and central problems of contemporary politics, Mills is likely to be misunderstood and undervalued. Some of his admirers have vulgarized his ideas to create a pop sociology for the anti-American left. And his enemies have either denounced him as a crypto-communist or dismissed him as a mere journalist.

Certainly Mills was a radical—one of the very few among professional sociologists—but he was far more than a journalist. Unlike most of his contemporaries he was thoroughly trained in philosophy and in the classic tradition of sociological theory. And, having absorbed these classics, and not some instant theoretical system dreamed up in a Harvard seminar, he then sought to do what the masters of sociology had done—to confront the big issues of his time, to ask what sort of world he was living in, to find out where the power lay and to ask what could be done about it.

Mills was born in Waco, Texas, and educated in Sherman, Fort Worth and Dallas, before going to the University of Texas as an engineering student. Happily, he abandoned engineering

[1] See bibliography for list of some of Mills's works and also Gerth and Mills, 1948, 1954.

after a year, and his BA and MA were taken in sociology and philosophy. He took his doctorate at Wisconsin under Howard Becker in 1941, and produced a dissertation on sociology and pragmatism. In 1941 he was appointed associate professor at the University of Maryland, and from there went to work under Lazarsfeld at Columbia University in 1945. He retained an appointment at Columbia for the rest of his life, and from his base there did research, wrote books and reflected on his world. From all accounts, his colleagues did not like him and he had little time for most of them.

Five sets of influences went to the shaping of Mills's sociology. The first was the philosophic heritage of pragmatism with which he was concerned in his doctoral thesis. The second was the empirical study of social stratification and mass communication. The third was his contact with the brilliant group of refugee scholars who arrived in America in the thirties and who combined sociological, Marxist and Freudian insights in their attempt to explain the rise of Nazism. The fourth was Mills's own personal encounter with the Cold War, and the fifth, his reflection on the political timidity of his colleagues.

It is ironic that the term pragmatism has come to mean an approach to science and action which dispenses with abstruse philosophical discussion. For, when we say that Mills was influenced by pragmatism, we mean precisely that he was familiar with the works of the most intellectually rich philosophic tradition in America. Mills, who had read Peirce on 'The Fixation of Belief' and on 'How we make our Ideas Clear',[1] could hardly have accepted the naïve statistical empiricism of many of his colleagues as a sound basis for social science. Nor could he, familiar as he was with the psychology of Dewey and of Mead,[2] have failed to appreciate the complexity of the relation between individual action and social structure. From pragmatism Mills obtained the kind of philosophic education which made him immediately appreciative of European thinking about history and the social sciences when he encountered it a year or two later.

Yet for all his philosophical sophistication, Mills pursued empirical research of an orthodox kind while at Columbia. He made studies of trade union and business élites, as well as of

[1] See C. S. Peirce, *Collected Papers*, 1958.
[2] See George H. Mead, *Mind, Self and Society*, 1934.

various middle-class groups. He also studied the relative influence of the mass media and of opinion leaders. Even before he went to Columbia, however, he had written extended reviews of Lloyd Warner's Yankee City studies and of Burnham's *Managerial Revolution*. The question which underlies all these studies of stratification is simply 'where does the power lie?' Eventually they all take on a new meaning as they are brought together in *The Power Elite*.

But well before he began these studies, Mills had met refugee sociologists who were asking different kinds of questions about American society, and he was profoundly interested in what they had to say. More than that, it would not be an exaggeration to say that Mills, the Texan, was the last sociologist in America to speak with the authentic voice of the European refugees.

For the refugees, sociology had been subjected to a real test, namely, its ability to explain the rise of Nazism. And the sociology which best seemed to survive that test was an amalgam of Weber, Marx and Freud. Different authors produced their own syntheses but the constituent elements were the same, and it was this version of the classical tradition which Mills learnt from Hans Gerth at Wisconsin.

The other thing which the refugees had in common was their message to the Americans: 'it can happen here'. Mass society in America was seen as tending towards totalitarianism and fascism, and German militarism was seen as having a parallel in the rising influence of the Pentagon. Mills himself saw in Neumann's *Behemoth* many trends which were paralleled in his own America.

These first three influences help us to understand the position at which Mills had arrived when he wrote *The Power Elite* and *Character and Social Structure*. At this point he was able to give an account of American society, before going on to confront the problems of the Cold War.

Mills's first major book had been *The New Men of Power*, in which he analyses the background and the role of trade union leaders. Its significance, however, in any attempt to assess Mills's final position, is that he came to reject the optimism which he expressed in it about the trade union élite.

Thus, while in *The New Men of Power* (1948), he writes 'What the US does or fails to do may be the key to what will happen in the world. What the labour leader does or fails to do may be the key to what happens in the US', by 1960 he is rebuking the English New Left:

What I do not understand about some New Left writers is why they cling so mightily to the 'working class' of advanced capitalist societies as the historic agency, or even the most important agency in the face of impressive historical evidence that now stands against this expectation. Such a labour metaphysic is a legacy from Victorian marxism that is now quite unrealistic.

The really impressive historical evidence to which Mills referred included the research material which he had gathered in his studies of social stratification. Early on, his main pre-occupation in the study of stratification had been to discover where the power to change or stabilize society lay. In early reviews he had dismissed Lloyd Warner's studies of status in Yankee City as irrelevant and Burnham's assertions about the growth of managerial power as untrue. And his own studies of trade unionists and white-collar groups convinced him of their political impotence. At most their representatives were found at the middle levels of power, while the big questions were settled elsewhere.

In deciding who the real rulers of America were, Mills considered the evidence about the ownership and control of corporations which had been collected in response to Burnham's thesis. He considered the influence of the New Deal, and he considered the rise to political power of men like Eisenhower after the Second World War.

Clearly, the managers had not succeeded the owning élite in effective control of the corporations. Political organizations and institutions did have some influence, though it was the men who manipulated the party machines rather than the congressmen who were really powerful—and many of these were members of the business élite. And finally, in a state of perpetual preparedness for war, the 'warlords' came to play a very important role in determining the level at which the economy would run.

This ruling group, then, was not quite the executive committee of the bourgeoisie, which classical Marxism would lead one to expect at the helm of a capitalist state. But the direction in which it deviated from the Marxist élite was not that which followed from the decentralization and dissemination of power, as Burnham, Galbraith and Riesman had in different ways suggested. Power was now in the hands of an even more irresponsible élite than before, and against this élite neither the new men of power nor the white-collar group could hope to exercise even countervailing power.

As a theory of stratification, the power élite model is, in fact, somewhat difficult to sustain. Critics of the right and of the left have argued convincingly that it is not clear what the interests of the various elements of the power élite are, and that until this is made clear it is not proved that they can act in unison. Marxists argue that this élite is tied to the interests of a capitalist ruling class, while right-wing critics suggest that, in a composite élite of this kind, conflicts of interest arise which provide an intra-élite system of checks and balances.

But this does not really dispose of the argument of the power élite. What does remain is a picture of the breakdown of democracy. For however the élite itself may be divided, it may still be argued that for the masses there can be no effective voice in arriving at the big decisions. Mills believed that, even where there were apparent democratic processes, the opinions of the masses and their consent could be readily engineered by the élite who controlled the media.

What Mills offers us is a manipulative model of society as a model of the social system towards which America is tending. It is a real alternative to a number of the other models on offer. It involves a rejection of the Talcott Parsons conception of 'normative consensus'. It involves a rejection of the Lipset-Bell notion that the absence of radical conflict in advanced societies arises from the incorporation of the working class into a political consensus. And it involves equally a rejection of Coser's model of a society, built upon cross-cutting and counterbalancing conflicts. Mills's society is plainly one in which the élite gets its way and engineers the consent of the democratic masses.

Mills's notion of the mass society is particularly interesting, but it is obviously deeply dependent on social-psychological assumptions. For to be a part of a mass and subject to manipulation, a man must have undergone social changes which have affected the working of his psyche; so a central problem in Mills's work is how men are socialized into political society. It was this problem with which he was concerned in his collaborative work with Gerth, *Character and Social Structure*.

In their preface Gerth and Mills write:

> No matter how we approach the field of social psychology we cannot escape the idea that all current work that comes to much fits into two basic traditions, Freud on the side of character structure and Marx, including the early Marx of the 1840s, on the side of social structure.

What this means is perfectly clear in the book that follows. Sociology must have an adequate theory of the relation between personality and society. The Freudian account is a good starting point but today we must extend Freud's notion of socialization into the kinship order, to show how man is socialized into the leading institutional orders later discussed in *The Power Elite*. In this analysis, Freud can be enriched with the ideas of Mead, and Marx with those of Weber.

The big issues with which *The Power Elite* has to deal became for Mills increasingly the issues of peace and war. This is hardly surprising, since Mills was writing *The Power Elite* at a time when M. Bidault was appealing to President Eisenhower to use the atom bomb at Dien Bien Phu, and it seemed only a logical extension of the argument of *The Power Elite* to say that the concentration of power in the hands of a tiny élite made nuclear war more likely. This was the theme of *The Causes of World War Three*.

So preoccupied with power stratification is Mills by this time, that he does not consider either the interests of the hostile parties, or the means available to them in the Cold War, as likely causes of war. The sole cause is seen as lying in the concentration of power itself.

Once again, however, literal concentration on Mills's title is misleading. He may not have given an account of the causes of World War Three. But he has drawn attention to what, after all, is the central political fact in our lives—namely, that whether or not we are plunged into nuclear war depends on the decision of very small groups of men over whom we have no control whatever.

Again, although he could no more offer a cure for the drift to war than account for its cause, Mills felt that the most important thing which he had to do was to draw attention to the responsibility of the intellectuals. If there was no reason to be sure that the power élite would understand the issues which it faced, sociologists surely had a responsibility to make known what they knew. Instead of compromising themselves by becoming advisers to the power élite, Mills urged them to accept the utopian course of speaking the truth as they saw it, in the hope that somehow, somewhere and sometime it would be listened to.

Instead of accepting this role, Mills's colleagues seemed to him to be retreating into grandiose theoretical system-building or into small-scale empirical studies, and failing to expose the interconnections behind the global issues which faced us. Against this, Mills put a conception of sociology as being concerned to turn private troubles into public issues, or as trying to show the relations between history and biography in society. His statement of the case for this kind of committed sociology in *The Sociological Imagination* is perhaps the finest thing that he wrote.

In his last years, although on leave to recover from a heart attack, Mills devoted himself to finding out something about those with whom his own national power élite seemed likely to go to war.

In the case of Cuba he used the statistics of poverty to state the Cuban case to the American people under the aggressive title *Listen, Yankee* (Mills, 1960). In the case of Russia he began the task of rendering Marxism (which he could not accept himself as the last word in sociology) meaningful to his fellow countrymen, as an ideology that could move millions of men.

The intellectual task which Mills here set himself was a huge one and his last two books were really a very incomplete statement of his own views. One wonders what he would have said about the development of the Sino-Soviet rift. And one wonders whether the insensitivity to the race relations problem, which he shared with so many of his New Left friends, would have been overcome had he still been alive in the summer of 1967.

Of one thing we can be sure: Mills would not have settled for a quiet, professional definition of his role. Like Comte and Marx and Weber before him he saw it as his task to make sense of his time. American sociology needs more like him. British sociology has not yet been challenged by such a man.

Theoretical themes and contemporary sociology

Part III

16

Sociological theory: retrospect and prospect

My *Key Problems of Sociological Theory* was written in the early 1960s. It represents my attempt to find an approach to problems of methodology and theory in sociology which is radical and critical, but which nonetheless does not forsake science for dogma. It draws very heavily upon the methodological and theoretical writings of Max Weber and, not surprisingly, has won a sympathetic response from those who have been educated in the German-speaking world. More recently it has aroused interest amongst those who have been affected by the rise of a phenomenological approach to sociology in the United States.

A book such as *Key Problems* may be usefully described, and its purpose explained, by indicating the schools of method and theory to which it is opposed. If I were asked, therefore, to name the schools with which my own approach could be contrasted I would mention empiricism, functionalism and positivism. It is not possible to understand the approach to sociology which is described in these pages unless the inadequacies of these three approaches have been understood.

The form of empiricism with which I was preoccupied at the time of writing was that which dominated British sociology. It might best be described as the 'social book-keeping' approach. It was concerned with recording the facts of social inequality and it was located primarily in the London School of Economics. The criticism which is made of it, however, has nothing to do with its political orientation. It is simply that it fails to make explicit the nature of the sociological variables which it is discussing. Since the book was written the social book-keeping approach has become somewhat old-fashioned and, particularly since the widespread application of the computer to data processing in the social sciences, many sociologists have claimed that they are operationalizing *sociological* variables and testing them in a scientific and quantitative way. One thing, however, remains as true as it was when the book was written, and it is this: the relationships and structures which are most conveniently and elegantly expressed in quantitative and mathematical form are by no means the only ones and the most important ones for the sociologist. In fact the barbarization of social research can only be prevented if some sociologists are willing to work speculatively and inexactly beyond the bounds of exact quantification.

Functionalism has grown more rather than less popular since the book was written. Indeed it has been suggested by no less an authority than the president of the American Sociological Association that all sociology, if it is sociology, must adopt a functionalist approach (Davis, 1959). If this means nothing more than that sociologists are always concerned with the inter-relationships between institutions and other elements of socio-logical analysis it is nothing more than a platitude. If, however, it implies the resort to the language of the organic analogy which is discussed here it is to be as strongly resisted as ever. So also is the more mechanistic language of the systems theory in terms of which Parsons now states the propositions of structural-functionalism. Either these languages make implied reference to hidden value judgments, or they are particular ideal types having little reference to the real world of social interaction.

It is paradoxical that Parsons should be the leading advocate of this type of theory, because he, more than any other author, was responsible for the popularization of the term 'action frame of reference' to characterize the most fruitful approach to socio-logy. Moreover it was he, above all, who showed why positivism failed in its approach to sociological method. It failed because it saw the relationship between the individual actor and the normative order and the relationship between one actor and another as a simple and deterministic one. Yet Parsons comes to absorb all the action elements (the actor, his goals and the means to his action) under one heading of the normative; and this order comes to be seen as the sole determinant of all social action. The approach adopted here remains faithful to Parsons's original insight which he derived from Weber. Social relationships, the relation of the individual to the normative order and to authority are 'doubly contingent'. What is necessary from the point of view of those in authority is not scientifically necessary. We are social beings, and we may disobey.

The perception that social facts can only be understood in terms of a subjective language or from the point of view of a hypothetical actor is perhaps the most important in this book. It has always seemed to the author that the attempt to discuss sociological questions in any other language must lead to obscurantism. All other languages leave the empirical referents of sociological terms uncertain. The approach adopted, therefore, can be described in broad terms as a phenomenological one and is utterly opposed to the kind of methodological collectivism preached, though not practised, by Emile Durkheim.

In fact the phenomenological perspective (i.e. the recognition that, while natural science is concerned with having concepts about objects, social science is about objects which themselves have concepts about each other) does face serious philosophic difficulties, and it is the merit of Alfred Schutz that he has sought to give it an adequate philosophical underpinning. It does seem, however, that the phenomenological movement in the United States has lost its way. While the best of the phenomenologists (e.g. Berger and Luckmann) continue to build the actor's definition of the situation into an approach to the study of social structures, others seem to do nothing more than describe the actor's perspective so that, instead of sociology, all we are offered is 'the phenomenology of everyday life'.

It is with some justification that Marxists have criticized phenomenology for its failure to get beyond the study of various forms of false consciousness, for there is in much contemporary work of this kind a great danger of trivialization. There clearly is a sense in which we want to get beyond the illusions which actors may have about their social condition to the study of the social structures which really exist. But Marxists concerned to delineate the world as it really is, or the world according to the perception of a true consciousness, are too often tempted to retreat into some kind of methodological collectivism or into dogmatic assertions about social and historical laws. There *is* a way of distinguishing between transient and illusory social definitions of social structures and the actual structures which affect men's lives. It was in dealing with this problem that Weber distinguished between the actual intended meaning for an observed actor and the meaning for a hypothetical actor around whose action orientation ideal types of social structure were to be built. There is an important area of debate here, but the problems inherent in it will not be solved so long as Marxists represent Weber, together with the whole phenomenological tradition, as never rising above the study of false consciousness.

The debate between the Weberian and the Marxist tradition seems to the non-German sociologist to have become confused in another way. Very often the methodological points which Weber makes are said by those who are fully involved in German intellectual and political history to have arisen in the course of various explicitly or implicitly political arguments. Moreover, this awareness of the entanglement of sociological and political issues has been intensified in recent arguments about the so-called 'student revolt'. But, while this point is to be made, the outsider notices a tendency, particularly on the part of Marxists, to refuse to discuss anything but the political origins of methodological ideas. Perhaps an outsider, more than a little sympathetic to what good Marxists are about, might usefully suggest that when this essential task in the sociology of knowledge and the history of ideas has been accomplished, the methodological problems which Max Weber treated remain, and that more than most sociologists, Weber's intellectual insights took him beyond what it was, from a political standpoint, convenient for him to believe.

Finally it is worth recording that my subsequent work has made me far more appreciative of one other aspect of the Weberian methodology. This is the emphasis which it places on ideal types as distinct from substantive theory. Weber himself may have confused the issues here by appearing to suggest at times that ideal types were theories subject to a direct test of falsification. In this respect he seems to have been going too far in establishing a bridge with the positivist tradition. The important point, however, is precisely that typology is an essential precursor of effective theorizing. It is only when we have yardsticks available, only when we have an idea of what the relevant elements and the relevant questions are, that we know how to describe and to measure the concrete instance. Substantive theorizing on a comparative and historical basis then follows. Contrary to the popular view that what sociology needs is more observation and more empirical generalization, it has seemed increasingly to the author that what sociology needs above all else is the exercise of the sociological imagination, so that ideal types may be formulated which are as fruitful in the study of our own times as those formulated by Weber, Marx, Simmel and Durkheim were in theirs. My own concern now is the comparative and historical study of race relations. It is my hope, however, that much of the discussion I began in *Key Problems of Sociological Theory* may serve to stimulate colleagues to resume the enterprise of typological analysis which Weber began, rather than seeking an American future in purely empiricist, positivist or functionalist studies.

17

Ideal types and the comparative study of social structures

Despite the scientistic and positivistic orientation of much socio-logical research and writing since the war, it has become clear that the basic methods of the social sciences cannot be the same as those of the natural sciences. One particular aspect of this prob-lem is the use by sociologists of what Max Weber called ideal types and Schutz called typifications. The aim of this chapter will be to clarify the meaning of the notion of types, so as to make it clear why and in what ways they may be used. This is done in the belief that, at the very least, there is a phase in the research process in sociology which involves type-construction, and that this phase looms much larger in sociology than in other subjects; but more than this, it may be the case that it is in the nature of the subject matter of sociology that type-construction is so central to what good sociology does that it may be the defining feature of the sociological method.

It is of particular importance at the present time to make clear the goals of typological analysis because, in the changed intel-lectual climate of present-day sociology in which positivism now finds itself under attack, there is a danger, though there is no logical necessity for this, that sociologists will emphasize a form of subjectivism, which, even though it is not the intention of the writers involved, might trivialize the subject and direct it solely to the study of interpersonal encounters and transactions. It is assumed here that even though such encounters and transactions are a legitimate field for sociological analysis, at least as much, but probably far more, attention should be paid to the analysis of historical political structures, within which, it may be acknow-ledged, interpersonal encounters occur and sometimes subtly re-define and alter or serve to indicate impending change in the over-all institutional framework. Like Max Weber we accept the complexity of the methodological and epistemological problems which face the social scientist, but like him also, we believe that this should lead to the creation of more complex constructs for the analysis of social and political reality, not a turning away from it. We agree, that is to say, with Alvin Gouldner's strictures on Howard Becker Junior, who Gouldner argues, 'is committed to a kind of inter-personal social psychology, which, with all its humanistic merits, fails to see that men—superiors as well as subordinates—may be powerfully constrained by institutions, by history and, indeed, by biology' (Gouldner, 1970).

In fact the problem of ideal types is discussed in the work of Max Weber, and his phenomenological successors, in eight different contexts. It is necessary to set these out here in order to draw attention to the centrality of the use of types in comparative and historical sociology and to show how other usages are related to this one. The eight contexts are as follows:

1   In his essay on objectivity, Weber was emphasizing the difference between history and science and took up a position much like that of Rickert. The essence of the ideal type here is that it arises out of some question which has relevance for value for the sociologist, and, while it illuminates history, does so by 'artificially accentuating' certain elements of reality. Types here are distinguished sharply from laws and cannot be thought of as having predictive value.

2   In his controversy with Dilthey, which happened to be at the centre of his thinking when he wrote the chapter which was to become the first chapter of *Economy and Society*, Weber argued that human behaviour could be understood as meaningful, through the use of ideal types of what Parsons calls 'action-orientation' or, in a non-psychological sense, of motivation. A type, in this sense, is an account of what an actor's ends are, how he sees the world and what rules govern his behaviour in seeking to attain his ends. (Weber tended to emphasize rational behaviour in a rather narrow sense, but there is no reason why types of action orientation should be confined to those cases in which the means chosen to attain the ends are those which empirical science declares to be the causal means of attaining the state of affairs envisaged as the end.)

3   In an attempt to link this explication of Dilthey's method of understanding with normal scientific procedure, Weber suggested that the 'plausible stories' suggested by the ideal types

could be tested and meaningfully adequate explanations turned into 'causally adequate' ones. This is a notable departure from Weber's earlier usage of the notion of ideal types, for there, as we have pointed out above, ideal types could not be verified, falsified or tested. Furthermore, Weber insists not merely on linking the notion of the types to testable theories, but envisages a particular type of testing. He says that there must be proof that 'there exists a probability that action in fact normally takes the course which has been held to be meaningful' and that for this 'there must be some determinable frequency of approximation to an average or pure type'.

4 Weber had, in his early essay, specifically rejected the position of Simmel, who had held that the sociologist was concerned with the forms of social relations rather than their content. He says, 'the term "social" which seems to have a quite general meaning, turns out to have, as soon as one carefully examines its application, a particular specifically coloured, though often indefinite meaning. It generally rests on nothing but its ambiguity. It provides when taken in its "general meaning" no specific point of view, from which the significance of given elements of culture can be analysed.'

5 Despite this it becomes clear in the latter part of the first chapter of *Economy and Society* that from the subjective point of view of a hypothetical actor (i.e. in a statement about how an actor relates his knowledge of the world and the rules which govern his behaviour to his goals), there are certain formal aspects of the actor's orientation to, his expectations of, his compliance with or control over the behaviour of others which recur in the variety of different contexts. These forms of social interaction may be elaborated and specified to a considerable degree, and are the ultimate means in terms of which the sociologist seeks to compare historical events and to understand historical processes. *Per contra*, forms of social organization and action which are found to occur in different historical circumstances are shown to be deducible from the range of possibilities which the analysis of the elementary forms of social action, interaction and social relationships opens up. This is the main significance of the whole text of *Economy and Society*. On the face of it, this would appear to mean that Weber is backtracking on his rejection of Simmel, as surely as he had

withdrawn from his position on the testability of the types. In fact, however, there is a marked contrast between the work of Weber and that of Simmel or of our contemporary who has found his way to a position so similar to Simmel's, namely Erving Goffmann. Both Simmel and Goffmann can be accused of falling back on that kind of interpersonal psychology which Gouldner condemns. Sometimes in Simmel's work, it seems, despite its devastating insights, to be little more than a sociology of parlour games. Weber, on the other hand, is concerned with more complex games like those called 'booty capitalism', 'capitalism rationally oriented to market opportunities', 'plantation slavery', 'traditional and legal domination' and 'patrimonial or bureaucratic administration'.

6 Alfred Schutz, amongst critics of, and commentators on, the work of Max Weber (in the work which he claimed was designed to give a philosophic underpinning to Weber's sociology) suggested that Weber had not made sufficiently clear what was involved in one actor's making statements about the motivation of another. He sought to emphasize that although I might be able to read directly the record of the behaviour of my consociates (i.e. those with whom I had face-to-face contact), even here I could not speak with certainty about my consociates' motivation. All I could do was to make 'typifications' of it and such typifications were likely to lose the rich particularity of those used in interpreting the behaviour of consociates, when they were extended to giving an account of the behaviour of those with whom I was not in direct contact. The more remote the relationship, the more abstract and general it became. Schutz seems to have believed that Weber's ideal types were more of this latter kind. They might apply either to actions or to persons. In so far as they applied to persons they approximated to what social psychologists called stereotypes.

7 A further and even more fundamental criticism of Weber made by the phenomenologists is that he apparently gave no account of how it was that observed individuals could be assumed to have a shared and intersubjective world. The notion of typification is, therefore, extended to include not merely shared concepts of the action or person of other human beings but also to any concept or word which enables two

actors to agree that the experience that they have at a particular place or time is the same experience. On this basis Berger and Luckmann have argued that a sociology of everything that passes for knowledge in everyday life is an essential prolegomenon to sociology. Less cautiously some later phenomenologists seem to have assumed that this phenomenology of everyday life *is* sociology.

8   As the stream of phenomenological thought becomes merged and confused with that of George Herbert Mead and what is called symbolic interactionism, words and concepts take on a particular significance. Without them, action is impossible, but at the same time the world of objects takes on a much more flexible and transitional character than would otherwise be the case. Thus what is called 'labelling' theory in the sociology of deviance, emphasizes that the distinctive character of a criminal act lies not in its intrinsic quality but in the fact that it is an act which some person or persons have chosen to label as criminal. Hence many deviance theorists tend to equate the notion of ideal types with this kind of account of inherently shifting and unstable transactions and encounters. An interest in history and politics is replaced by a concern for more intimate and personal concerns. It is perhaps no accident that this movement begins to achieve its greatest popularity, when, in the advanced capitalist societies, radical politics have given way to withdrawal into some kind of counterculture, which simply refuses to accept the language and symbolism of the society at large. Gouldner aptly characterizes this approach to the contemporary world as being not that of man-fighting-back but of man-on-his-back.

The problems which we are discussing here are not simply the problems of an esoteric group of people called sociologists. They are problems which must occur to anyone who is concerned with analysing the social world and living more effectively in it. It is, therefore, worth restating the eight problems mentioned above as problems which occur in common-sense thinking about social and political topics, and, that is to say, amongst people for whom Weber and Simmel, Schutz and Mead are unknown names:

I   It is a fact that in the social sciences we choose our starting point in any concrete investigation. We declare something to be problematic or of value, and then look only at relevant aspects of our experience in order to understand what causes it or gives it meaning. This is quite different from the procedure widely recognized as scientific in which the scientist chooses from the manifold of experience those aspects which are recurrent and sums up his experience in terms of these.

2   It is true that it is difficult, if not impossible, to talk about, let alone explain, human behaviour without imputing motives to individuals. It is also true that the notion of social relations and social groups can best be understood, not by asking what sort of 'things' they are, but by describing them from the point of view of a hypothetical participant in such groups and relations.

3   When we impute motives, however, we are never sure that we are right. If two people disagree on the motivation of another they will try to devise tests to see who is right. In making these tests, greater refinement of common-sense testing might appear to be achieved, by assigning probabilities to different patterns of motivation, or by saying that the behaviour concerned approximates to that which one would have predicted, but deviates to a certain degree.

4   In any study of social life it is interesting to notice that situations which appear at first to be widely different in terms of their content, are in fact rather similar. For instance, in the world of gangsters and in academic life, where survival in the one case and reputation in the other are precarious, patterns of social relations may emerge similar to those of a feudal social system.

5   More serious attempts to understand history through comparison suggest that widely different social systems depend upon the operation of social structures, which, if they are not identical or similar, are at least comparable, and one has only to press the argument a little way to find oneself discussing what the criteria are in terms of which comparisons are made.

6   There is a problem of explaining how one individual can ever make statements about the motivation of the behaviour of another. Since one man cannot see into another's head, statements about motivation are not subject to testing directly against sensory evidence in the same way as statements about physical objects are. On the other hand, we feel that we know someone when we encounter him directly and must have some sort of

stereotypes to remember people at a greater distance in space or time, or to think about a lot of people all at once.

7   If one stops to think about it, it is difficult to see how people can be sure that the world they are experiencing is the same world that others are experiencing, but it does occur that I sometimes say, 'I see a dog' and someone replies, 'that's right, so do I'. This leads to the conclusion that because men are capable of using words they do not commonly face up to the problems of solipsism which philosophers worry about.

8   There are a number of social words or labels which are not used in agreed ways or, having been so used for some time, are suddenly called into question.

The aim of this chapter is to suggest that the very core of significant sociology must lie in the comparative study of social structure, and that the best and most comprehensive example of work of this kind is that of the comparative sociology of Max Weber. In order to justify this proposition, however, it is necessary to disentangle the notion of ideal types, listed as 5 above, from other usages, which arose out of Weber's involvement in particular controversies. It is necessary to distinguish between Weber's method and any type of functionalism and systems theory. And it is also necessary to say something about its relation to the methodological doctrines listed above as 6, 7 and 8.

The first point to be made about Weber's comparative and historical sociological concepts is that the importance of his argument is regarded as being invalidated by being dependent on the positions which he took up in the controversy with Dilthey. In fact they are not, although it is true that Weber did see that argument as being relevant to his own opposition to the reification of social concepts. The best point to begin any kind of comparative sociology, therefore, is with the concept of a social relation.

The basic problems which must be faced at the outset of any systematic discussion of sociology are epistemological and theoretical ones. We must start with the fact that, despite Durkheim's apparently contradictory view, social facts are not apprehended as things and cannot be treated theoretically as things. If we do try to treat them in this way, we end with reified social entities, whose definition in empirical terms is totally arbitrary, so that the sociology, which is stated in terms of them is incapable of any sort of testing, and is usually nothing more than a claim on the part of the sociologist concerned that the social order which he desires is empirically necessary. What Weberian sociology leads us to do on the other hand is to explicate our social concepts in terms of social action and interaction and having explicated them in this way to indicate what the empirical referents of the whole complex construct are. To say this is not to say that social relation and social group concepts must be reduced to action elements and these elements tested. Rather it is true that, from the point of view of sociology, concepts referring to motivation or patterns of action-orientation are tested by reference to whole complexes of behaviour, which together form the empirical referents of relational terms. Our problem in sociology is, in the first place, a theoretical one of explicating complex concepts about social relations. Once we have done this we can turn to the more complex business of analysing the situation of an actor who acts in a world of social relations.

Pursuing this theoretical task, we have to ask first where we get social relation terms from and how it is that we are able to understand them, both individually, and in their interconnections one with another. On this there are two opposite positions to be avoided. One is that which was tentatively advanced by Georg Simmel, namely that there are certain social categories which are given to us in our perception of the behaviour of others which enable us to read it as social, just as there are categories given in the perception of nature. The other is that what the sociologist has to do is simply to comprehend and take over the social categories which they find men using. Our own position is that there is no social language given in perception, and yet that it is our task as sociologists to speak in terms of a language more shared and more justifiable than the variety of social languages used in everyday life. We should seek to do this by making our concepts clear and by obtaining agreement amongst as wide a community of sociologists as possible.

What then are the theoretical elements involved in the concept of a social relation? They appear to be as follows in the simplest case of a dyadic relation. In the first place there is an actor, whom following the Parsonian convention we may call ego, who orients his behaviour in relation to that of another (using the same convention, called alter). This orientation of behaviour may involve merely taking account of a particular statistical probability, based upon past observations of alter behaving in a particular way, or it may involve actual demands being made by ego and on alter with which he expects alter to comply. But, even if we confine ourselves to the latter case, there are a number of contingencies possible. The first of these contingencies is the degree to which alter understands what is expected of him and the second obvious one, the degree to which he complies. At this point Talcott Parsons narrows down the field for the sociologist by positing a completely 'institutionalized' social relation in which ego communicates successfully with alter and alter complies, both because he has a need-disposition to act in accordance with certain norms, and because he wants the approval of ego. Even Parsons, however, notes a limiting case in which communication is imperfect and he refers to this as a polar or limiting case, representing what he calls, using the term in a special sense, 'anomie'. We should try, in order to produce at a later stage a full range of social concepts, to see whether there are not at this level certain other possibilities also.

We might, perhaps, begin by positing situations in which there are varying degrees of communication and varying degrees of conflict. This we could express diagrammatically (see Figure 2) by saying that any particular social relation must be thought of as falling somewhere within a triangle within which the three corners represented complete harmony, complete conflict and complete

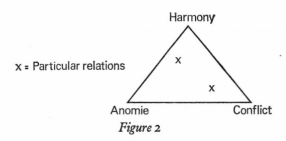

Figure 2

anomie. This is somewhat illuminating in discussing such topics as industrial, marital and international relations. There may be more or less understanding by the parties of each other's demands and there might be more or less potentiality for conflict. Peace-loving conservatives are always liable to try to explain away non-compliance on the part of alter as due to misunderstanding.

Since, however, this often serves to mask a real conflict, one should always raise the question of what would have happened had there been complete understanding. In fact, in marriage and in industrial relations and international relations the truth usually lies between the extremes. Understanding is only partial and, independently of this, compliance is only partial. There may, however, be a further dimension to social relations when they are discussed on this micro-level. This is whether or not the demands of ego are regarded as legitimate, and, whether they are or not, whether alter complies. Clearly there are cases in which alter's demands are regarded as legitimate by ego and he complies, and there are also clearly cases in which the demands are not regarded as legitimate and non-compliance is the result. What are too often overlooked, however, are those cases in which the demands are not regarded as legitimate, yet there is compliance, and those cases in which there is an acceptance of the legitimacy of the demands, but non-compliance. Thus we have four cases: (*a*) legitimacy with compliance, which represents even more fully Parsons's completely institutionalized relation; (*b*) non-legitimacy which when it is coupled with non-compliance is again the pure case of conflict; (*c*) the case of non-legitimacy but with compliance which we may refer to as the case of forced compliance and (*d*) the case of acceptance of legitimacy without compliance which we may call the genuine case of deviance.

Since the compliance-non-compliance dimension occurs in both the classifications mentioned above, we should have an eight rather than a sixteen box table (see Figure 3). The fact that compliance may or may not be the result of a subjective acceptance on the part of alter that a demand is legitimate is clearly brought out by Weber. The main reason for the emphasis on the word 'subjective' here is Weber's belief that all claims to legitimacy have only a relative validity and that sociology must include cases where the feeling exists as well as where it does not exist and even where it does not exist take account of the possibility of compliance resulting from material self-interest (e.g. being paid or from the exercise of violence or power).

It must be admitted, however, that Weber's definition of a social relation is confused. Wanting, as he does, to bridge the gap between *Verstehen* and positive science, he confuses the theoretical definition of a social relation as 'the behaviour of actors in so far

Ego makes demands on alter

Communication

Perfect communication Perfect compliance		Imperfect communication Perfect compliance	
Demands regarded as legitimate	Demands regarded as illegitimate	Demands as comprehended regarded as legitimate	Demands as comprehended regarded as illegitimate

Perfect communication Imperfect compliance		Imperfect communication Imperfect compliance	
Demands regarded as legitimate compliance of non-normative kind	Demands regarded as illegitimate conflict	Demands as comprehended regarded as legitimate	Demands as comprehended regarded as illegitimate

Ego's behaviour oriented to a statistical probability of a particular line of conduct

Competitive ecological and economic interaction

COMPLIANCE

Note: Each of the three elements or dimensions are repeated here in either-or terms. It should be remembered therefore that there can be degrees of adequacy in communication, legitimacy and compliance.

Figure 3

as, in its meaningful content, the action of each takes account of that of others and is oriented in these terms', with the notion that, 'the social relationships consist entirely and exclusively in the existence of a probability that there will be a meaningful course of social action—irrespective, for the time being, of the basis for this probability'.

Before turning to the question of verifiers and falsifiers of statements about social relations, we should notice that related to the problem raised by this definition is that concerning the taking account of the behaviour of another. That might be a matter of taking account of a probability, or it may mean making a demand on alter. This means that before we follow Weber in discussing types of legitimate order governing social relations, we must recognize the relatively sub-social case in which the orientation of ego is to nothing more than a statistical probability, and also the case in which there is no claim to legitimacy recognized.

What we are talking about when we talk about social relations then and what we have to demonstrate, are empirical facts about human behaviour which we interpret as indicating orientation of one individual to another, either in a calculating probabilistic way, or in the sense of making or receiving demands, as indicating belief or non-belief in a legitimate order governing the interaction, or as sanctions employed to obtain compliance. Thus if we have fully explicated the concept social relation theoretically, we should know what sorts of empirical evidence are necessary to verify, falsify or otherwise test that which we have to say. In Weber's opening chapter in *Economy and Society* the question of verification is not discussed at this point, but earlier, in relation to the establishment of causally adequate explanations of action. We have noted that Weber had said in this earlier context that causally adequate explanations of behaviour must be used to check that explanations adequate on the level of meaning were anything more than plausible stories, and that such causal explanations involved showing that 'there exists a probability that action in fact normally takes the course held to be meaningful'. This is in fact a misleading formulation for, as Winch (1958) and others pointed out, it adds nothing to the validity of an explanation on the level of meaning, to show that a particular act is likely to recur. It will be remembered that Weber himself, in his earlier essay, took the view that while natural science studied that which was recurrent, the sociologist studied sequences of events which were relevant for value. Now he appears to be abandoning this position and probably was doing so with a view to relating sociology to mainstream positive science.

There is, however, another way of looking at the question of how we distinguish between mere plausible stories about motivation and those which are valid from the point of view of the observer. This is that once we have set out explicitly our account of motivation, we may return to the original behaviour-in-context which seemed to need explanation and look at many other aspects of the behaviour which we had not considered before. In this case we would not make a prediction in the form, 'wait until this happens again and see whether the behaviour as a whole does not have this form', but, 'go back to that same behaviour sequence which you were looking at before and see whether there are not observable elements of e_1, e_2, e_3, etc.' That is to say that we do not prove motivation propositions by showing that acts were frequently repeated. We prove them because they have multiple empirical referents and there are, therefore, always unobserved aspects of a single behaviour sequence to which we can return to prove our proposition. In this way explanations in terms of the meaning of an action are tested, and, if they pass the test, are regarded as being valid explanation. If this does happen, then it is possible to say that something akin to the scientific method has been adhered to. But if the validation of statements about motivation takes this form, then statements about social relations, as we have defined them, are testable in the same way. Thus, for example, we may say that a free market relationship exists among a plurality of actors, and then look to see whether, in fact, there is a group of people who hold a particular type of good desired by another group; whether, if the money or services which a particular buyer offers are not acceptable, the suppliers look for other buyers; and vice versa, when the price demanded by the suppliers is too high, the buyers look to other suppliers offering a lower price. These are the bald elements of a market situation, of course, and it would be possible to introduce all sorts of nuances into our definition to make it more discriminating. What is important, however, is that an ideal type of a social relation has the same operational features as a type which relates only to individual action or motivation. It is possible to make models of both types and, since they have multiple empirical referents, to see whether a return to the original problematic situation does not reveal that those elements are present.

Social relation concepts then, do not need to be reduced to individual action concepts. The real point which Weber makes is that they should not be reified. Durkheim's notion of social facts as things does this, but neither Weber or Marx do. Thus when Marx is writing about the estrangement of labour he says:

> The alien being to whom labour and the produce of labour belongs, in whose service labour is done, and for whose benefit the produce of labour is provided, can only be man himself.
> If the product of labour does not belong to the worker, if it confronts him as an alien power, this can only be because it belongs to some man other than the worker.
>
> (Marx, 1956, p. 79)

Both Marx and Weber may be said to have a humanistic perspective or to be 'methodological individualists', in the sense that the elements in their theoretical constructs of social relations are assumed to be individual hypothetical actors orienting their conduct to one another, in one of the ways mentioned in Figure 2. They are not methodological individualists, however, in the sense that they believe that all propositions about social relations can be reduced to verifiable or testable propositions about particular historic individuals. It is possible to distinguish between ideal types of individual action and ideal types of social relations, and propositions referring to either of these may be tested. We, as sociologists, are primarily concerned with propositions about social relations, although there is the more complex case of action carried out in the context of social relations, which involves an even more complex construct.

Once we have reached the point of saying that we can have ideal types of dyadic relations, which can be used validly, once they have been tested against their multiple empirical referents, what follows? Simmel, at this point, trivializes his own position by following his discussion of the dyad with a discussion of the general effects of increasing numbers on the quality of social life, and Parsons may perhaps be represented as simply building up the theoretical model of a whole social, cultural and personality system around the notion of the completely institutionalized social relation. What Weber does next, however, is to go on to a discussion of the group and of other multi-person structures. It would not be possible here, and it would be redundant, to set out what is involved in the more complex concept of a group. Weber has done so at considerable length in the second half of the opening chapter of *Economy and Society*. What we should note, however, is that it is the set of concepts which he develops on this level which are of greatest moment in his comparative and historical work. He retains at the multi-person group level all the contingencies and possibilities which exist in dyadic relations (e.g. power, legitimacy and so on), but also distinguishes between groups which have characteristics such as the representational and leadership quality of the acts of their members; and other multi-person structures, like markets, which do not necessarily have these characteristics, but which arise out of the self-oriented (as opposed to collectivity-oriented) action of a plurality of individuals. On the level of the group, as well as on the level of social relations, Weber rejects any commitment to functionalism. What he does is simply to work out the range of theoretical possibilities there, given the elements out of which his types are constructed. Again, of course, on the social group level as on the social relational level, there is a limiting case of perfect harmony, but in the real world conflicts about expected role behaviour in the group, lack of clarity about legitimacy and so on are bound to arise, and Weber keeps open the road which leads to the fullest possible range of structural types.

How far can one go and how far should one go in the establishment of sociological concepts beyond this point? To what extent should one develop a model of total social systems, within which groups play a part as means to over-all ends, and in which different individuals and groups perform functional roles? Parsons apparently believes that one can, but is relatively unclear in *The Social System* as to whether this larger system arises out of the very concept of a social relation or whether, beyond that level, and the level of the group, an account of a comprehensive kind can be given of the total pattern of social relations and cultural patterns which constitute the social system. The lack of clarity also remains in his later work. During the phase of this co-operation with Bales, the small group is seen as containing all the functional subsystems necessary for a society, and his central theoretical propositions seem to be tested against the behaviour of small groups. Later, however, he extends the theory to cover historical societies.

What Weber does is to set out to develop a language in terms of which the structures to be found in the major areas of life can be discussed, and he proceeds to a masterly analysis of the structural problems in those areas. Thus we have sections of *Economy and Society* dealing with economic structures, political and legal structures, class structures, and so on. But while most of his analysis of these separate institutional areas is unsurpassed, he is not particularly concerned to develop a general theory of their interrelations. What he does is to look at the empirical evidence of the actual relationships which have been found to hold at different periods in history. Referring to the organicist sociology of Schäffle, Weber writes:

Schäffle's brilliant work, *Bau und Leben des sozialen Körpers* (attempts) to understand social interaction by using as a point of departure the 'whole' within which the individual acts. His action and behaviour are then interpreted somewhat in the way that a physiologist would treat the role of an organ of the body in the 'economy' of an organism. . . . How far in other disciplines this type of functional analysis of the relation of the 'parts' to the 'whole' can be regarded as definitive cannot be discussed here; but it is well known that bio-chemical and bio-physical modes of analysis of the organism are on principle opposed to stopping there. For purposes of sociological analysis two things can be said. First this functional frame of reference is convenient for purposes of practical illustration and for provisional orientation. In these respects it is not only useful but indispensable. But at the same time, if its cognitive value is over-estimated and concepts illegitimately 'reified' it can be highly dangerous.

(Weber, 1968, I, Chap. I)

Thus it would appear that, just as in biology the general study of the functioning organic whole has to be followed by biophysical and biochemical modes of analysis, so functional sociology is only a starting point, and the really telling discoveries are likely to be made on some kind of sociological equivalent of biophysics and biochemistry. This would seem to suggest that the comparative study of institutions in different societies is the all-important factor in sociology, while a notion of the functional whole of a single society or societies in general has value only for purposes of provisional orientation. But, additionally to this, Weber argues that the concepts which we use when we go further in sociology have the additional quality of being meaningful and of yielding understanding.

> In the case of social collectivities, precisely as distinguished from organisms, we are in a position to go beyond merely demonstrating functional relationships and uniformities. We can accomplish something which is never attainable in the natural sciences, namely the subjective understanding of the action of component individuals.
>
> (Weber, 1968, 1, Chap. 1)

Once the limitations of functionalism are exposed in this way, the way forward for sociology becomes clear. It must make comparative studies of social structure in a way which was explicitly rejected above all by Malinowski. No doubt Malinowski was right in opposing the antiquarian use of the comparative method by anthropologists like Frazer. But there can be little doubt, when one turns to history, that the institutional forms of one society are, in fact, comparable with one another if we analyse them with the use of sufficiently abstract concepts. Frazer may have been wrong in comparing, say, sacrifice between one society and another; Weber was certainly not wrong in comparing political, industrial, administrative, legal and religious structures. In fact it is only when such work has been done that the relationships between one institutional area and another can be fully explored. Thus, if we look at governmental administration in a former colonial territory today, it is not sufficient merely to look at it either in terms of some absolute form or in terms of the part which it plays in the functional whole, which to some extent that society might be. It is also extremely useful to know that when bureaucracy develops imperfectly there are certain known directions in which the particular historical form might deviate.

This brings us back to the question of the testability of ideal types. If we refer back to 3 (page 193) in the list of ways in which the notion of ideal types is used it will be seen that Weber seemed to regard his ideal types as testable. In developing his notion of the comparative forms of institutions and structures, however, we find Weber once again insisting that actual social structures are unlikely to conform to the pure type and that this type is only a yardstick against which concrete cases may be measured. This is surely true. Theory does not describe reality. It illuminates it by bringing what is into comparison with what could have been or what is the case elsewhere. What Weber achieved, and what no other sociologist has achieved in the same degree, was the establishment of a range of structural possibilities in all the main institutional spheres. What is important is not simply his account of bureaucracy, for instance, but the development of that concept against the more general background of historical possibilities. So, also, in each sphere the sociologist should not approach a society with no previous experience. He has had experience in reading the accounts of other societies which gives him the means to the comparison and analysis of any new institutional form which he might encounter. Any reading of contemporary sociological writing will show how badly such comparative tools are needed. To quote but one example, the study of race relations in America or Britain could not possibly be so insular and, in a bad sense, subjective, were there available a set of concepts which might be used in the field which have the analytic and explanatory power of Weber's ideal types.

It may be argued that the ideal types which the sociologist uses are in fact not very different from the pure experimental cases which the natural scientist uses. He does not claim, any more than the sociologist does, to give a complete description of the world. He sums it up by seeing what happens in ideal or controlled experimental conditions and, having thus established the pure type, measures the extent to which actual events depart from this pure type, and then seeks to explain the unexplained residue. Against this, however, it must be admitted that the cases are rare indeed in which it is possible to find or to create a pure type of social structure in history. The awkward fact which we have to face is that, although ideal types are essential in sociology, they cannot themselves ever be proved as natural laws can in science. But this does not mean that they are illegitimate instruments of analysis by any means. What it means is that the creator of sociological typologies needs a degree of creative insight and sensitivity which he would not need if we had available foolproof historical methods. It is for this reason that the phase of type-construction is so much more important in sociology than it is in the natural sciences. Indeed it can be argued that type-construction *is* sociology and that the interpretation of particular periods and societies in terms of the types is really the province of history.

Two other questions remain. These are those of the relation between ideal types and quantitative evidence, and of their relation to the categories which men use in everyday life. On the first of these questions it should be pointed out that the analyses of patterns of culture and social relations do not lend themselves immediately to quantification. It is true of course that once the various elements of an ideal type of social structure have been made clear, some of these might be quantifiable, and that worthwhile work might be done in measuring the deviation from the pure type of that element in a particular case (e.g. Weber makes it one of his criteria of pure bureaucracy that all official acts are recorded in the files; the extent to which this is the case in a concrete instance can very readily be measured). Moreover, it is also true that in the application of ideal types there is a great deal of sheer factual material which needs to be gathered and stated in quantitative form. In these matters, however, the words of the Webbs still have relevance:

> The accumulation of many observations, though possibly only qualitative or capable of only imperfect measurement may amount to quite effective verification; verification it is true . . . of a low order of probability; such as that on which most of the world's action proceeds.
>
> (Webb, 1932)

We should never sacrifice what is at the heart of sociology in an attempt to gain knowledge of the social structures and relationships which affect men's lives, in favour of quantitative accuracy pursued for its own sake. Much that has happened in American sociology since 1945 is subject to precisely this accusation. What

Lazarsfeld calls 'variate language' cannot readily accommodate the qualitative complexity of the study of social structures.

So far as the point of the categories of everyday life is concerned, we must insist that though the sociologist must take account of these as data, the object of sociology as a subject is to give an account of these in the shared language of sociologists of the matters concerned. It is true that the categories of everyday life change and that it is desirable in a changing world to have sociological models, which can accommodate change. But this is precisely what the Weberian typologies do. More than merely recognizing the possibility of change, they seek to give an explicit account of the logical and theoretical possibilities so far as the direction of change is concerned. The aim of the sociologist is to give a structural account of types of social structure and types of social institution. These change, and a sociology which is of any value will give an account of that change. It is also true, as we pointed out at the beginning of this chapter, that personal encounters and transitions take place within this over-all structural framework. It is interesting to pursue these, but they cannot be substituted for the analysis of social structures.

In conclusion, this chapter should be seen as a plea for a return to comparative and historical sociology and a sociology which is geared to the understanding of the political problems of our day. The sort of sociology we have been discussing is the sort which will enable us to make public issues out of personal troubles, rather than ignoring the troubles as empiricist sociology does, or turning public troubles into personal issues which is what much modern phenomenological sociology is inclined to do. Surely this is what is needed in a world, in which long-established forms of order in the formerly colonial world, as well as in the metropolitan countries themselves, have collapsed and new forms are emerging every day.

18

Thirty theses on epistemology and method in sociology

1   Whereas natural science is an activity in which men formulate concepts in order to understand the behaviour of classes of objects or things, the human studies are concerned with the study of a particular class of objects which themselves have the curious characteristics that they may be thought of as having concepts about each other and about other objects.

2   W. I. Thomas suggested that sociology was concerned, not with simple objective facts, but with the actor's 'definition of the situation'. Alfred Schutz (1964, 1967) has suggested that the main focus of the human studies should be on 'the phenomenology of everyday life', i.e. on the forms and categories in terms of which men habitually organize their perceptions and their experience and so make a shared and intersubjective world possible.

3   This phenomenological perspective has combined with the perspective of symbolic interactionism, deriving from the notion of George Mead that the self is a social product, to produce the doctrine in some spheres of sociology, notably in the study of deviance, that mere statistical 'facts' are misleading and that what matters most is the decision to label particular acts as belonging to one category rather than another. In an extreme form this might lead to the view that there is really no such thing as crime, only a decision on the social, cultural and linguistic level to label certain acts as criminal.

4   This extreme form of subjectivism produces a reaction amongst some sociologists, who point out dangers, for instance, in the sociology of politics or class conflict, of holding that what is significant is not what actually and objectively exists but what people think exists. This often leads to a reversion to the crude epistemological doctrine of Dr Johnson and Lenin which proves the objective existence of the material world by kicking a stone or by any other operation on that world.

5   It is an odd historical fact at this point in history that the same sociologists who support labelling theory in criminology also insist upon materialist and objectivist perspectives in the sociology of politics. This has to do with the fact that in the sphere of politics it is the 'authorities' who seek to will away the sufferings of the masses by re-labelling them, whereas in the criminological field it is those who are against authority who wish to deny the reality of the object which causes concern.

6   The problem of social reality and its nature has been some-what obscured in this discussion by an oversimplification of the consequences for sociology of the doctrines of Mead and Schutz (and of Weber, to whose work Schutz originally sought to contribute a footnote). To do Mead and Schutz justice, their own position was complex enough, but both of them were in the first instance philosophers and they did not, therefore, develop fully the implications of what they were saying for strictly sociological analysis.

7   The epistemological problem of the sociologist is only understood if it is recognized that what the sociologist seeks to study as his most elementary unit are social relations, or, if one wishes to avoid the apparently static connotations of that term, forms of social interaction.

8   One does not say that social relations form the ultimate *data* of sociology, for they are not 'given' in perception. They are constructed by the observed actors who are party to them, by other observed actors, who observe the behaviour of the involved parties from the outside, and by sociologists, who observe the behaviour both of the involved actors, and of those for whom the construct which they make to explain the behaviour of others becomes an agreed part of their social environment.

9   Concepts like 'role' are more complex than the concept of social relation. They assume, not merely that certain behaviour is required, but that there is some agreement about what is required by a multiplicity of parties (even though there may also be disagreement). Such agreement presupposes not merely a social relation but a whole network or system of social relations.

10   The explication of paragraph 8 above is central to the understanding of what sociology is about, to the formulation of meaningful research plans and above all to the resolution of the problem of 'false consciousness' posed in paragraphs 3 and 4.

11 (a) We must begin with what is assumed both by other actors, and by observing sociologists, about the behaviour and the ideas and the motivation of the actors who are parties to a social relation.

(b) The first assumption which we make about these actors is that they believe they understand one another. Such understanding includes (*i*) a belief that they share the same world of objects or that, at least, if there should be disagreement, there are techniques for resolving such disagreement, and for arriving at agreed statements about the world, (*ii*) a belief that each party is able to understand his own behaviour as meaningful and that, by making an analogy between his own behaviour and that of others, is able to grasp the meaning of the others' behaviour.

(ci) Much of the work of Alfred Schutz, especially his comments on the methodology of Max Weber, is concerned with the problems mentioned in paragraph 11 (b). He argues that the process of the actor understanding his own behaviour begins with a sheer ongoing experience (the notion of the *durée* in Bergson), involves attending to that experience, when, by definition, it must already be understood as being in the past tense, and seeing particular behavioural events as parts of projects, in which the individual first fantasies a state of affairs, and then chooses a course of behaviour which is understood as a means to the attainment of that state of affairs.

(cii) Further, Schutz outlines the process whereby one individual comes to claim to understand the behaviour of another as meaningful. He argues that in one respect we have a more immediate understanding of this behaviour than we have of our own. This is that we observe it as it actually occurs, i.e. in the present tense. But, when we go beyond the behavioural record to impute motives, there can be no guarantee that our account of the other individual's behaviour and its meaning is accurate.

(d) What human beings continually do when they impute motives is to set up hypotheses about motivation. These never tell the whole truth (and we should re-emphasize that those who set them up could never know whether they did or not), but take the form of oversimplifications which have an implicit *ceteris paribus* clause attached to them. Schutz, however, distinguishes between the degree to which it is possible for an actor to get near to the truth in the case of his interaction with his consociates, with whom he has face-to-face relations, his contemporaries and his predecessors and successors. The more we move away from face-to-face relations, the less chance we have of verifying our interpretations through the winks and nods which accompany behaviour and speech.

(e) Schutz makes too much of this distinction and seems to suggest that there is a difference of principle, and not merely of degree, between the interaction which an individual has with his consociates, as distinct from his contemporaries and his successors. The view taken here is that interpretation always takes place through the formulation of ideal types, whether amongst consociates, contemporaries or predecessors and successors, even though there may be some considerable interest to the human studies in studying the winks and nods of social interaction, such studies being particularly important in making anthropological and ethnomethodological studies more sensitive.

(f) The kind of interpretation of the behaviour of another which posits a simplified pattern of motivation is what Weber called an ideal type and what Schutz and his followers call a typification. Schutz, however, suggests that the social world for the actor consists of such typifications, and that the notion of typification may be extended to the notions of objects with which men operate in the course of their social interaction. It is only through their capacity to make typifications of the experiences which they call dogs, trees and tables as well as of the 'actions' of other individuals that men can detect meaning in the world at all, let alone have the sense of having a shared and intersubjective world.

12   One line of development which the work of Schutz suggests is the analysis of language, since the whole of self-understanding, as well as mutual understanding in interaction depends upon shared systems of meaning. This has led some sociologists to turn away from the study of social relations to the study of language, culture, myth and 'everything which passes for knowledge in everyday life'.

13   By contrast with the view that sociology should develop along the lines suggested in the previous paragraph, we take the view that such studies are only a prolegomenon to the truly sociological studies and that sociological studies of social relations[1]

---

[1] This seems to be understood by Berger and Luckmann in their *Social Construction of Reality*, 1967.

can be made which assume the existence of a language understood or understandable with a fair degree of precision by a plurality of actors as well as by a sociological observer. One of the difficulties about phenomenologically oriented sociology is that it tends to talk about the understandings which are presupposed in social interaction, without talking about the social interaction itself. An account is given of the runners at the moment that the starter fires his pistol, but no account is given of the race itself.

14   (a) A 'social relation', which is something which most actors believe to be one of the kinds of entity which form part of their world, is more complex than a typification or ideal type of a course of action. It assumes one actor, A, who has expectations of the behaviour of another, an understanding of those expectations by another actor, B, and a response by B in terms of his own behaviour to his understanding of A's expectations.

(b) A's expectation of B covers two cases at least:
(i) that in which he guesses at B's understanding of the world, including B's own behaviour and B's motivation, and then seeks to intrude into B's orientation to action a new element, namely a typification of his (A's) expectations. He may seek to be more or less 'honest' in the typifications which he seeks to produce, in some cases, for example, trying to prevent B perceiving what are his true motives as he himself understands them.
(ii) that in which A does not understand B's behaviour, but is aware of what he is likely to do, in terms of statistical probability assessed on the lines of past behaviour. This is a common and important aspect of market behaviour, and should not be ignored simply because on one level it operates without seeking understanding. It is still the case here that A sees his own behaviour as meaningful, and we should wish to include this case under the general heading 'meaningful social interaction'.

(c) B's understanding of A may be more or less adequate. Not merely is it the case that A might seek to conceal his true purpose from B, but B can only have a typification of A's expectations. There may be some process of clarification in which B asks explicitly or implicitly, 'Is this what you want me to do?' and A replies, 'No, you haven't quite got the hang of it.' Even after this process has gone on, however, we may doubt whether the communication of expectations is ever perfect. Nonetheless, it is important to emphasize that, even if B misunderstands A, social interaction is involved. The social interaction would only be arrested if B was simply unaware of A's expectations or of A's having expectations.

(d) Given that B has some understanding of what A expects, he may do one of three things. He may plan his own action project so that he performs in accordance with A's expectations and to his satisfaction. He may accept that A's expectations are legitimate and that he 'should' conform, and yet not do so. Or he may reject A's demands and pursue a course of action, or abstain from a course of action in a way which is inconsistent with A's demands.

15 From the point of view of other actors the social relation which we have been discussing appears, not as a subjective fact involving the orientation of *his* conduct to that of another, but as an objective external fact, a part of his environment which he can typify and treat as a thing, provided that he can agree with others on what social relations actually exist. It is a fact of course that there is less agreement on the use of social relation terms than there is on terms referring to physical facts, but it is nonetheless possible to typify social relations, just as it is the world of things and the action orientation of other actors.

16 The concept of social relations which we have just discussed is central to the work of four of the greatest sociologists, namely Simmel, Durkheim, Weber and Marx, though the problem is approached differently and in terms of a different language by each of them.

(i) Simmel asks how it is that human beings, confronted with the manifold of ongoing behaviour and events, interpret those events or some of them as social. He concludes that they have a capacity for using social categories, and that the prime task of the sociologist is simply to make clear what those categories are.

(ii) Durkheim's emphasis is on the externality of social facts. Indeed he wishes to treat them as things and to deny that they are individual, mental or psychological entities. Nonetheless, when he analyses these 'external' facts, it is clear that they are forms of social solidarity or types of social relations.

(iii) Weber appears to emphasize the subjective side, and is sometimes criticized by Marxists for directing our attention to a purely subjective or false consciousness. It is clear, however, that while Weber insists upon the fact that social relations can always be subject to analysis in terms of the subjective expectations of hypothetical actors orienting their conduct to one another, he also envisages the possibility of actors orienting their conduct to a world of social relations which for them are objective and external. Clearly his historical categories such as bureaucracy, adventurer capitalism, a plantation or a city are not simply figments of a single actor's imagination. They are objective facts, confronting the actor from outside.

(iv) Despite the association of the label 'Marxist' with doctrines which emphasize the objectivity of the material and the social world, it is clear that Marx himself did not take this as meaning that the social world was a superhuman one. In his discussion of the estrangement of labour, after he has analysed all the various aspects of alienation, he seeks its source in, and sees the external world as consisting of, the demands of other exploiting men and of an exploitative social system.

What appears to be agreed, therefore, between all the main founders of sociology is that social facts are both objective and subjective. They are objective in that social relations may appear as, and be typified as, 'things', but they are doubly subjective, in that the relations themselves have to be analysed in terms of typifications of subjective expectations and their fulfilment and non-fulfilment, and in that the actors who observe and typify the social relations cannot get beyond typification to an undisputed picture of social relations as they really are.

17 Thus far we have been concerned (a) with the orientation of the behaviour of one actor to another in a social relation and (b) an actor perceiving a world of social relations external to himself. We have yet to consider what chance there is of a sociologist being able to claim any kind of validity for the account which *he* gives of the action-orientation of an actor in a world of objective social relations.

18 Sociological observers are no more capable of gaining access to social relations or the motivation of other actors from the inside than are other actors. In so far as any sociologist claims that he understands these things directly through some process of sympathetic introspection, he simply puts himself on a par with the participant actors themselves and is not entitled to claim

any kind of privileged status for his conclusions. What the sociologist does do is to construct his own ideal types (a) of an actor's perception of the world of social relations which surrounds him and through this (b) of the pattern of mutual expectancies involved in these social relations. There is a sense, therefore, in which the sociologist's statement is a construct of a construct of a construct, rather than an immediate description of an observable thing.

19   The tradition of Thomas and Schutz has sometimes led to an oversimplification of this problem. Instead of recognizing that sociological statements are constructs used to explain constructs used to explain constructs, it has been claimed that sociology can simply describe the actor's definition of the situation. This is misleading in two respects. On the one hand it ignores the fact that sociology is about a world of social relations, which is assumed to have an existence independent of those who experience it as an environment. On the other hand, it presupposes that we can directly describe an actor's definition of the situation.

20   (a) The real merit of the sociologist's account of social relations, and of actors in a world of social relations, is that sociologists have reasonably clearly formulated procedures for resolving disputes amongst themselves as to what is the case. That is to say, using Weber's terminology, that, having given explanations which are adequate on the level of meaning, it is incumbent upon sociologists to distinguish between merely plausible stories and those ideal types which have been used to predict reality and have been able to predict it with some degree of statistical accuracy.

(b) Much confusion has been caused by Weber's use of the term 'causal adequacy' to describe the characteristic of an explanation which has been tested. So also has his confusion of the concept of ideal type, as it is used in this context, with his use of the same term to describe methodological devices used in history, which were quite different from hypotheses and laws. It is therefore necessary to emphasize the following.

In his later work Weber sought to distinguish the sociologist's use of ideal types of action orientation and of social relations, and of action orientation in a context of social relations, from any pseudo-technique based upon sympathetic introspection or intuition. He suggested that this be done by testing hypotheses about the subjective action-orientation of a theoretical actor or actors, by seeing whether those events which might be expected if such hypotheses were relevant, did actually occur. Confirmation might take the form of the statistical recurrence of the same event, the occurrence of a variety of predicted events, the statistical recurrence of a variety of predicted events, or the occurrence of at least some of a variety of expected events.

21 Weber also felt that he had bridged the gap between positivist sociology and the tradition which held the method of the social sciences to be one of *Verstehen*. Thus statistical statements about the probability of behaviour occurring might well be relevant to the sociologist, but would only be so if they could be explained in terms of subjectively understandable courses of action orientation. On the other hand, statements which were based on *Verstehen* were to be accepted if, and only if, they yielded true predictions about events.

22 Just as the sociologist is able to distinguish between those of his own 'meaningfully adequate explanations' which merit retention and those which do not, so he is also able to distinguish between those of the observed actors' 'definitions of the situation' which have objective validity and those which do not. He does this by subjecting these interpretations to the same tests as he would interpretations by another sociologist. It may be that no ultimate validity or truth can be attributed to the interpretations which pass these tests, but tests there are, and there is a distinction between those interpretations which stand up to them and those which fail. If, therefore, there is any ground for assuming that a distinction can be made between true and false propositions made by sociologists, a distinction can also be made between completely arbitrary actors' definitions of the situation and definitions which have objective validity. What this means is that the phenomenological perspective does not imply an incapacity to distinguish between true and false consciousness.

23 What we have seen here puts into perspective the observations of the Marxist sociologist of literature, Lucien Goldmann, who writes as follows:

> The weakness of phenomenology seems to us to lie precisely in the fact that it limits itself to a comprehensive description of the facts of consciousness. . . . The real structure of

historical facts permits, however, beyond the conscious meaning of those facts in the thought and intentions of the actors, the postulation of an objective meaning which often differs from the conscious meaning in an important way.

(Goldmann, 1969, p. 32)

24 It should be noted that throughout we have insisted that the task of the sociologist is to study social relations and patterns of social relations. Mere statistical facts as such are of no interest to him. They are of interest only in so far as they indicate the extent to which an explanation of behaviour in terms of patterns of action orientation, or of social relations or of patterns of action orientation in an environment of social relations, are validated by events. The recent positivist interpretation of Weber, as put forward by Lazarsfeld and Oberschall (1965) who see Weber as simply making a series of probabilistic statements is therefore gravely misleading.

25 (a) In contrast to the Weberian tradition, the tradition of Durkheim is used to validate purely statistical studies of correlations between one type of behaviour and another as sociological. This, however, is equally misleading, as we can see by considering Durkheim's justification in the *Rules* of a sociological use of statistical rates, and his exemplification of what he meant in his work *Suicide*.

(b) When Durkheim begins defining the sociological subject matter he points first to norms and rules, i.e. to ideal forms of social relation to which men feel themselves obliged to conform. But, having done this, he recognizes that actual behaviour does not conform to these rules. His problem then is this. Either nonconformity is due to the fact that men simply randomly disobey, or it is due to the fact that some as yet unperceived pattern of social relations is determining their conduct. There is no doubt as to Durkheim's answer. He believes that there are underlying 'collective currents' not 'fixed' enough to be discoverable as norms, yet nonetheless influencing human behaviour in an 'external' and 'social' way. The degree of this influence is shown in the statistical rates of such pathologies as suicide and divorce, but the discovery of the statistical rates only poses a problem for the sociologist. Crime, Durkheim tells us, is to be understood as a 'normal' phenomenon, i.e. it is produced by underlying patterns of social relations. The task of the sociologist is to discover these patterns of social relations.

Thus, although Durkheim is often praised for his statistical skill in his study of suicide, he would not have regarded this as more than a technical matter. The important point for him was that, if there was a proved statistical difference between two social categories such as Protestant and Catholic in the degree of their suicide-proneness, this suggested an underlying and undetected pattern of social solidarity amongst the two groups.

26 The greatness of the work of Weber and of Durkheim lay in this. Both of them saw the value of statistical methods of organizing and analysing evidence of the association between one event and another. This did not, however, mean that either of them were ever interested in statistics for their own sake. What interested them was the construction of social theories about actors in a world of social relations, i.e. ultimately making constructs about constructs about constructs. Both sought to hold together the generally applicable forms of inductive reasoning of positivist science and the meaningful understanding of social relations. Their greatness emerges when one realizes the extent to which this holding together breaks down in modern writers of the phenomenological and the positivist tradition. Neither the phenomenology of everyday life, nor mere studies in social statistics, are of themselves sociological.

27 There are two further points made by Talcott Parsons about the adequacy of the methods which we have outlined which merit discussion here. One is the relation between what we have been saying and a sociology which is cast in terms of the notion of a social system. The other concerns the relation of the kind of objective-subjective sociological concepts we have been discussing to those of psychology. In his notable introduction to *The Theory of Social and Economic Organization*, Parsons (1964) seeks to correct Weber on these two points. We wish to retain Weber's perspective and reject the criticisms.

28 The notion of system and that of the actor orienting his action in a world of social relations are of course by no means incompatible. For many purposes indeed it is useful to notice the extent to which, once an ongoing pattern of behaviour exists, it becomes a boundary-maintaining system which returns to state if it is disturbed. But it is not consequentially justifiable to pre-

tend that all social-action orientation is systemic in this sense and without internal conflicts. Nor is it adequate from a sociological point of view to cease talking about the meaningful orientation of action and concentrate only on the generalized attributes of systems.

Parsons, like Weber, begins by writing within what he himself calls the action frame of reference and this, it would seem, would imply some of the epistemological and methodological positions outlined above. But when Parsons talks of social relations he quickly passes to what he calls the completely institutionalized case, in which there is a system in which B's fulfilment of A's expectations is doubly bound in by a normative order on the one hand and his emotional dependence on the other. The whole of what follows in *The Social System* (Parsons, 1952, Chap. 2) is concerned with the maintenance of this state of affairs. Finally in his mature work, Parsons ceases to speak of action and relations altogether, and simply discusses systems processes in the abstract.

What is lost in this subordination of the action frame of reference to the notion of the social system is the interpretation of social relations and action in a world of social relations as meaningful. The theory of social systems applies to supra-individual and supra-human things. What is said about social systems might equally apply to other types of systems, since it is never very clear as it is with hypotheses adequate on the level of meaning what consequences in the form of actual behaviour would follow if a particular hypothesis were true. In its exemplifications there appears to be only a gross fit between the propositions of systems-theory and events in the real world.

29   We do not believe that the analysis of human behaviour in terms of models of meaningful action-orientation of itself implies any reference to psychology. Patterns of action-orientation are the elements from which the notions of social relations are constructed, but from the sociological point of view they are explanatory constructs only. They are not to be thought of as having the form which they do because of some psychological imperative. On the other hand, it is true that since the human personality system is not infinitely malleable, particular patterns of orientation necessary to maintain a pattern of social relations require and presuppose and are limited by, psychological possibilities in the socialization process. In so far as this is all that

Parsons is trying to say, he adds valuably to the theory of social action, particularly in the case of the more enduring structures of social action.

But Parsons is saying something more than this. He is saying that for a social system to be a social system, social relations must be institutionalized, not merely in the sense that all elements of conflict have been eliminated, but in the sense that the participants have developed a 'need-disposition' on the psychological level to do what the system requires. Thus the ongoing social system involves not only mechanisms for socialization, but also for the control of deviance and the re-socialization of the deviant. Social order comes to depend upon two overlapping systems, one on the social, the other on the personality level.

The problem with this approach is that all conflict is then seen as due to disturbance on the personality level. This is how Parsons comes to account for deviance. By contrast, Durkheim sees crime as a normal phenomenon (i.e. something governed by its own norms of a social kind, rather than being the product of a personality disturbance) and Weber always envisages, as we have done, that conflict rather than system might be the outcome of the interplay between different patterns of action orientation in the world of social relations.

30   What we have attempted here is to outline the implications for sociology of the subject's being conceived as being about social relations, and of the necessity of taking account in our concepts of the concepts used by actors within social relations, or actors living in a world in which social relations appear as objects. We have shown how it means that this kind of sociology must be distinguished, from both the phenomenology of everyday life, and from mere statistical positivism and empiricism. Finally, we have shown that it is a kind of sociology far richer and far more closely related to the real world in a provable way than is contemporary systems theory. For this reason it is hard to see that there is likely to be much significant work going on in contemporary sociology, which has the profundity and the truly sociological quality, which is evident in the work of Weber and of Durkheim.

19

Sociological theory and deviance theory

Deviance theory has developed, as one of its most distinguished contributors had earlier suggested all sociological theory must, in terms of the middle range. On this level it would appear to have been far more fruitful than most. For we have had anomie theory, sub-cultural theory, conflict theory and a variety of other theories which straddle the boundaries of sociology, psychology and psycho-analysis. What has not happened, however, is any serious attempt to get beyond the middle range. This is more the pity, because the middle-level theories which are in operation seem to cry out for more general theoretical statement, and because it could be that what appear to be irreconcilable differences between schools actually turn on the fact that interest has been focused on different aspects of the structure of social interaction. Thus a general statement could be arrived at which subsumes within itself most of the present theories and which exposes the essential triviality and confusion of others.

The possibility of a general theoretical statement will, of course, depend in part upon the kind of general theory which we use. If we adopt a scientistic paradigm and emphasize the law-like nature of social behaviour, its systematic interconnectedness and its uniformity; if we assume that there are no problems involved in the interpretation of the behaviour of one actor by another; if we believe that no society can exist unless all men have so internalized society's demands that they want to do only that which they should do; if we fail to realize that social facts have a dual nature in that they exist both in themselves and in the conceptualizations of those who observe them; if we do any of these things then we shall, of course, find that there are circumstances and situations that our general theory cannot explain. We shall find diversity, conflict and randomness. We shall find misunderstanding and inadequate socialization. And we shall

225

find that the same act produces different responses in different circumstances. But there is no reason why our sociological theory should be so restricted. The restriction follows only if we imagine that sociology must work within the framework of systems and role theory on the one hand, and sheer statistical empiricism on the other. If, on the other hand, we follow through to their origins or to their logical conclusions the implications of symbolic inter- actionist and phenomenological theory, none at all of the obser- vations which appear so puzzling in deviance theory present any serious problem.

One hastens to emphasize at this point that the two schools of thought which we have mentioned cannot provide this necessary clarification and intellectual therapy, if they are taken in the sectarian form in which they most commonly appear, in and around the margins of the study of deviance. What we have to do, therefore, in order to achieve this intellectual clarification, is to go back to the root of the argument, to say what we mean by social interaction and social relations, and to be clear about the epistemological complexity involved in studying them. Such an exercise is long overdue and would, of course, for its satisfactory execution, need to be carried through on the same scale as that which led to Parsons's *The Social System*, but there is much material to draw upon in the classical sociological tradition, represented by Weber, Durkheim, Marx and Simmel, which Parsons himself eventually explicitly rejected.

Let us begin this analysis with an assertion. It is that sociology is concerned with the study of social relations. Our real problems begin with the explication of the phrase 'study of social relations'. If we imagine that such social relations are merely 'data', i.e. that they are 'given' in perception, we shall always be puzzled by the kind of 'data' thrown up in the deviance field. If, however, we realize that complex theoretical constructs are involved in the very notion of social relations and that the entities with which we are dealing, are contingent in multiple ways, the study of deviance will raise few problems of an unexpected sort. Social relations appear as entities to three analytically distinguishable types of people: to the participants in a social relation who know that relation from the inside, to other actors for whom the exis- tence of this social relation might appear as an environmental fact, that is, as something which might be used as a means, or regarded as a condition of, or an obstacle to, action; finally, to a sociologist who, on the one hand, seeks to understand the second actor's perception of a world of social relations, but, on the other hand, goes in directly to give his own account of that world. In no case, however, is what we are discussing a mere observable fact. In each case, even in the first, some kind of second order construct has been made by someone, before the consciousness of a social relation existing arises.

Alfred Schutz has probably given us the best account of what must be assumed to be involved in what Max Weber calls the orientation of the action of one actor to that of another. For him, the only direct experience of reality which human beings have is their own ongoing experience (Bergson's *durée*). We get further and further from this direct experience as, first, we attend to the act and perceive it only in the past tense, as, second, we seek to control it and use it as part of a course of meaningful action. As we get further and further from it we typify it and over-simplify it. Our concept of the experience is sharpened, but it may well also be false. Even at the level of the actor's interpretation of his own action, therefore, the possibility of false consciousness arises.

Much more, however, than our interpretation of our own experience in terms of our own action projects, the interpretation of the observed behaviour of others in terms of typical action projects is beset with difficulty and uncertainty. It is true that we do have more chance to exercise judgments and to check our hypotheses about motivation in the case of those with whom we are in direct contact, whereas the evidence which we offer for such hypotheses in the case of remote past or future actors tends to be far less adequate. But in all of these cases, what we have is not a true account of the observed behaviour as though we had seen it in the head of the other actor. What we have is a typification which may be clear but which may also be wrong.

The object of mentioning all this is not to complain about the nature of social reality, but to get it right. What we have shown so far is that even the mutual reading of each other's behaviour as indicating the existence of action projects, which goes on between two actors, may well be based upon error or, in a limiting case, it may not. How much more then, is it likely that there will be misunderstanding about a communication which seeks to impose a new element upon the action project which ego imputes to alter. Ego cannot be finally sure either that he knows what alter's project is or that alter fully understands the circumstances or demands which he, ego, now places in alter's way. It is surprising, therefore, to find Parsons saying at this point in his analysis of a social relation that the situation in which alter gets the message wrong would be only a limiting case. Surely the limiting case would be that single one in which alter got it exactly right.

Even yet, however, we have not come to the nub of a social relation. That nub is reached when we concentrate, not merely upon the fact of communication, but on the fact that what is communicated is a demand. There is, of course, the case in which ego might only place evidence in alter's way that there is a statistical likelihood that he will act in a certain way, in the hope that this knowledge will influence his conduct. This case, however, might better be dealt with when we are speaking, under the second heading, of the actor for whom social relations form part of his environment. For the moment, we need to notice that demands may be made, that they may or may not be regarded as legitimate by alter, but that even if they are, alter might still not conform. The case in which alter knows what is expected of him, and accepts that it is right or legitimate, seems at first to depend upon what Parsons calls the two-fold binding in of the social relation. It assumes that alter has been socialized into accepting a norm as governing his behaviour, or, to put it in another way, that he has internalized the norm, and that he cares about the attitudes which ego has towards him. It might well be argued that where this was indeed the case deviance would be impossible. In fact, however, there are a number of possibilities short of conformity which might occur, in which it could be said that, in some sense, alter regarded ego's demands as legitimate. The norms themselves could be unclear and ambiguous, allowing for loopholes, alter could be regarded as having only imperfectly internalized them, or alter might suffer from rigidities in his behaviour pattern arising on the personality level which prevent his responding flexibly to the demands made upon him.

Such cases of deviance need to be sharply distinguished from cases of conflict. Clearly there are cases in which alter knows full well what ego's demands are, but neither considers internalizing them, nor has personality difficulties as a result of knowing that they are being made. Quite calmly he rejects them, and probably takes whatever defensive or offensive action is necessary to prevent their affecting his life. This could, of course, take the form of violence. It could mean trying to deflect the demands or take avoiding action. It could take the form of argument or of some kind of symbolic act, which serves to signal the illegitimacy of the demand.

What is clear from what has so far been said is that some aspects of most explanations of delinquency and deviance are subsumed under what we have said about the possibilities inherent in a social relation. As soon as sociology stops confining itself to the notions of system and role which are built, as Parsons has clearly indicated, upon the case of a completely 'institutionalized' relation, this becomes clear. When we use the term social relation we should mean no more than a form of social interaction which might be thought of as lying somewhere between four points. These might be referred to as 'harmony' (Parsons's completely institutionalized relation), anomie (in the special sense in which Parsons uses that term in his discussion of social relations), deviance (not confined as in *The Social System* to deviance arising on the personality level) and conflict.

Immediately we might notice some of the implications of what we have been saying for existing deviance theories. So far as so-called anomie theories are concerned, we should note that the concept has a far wider range of uses than Merton's essay suggests. In fact, as we shall show later, the real interest of Merton's theory might lie in its sub-sociological nature or partly sociological nature, indicated by its concentration on the question of the availability of 'means'. Unfortunately, the notion is often taken, because of its Durkheimian pedigree, to refer to a wider range of states of normlessness and misinformation. Sub-cultural theory has produced rival theories which argue that the norms of the sub-culture have only the negative characteristic that those who follow them have been inadequately socialized (they are deprived or they don't know any better), that the sub-cultural norms are a sub-variety of a basic set made possible by the fact that the basic set are themselves ambiguous and full of let-outs and loopholes, that the sub-culture represents a group legitimi-zation of certain psychologically caused tendencies or that the norms are oppositional ones based upon a rejection of the main norms of the society.

Labelling theory, of course, has a more sophisticated origin than many of the theories so far mentioned. But it has been advanced in more or less sophisticated terms. When, however, it says no more than that the label of deviance which the agents of society attach to an act has only a relative significance, it would appear to be simply a variant of conflict theory, since the rejection of the label of deviance by alter would place it clearly in our fourth category.

Finally we should notice that sociological and psychological or psycho-analytic theories have too often been thought of as mutually exclusive. There might well be cases in which mis-informed, deviant or conflict-based action occurs without any personality mechanism being involved. In this case we posit only a rational adjustment on the part of the actor. Clearly there are also cases in which individuals violate norms because of rigidities of their behaviour arising on the personality level. But the third possibility, too often neglected, is that in which a reaction occurring originally within the context of a social relation, probably of traumatic kind, is repeated again and again in 'inappropriate' contexts, because of personality disturbance engendered by the initial trauma. It is the merit of Parsons that he makes explicit his sociological and psychological explanation in this way. It is the defect of Merton's essay that it is not clear as to whether his theory is to be thought of as constituting a sociological explanation, or whether it, too, has a hidden psychological dimension.

So far we have been concerned with the nature of social rela-tions solely as they appear to those who participate in them, and we have been looking particularly at the problems involved in saying that one actor takes account of the behaviour of others. We have not discussed what is involved in saying that two actors have a shared inter-subjective world of things both physical and social. We shall now have to consider what is presupposed in saying that such a world exists, and what the attitude of the actors is towards it. The problem of this shared world of objects is, so far as physical objects are concerned, a common problem for participants in social relations, and those for whom these social relations constitute an environment. So far as social objects like social relations are concerned, there is a problem only for the latter. As a matter of convenience, however, we consider the two problems together here.

The world of objects is not simply the empirical world of the scientists, nor is it value free. What has to be taken into account in constructing any kind of social action, therefore, is not what objects exist in the actor's world, but how those objects come to be defined and evaluated. Furthermore it must be recognized that because there is a subjective element in these definitions there is a real possibility that any two actors involved in a social relation might disagree as to the nature of their object world. This is true even of physical objects. It is much more true of social objects.

Physical objects might be viewed in various ways. They might be regarded as conditions of action, which act as obstacles to an actor's goal fulfilment. They might be regarded as merely neutral conditions. Or they might be regarded as manipulable objects, available for purposes of goal attainment. Cross-cutting these distinctions, however, are others. The objects might be regarded as purely neutral means. They may be regarded as means to highly desired ends and, therefore, secondarily desirable in themselves, or they may be regarded as ends in themselves. But, contrary to any of these alternatives, is the possibility that the particular objects might be regarded as sacred or holy and, therefore, non-manipulable.

Something might be said here about the implications of these remarks for the theories of Marx and Durkheim and through them for the Mertonian theory of deviance. For Marx it was characteristic of the object world of capitalist society, but most particularly of the world of social objects, that it was alien to man, that is to say that it confronted man as an external and oppressive force. Other social relations than those arising immediately from men's involvement with the means of production were seen to be dependent upon the social relations of production. The alien character of these social relations, like the alien character of the product of labour, could thus only be overcome if the actor were to take control of the means of production, and hence, control all social relations and the world of physical objects, as means to the attainment of his ends. By contrast with this, Durkheim distinguishes the whole world of social objects from that of the merely physical, and places them in the category of the sacred and non-manipulable. The difference between the position of Marx on the one hand and Durkheim and his functionalist successors on the other concerns the possibility of human agency in the business of social change. For Durkheim, the social is a reality *sui generis*, which, from the point of view of the individual, has a sacred and therefore unchangeable quality. Functionalist anthropologists like Radcliffe-Brown are what Popper would call holists, who argue that all social relations are systematically interconnected, so that in principle it is not possible to change any part of the whole without affecting the whole. Marx argues that, at certain points in history at least, men can intervene, but the effective point of intervention is in the social relations of production, other changes being possible in general terms only as a consequence of these basic changes.

All three of these theories as stated, however, have one feature in common. This is that they tend to be holist in Popper's sense. But, as Lockwood (1964) has pointed out in an extraordinarily acute theoretical essay, Marx's theory at least raises another possibility. This is that there might be not merely structural conflicts within one institutional order which spread 'functionally' and 'holistically' to the others, but that there might be a relative lack of fit between the various institutional orders, so that there would be no over-all system integration. If this is the case, then the problem of defining what is deviant becomes far more difficult than if we have the normative standard of a functionally interconnected system to refer to. The point is developed much further by Thomas and Znaniecki:

> With the growing social differentiation and increasing wealth and rationality of social values, the complex of traditional schemes constituting the civilization of a group becomes sub-divided into several more or less independent complexes. The individual can no longer be expected to make all these complexes his own; he must specialize. There also arises between the more or less specialized groups representing . . . systematic complexes of schemes a half-conscious struggle for supremacy. . . . It is clear . . . that no special complex, however wide, rich and consistent, can regulate all the activities which are going on in the group. Moreover the broad complexes which we designate

by the terms 'religion', 'state', 'nationality', 'industry', 'science', 'art', split into smaller ones and specialization and struggle can thus be characterized as that of a plurality of rival complexes or schemes, each regulating in a definite traditional way, certain activities and, each contending with others for supremacy within a given group. The antagonisms between social stability and individual efficiency are further complicated by conflicting demands put on the individual by these different complexes, each of which tends to organize personal life exclusively in view of its own purposes.

Lemert (1964, p. 67) who quotes this passage goes on to add:

In life-history retrospect, when the individual leaves the arena of primary groups and enters into numerous associations and unstructured situations with individual members representing disparate values, the patterned values acquired in primary groups are overlaid with social interactions which change the meaning of his early experiences.

Thus what the perspective of our second actor sited within an environment of social relations seems to point to is a theory of general anomie and conflict. By this is meant anomie in the broader sense of the term as used by Durkheim. The individual finds himself in a situation in which there is no single normative order which commands his moral allegiance absolutely. Moreover, since he approaches this order with a superego already moulded within one small world of social relations, and then finds himself forced to internalize and regard as legitimate, now this, now that other order, the external anomie of the normative order also becomes an internalized and socialized anomie.

Such a situation would also appear to give rise to the possibility of opportunistic appeals to moral authority by individuals calculatingly following their own self-interest. So, for instance, in a situation where quite manifestly everyone is simply fighting to survive or keeping his eye on the main chance, one finds a character like Tennessee Williams's Stanley Kowalski, in *A Streetcar Named Desire*, suddenly asserting, 'in Louisiana we get the Napoleonic Code'. Moreover, it is not merely in situations of obvious breakdown of the normative order that such claims may be made. A case can be made that, in a mass society, those who manipulate the mass media continually employ what one may call the Kowalski strategy on behalf of their masters. Another implication of the Thomas and Znaniecki perspective, however, is that in the sort of social circumstances which they describe, although a *de facto* tolerance of diversity arises, there must be an underlying set of rules which must be adhered to as a minimal basis for 'law and order'. In these terms it might be suggested that what happens with regard to the law of the roads might be generalized as a model for the whole of society. Here no one seeks to dictate what sort of car each motorist should drive, or what journeys he should undertake, but an elaborate system of rules and markings arises to prevent crashes. Sometimes Durkheim's conception of organic solidarity reads this way, especially when he seeks to counter Spencer by drawing attention to the underlying non-contractual element in contract.

Such an interpretation of what happens in the unintegrated society, however, does not fully explain what policemen are doing. They are not enforcing all laws by punishing every violation, but neither are they simply enforcing a basic set which is the underlying necessity for the functioning of a tolerant liberal and diversified society. What seems to be being suggested is that the police enforce some laws against some offenders some of the time, and that the basis of their use of their discretion is that they seek to impose the moral order of a plain and ordinary but respectable man on their fellows. This is to say that they represent a particular point of view in a society which is marked by deep moral differences, and that they use their power to impose that order on those who do not conform. The fact that all laws are not enforced against those who are policed does not mean that the load of these latter is lightened. It simply means an abandonment, in practice, of the rule of law so that law becomes an instrument through which one particular group in society imposes its views. The role of the mass media in helping to shape the code which is actually enforced is obviously also quite crucial.

Since the actual implications of anomie and conflict viewed from the point of view of the actor in a complex social environment are as complex as this, it is somewhat surprising that Merton's extraordinary oversimplified model should have enjoyed the vogue which it has, even more so because it is put forward as a theory of anomie and deviant behaviour. Clearly what Merton posits is a very distinctive type of society in which there are no over-all goals other than relative success compared with one's fellows. Within this, however, he posits the idea of 'legitimate' means, which are differentially available to different groups. Deviance is then seen as arising simply because legitimate social means are not available, at least in effective terms, to all. They, therefore, either stick to the means ineffectively or they revert to rational calculating and utilitarian rather than normatively governed action. This may, it is true, be a little more sociological in its approach than opportunity theories which simply suggest that deviance is caused by the availability of means and opportunities and can be cured by their removal. It hardly does justice, however, to the complexities inherent in the structures of advanced industrial societies to which we have drawn attention above. It does not, therefore, make sense any longer to treat the sociology of deviance, as Clinard does, as something which began with Merton's essay on 'Social Structure and Anomie'.

We must now turn to our final reference point, namely the perspective of the sociologist who studies social relations and social deviance. Here one finds that the lesson which many young sociologists have learned from phenomenology and symbolic interactionism is simply that the sociologist must begin his studies from the perspective of the observed actor, and that such an approach for the first time illuminates a field in which the veneration of hard data in the form of criminal statistics has prevented any effective knowledge ever being gained. I want to suggest that, while this position has some validity, it is of a far more complex kind than many deviance theorists imagine. To understand this it is necessary to consider the epistemological complexity of what sociologists are doing or can do. The sociologist observing the world of social relations has two possible sources of information. One is the direct observation of events in the social world, the other is the view of these events which is obtained and stated by other actors who observe them. The former has fallen into disrepute in many fields, but not least in the study of social deviance, because the observation of events in the social world was identified with the study of statistics, and these rarely seemed to tell one anything which was socially significant at all. Clearly what matters to a sociologist in any sphere is not how many people perform a particular act, but what relationship that act has to what other people expect of the actor, and how they evaluate this conduct. Durkheim, it should be noted, was well aware of this problem, and would take no delight at all in being hailed, as he often is, as the founder of modern statistically-based sociology. What he was concerned with were the external demands made upon the individual but, acutely recognizing that these demands were not always fixed and explicit, he suggested that statistical trends might give us an indication of underlying patterns of social constraint. Thus, his enigmatic observation that crime was a normal phenomenon. What this meant was simply that the sociological approach to any form of social pathology was to interpret it in terms of the constraint imposed on the individual's behaviour by his participation in an ongoing, if not explicitly recognized, pattern of social relations.

It should be noted, however, that Durkheim did not say that the sociologist had no resort except to the observed actor's definitions of the situation or his social theories. He clearly believed that it was possible for the sociologist to develop his own scientific and objective picture of the world of social relations, even to the extent of holding that the sociologist might observe such a pattern even when the participating and observing actors were unaware of it. A similar view is held by many Marxists who oppose the subjectivism which they think to be inherent in phenomenology. Thus, for example, Goldmann writes:

> The weakness of phenomenology seems to us to lie precisely in the fact that it limits itself to a complete description of the facts of consciousness. . . . The real structure of historical facts permits, however, beyond the conscious meaning of those facts in the thought and intention of the actors, the postulation of an objective meaning which often differs from the conscious meaning in an important way.
>
> (Goldmann, 1969, p. 32)

I would not, myself, wish to accept Durkheim's positivistic and scientistic certainty about the existence of an objectively describable world. Nor would I admit to feeling convinced about Goldmann's 'real structure of historical fact'. What I would do, however, is to claim that the sociologist can point to a distinction between that view of the world of social relations which has been arrived at by the procedures of sociological enquiry, and is agreed, at least by a partial community of sociologists, and that view which itself arises in the course of social experience and which has not been subject to the critical tests used to establish the sociologist's account. The real problem is to show whether or not there is any reason to suppose that the sociologist's agreed account has anything to commend it in preference to the popular participating layman's account.

I think that the sociologist's perspective has two things to commend it. One is that the procedures for arriving at the sociological account are agreed and public, whereas those of the participating layman are not. The other is that the sociologist is capable of giving an account in terms of the participant and observing actor's position and interests in the social world as to why he holds the view he does, while the reverse is not true.

The first of these reasons is, of course, not an entirely satisfying one. It fails to give us any guarantee of objectivity if that is what we want and it may be based upon an arbitrary agreement on the part of the sociological community to declare certain kinds of tests satisfactory. But this is true to some extent of all science. So far as the second reason is concerned, what we would be claiming is that the sociologist could show that the participant actor's view was not simply that of a detached observer but included many evaluative attitudes, prejudices, distortions, hopes and so on, which could themselves be understood as functional from the point of view of that particular actor's social position.

It might, of course, be argued, that that part of the sociology of knowledge which deals with the sociology of sociology shows that sociologists are also subject to these pressures, and to a limited extent this must be accepted. What is clear, however, is that the norms governing social enquiry are more readily accessible to analysis, and that it is part of the ethos of the sociological community that they should be subject to analysis. The views of social reality which are offered, say, in the mass media, are by no means subject to this institutionalized constraint. Our object here, however, is not to raise all the problems of the sociology of knowledge. It is to apply this critical view of the sociologist's account of the world to problems thrown up in the study of deviance. What we should wish to say about these is that it is by no means sufficient to say that the labelling of an act as deviant by a policeman, a court, or a newspaper has only a relative quality. It is possible for the sociologist to give a direct account of the structure of the act, and of its relationship to other actors, and it is also possible to look into the important question of why the labeller did the particular piece of labelling which he did.

The important first task is to consider the structure of the act and its relationship to the legal and normative order about it. The sociologist should take note of such facts as whether the act was legal or illegal, and whether the deviant actor was clear about the rule involved, whether he had completely internalized it and whether his relationship with the rule and with those who enforced it involved or did not involve personality strain. There has probably developed a too great willingness to ignore these issues since it became fashionable to suggest that deviance was purely a matter of labels.

With this done, however, the next and perhaps most important task is to explain the discrepancy between the sociologist's own description of the act, and that of the labelling participant actor, by analysing the position within a wider structure of social relations which that labelling participant actor occupies. This is where the sociology of deviance needs to be complemented by a sociology of the law-enforcing agencies, of the mass media, and, above all perhaps, of politics. What emerges from all that we have said above is that that which is commonly called deviance covers a multitude of different situations within the complexity of the structure of social interaction. It includes disagreements between related actors over the definition of the world, particularly of the social world; it includes false consciousness on the part of the actors about their own motivation and that of others; it includes that particular kind of anomie which is probably better called mis-communication; it includes an ambiguity in the normative demands laid upon the individual, their incomplete or inadequate internalization, and resistance to them on the personality level; it includes what is more properly called conflict. Looking at the matter from the point of view of observing actors outside of the social relations they observe, we have seen that the study of deviance also includes what is sometimes called the study of alienation, the study of system integration and non-integration, and the study of the availability of means. Finally we have seen that, if the sociologist is to regard his own position as anything other than a completely relativistic one, he must be able to describe social relations directly and show why it is that the accounts of social acts and relations given in practical life differ sharply from his own.

In conclusion, as part of my plea for the systematization of deviance theory, I would like to plead for a critical reassessment of all existing doctrines, and, not to be too critical, cults. I refer only to the doctrines of Robert Merton and the textbook version of George Mead by way of example. Both of these are stated and restated and, though they are sometimes criticized, the criticism rarely leads to their restatement in a non-cultic language in which they can be effectively generalized and used.

Merton's anomie theory, of course, is based upon a particular passage in Durkheim's *Suicide*, which is in some ways the most questionable version of his general doctrine. The greatness of Durkheim, contrary to common belief in the post 1937 world, was that he did not confine the study of sociology to what Parsons calls 'completely institutionalized social relations' or to completely integrated social systems. He saw that there was a wide range of other possibilities open and to many of these possibilities he gave the name of anomie. Anomie was a state in which the individual was not significantly morally involved with others. It was a state of normlessness in which the individual did not know his way about. It was a state in which there had been a differentiation of social functions without consequent integration. It was a state of lack of social system integration which was reflected in despair and lack of integration on the personality level. In one particular passage of a peculiarly conservative kind, however, Durkheim states his position in another way:

The relative limitation and the moderation it involves, make men contented with their lot while stimulating them moderately to improve it and this average contentment causes the feeling of calm, active happiness, the pleasure in existing and living which characterizes health for societies as well as individuals . . . loving what he has and not fixing his desire solely on what he lacks, his wishes and hopes may fail of what he has happened to aspire to without his being wholly destitute. He has the essentials. The equilibrium of his happiness is secure because it is defined and a few mishaps cannot disconcert him.

But in the state of anomie:

Reality seems valueless by comparison with the dreams of fevered imaginations; reality is, therefore, abandoned, but so too is possibility when it in turn becomes reality. A thirst arises for novelties: unfamiliar pleasures, nameless sensations, all of which lose their savour once known. . . . We may even wonder if this moral state is not principally what makes economic catastrophes of our day so fertile in suicides.

(Durkheim, 1952, p. 250)

Merton sees his own society as tending in the direction which Durkheim describes, but the real problem for him is that in the nature of the case, not everyone can fulfil his desires. The reason for this is that there is a lack of legitimate means.

It would be interesting to know what Durkheim would have thought of the notion of legitimate means in a society which set the sights of every individual on limitless success. Probably he would have regarded the very notion as a contradiction in terms. And indeed it is. For what Merton is really doing is to accept what Durkheim calls anomie as given, and then to turn to another question, namely the availability of means. The fact that this ties in very well with the interests of those sociologists for whom the prime problem in modern societies is simply inequality has led to an uncritical acceptance of Merton's so-called anomie theory.

Given the problem posed by inequality in a society hell-bent on success in a competitive order, there are, of course, two things which people can do. They can either stick to what non-utilitarian norms and taboos there are and centre their lives about these, thus opting out of the competitive struggle, or they can become completely rational utilitarians. This is obvious enough. Why those who behave in either of these ways should be thought to be deviant is far from clear. What is clear is that these two responses to the strain of living in contemporary America have nothing whatever to do with the two other types of response to which Merton refers, namely rebellion and retreatism. What he refers to as rebellion is the behaviour of those who refuse to limit their lives to competing individually for success, but resort to mutual aid and collective bargaining, i.e. members of the labour movement. What he refers to as retreatists are those who seek to avoid involvement in the competitive struggle as much as they can, by self-denying behaviour and by symbolic expressions which signify their rejection of competitive values. Merton saw this group as represented by hoboes and bohemians. Today they form a goodly part of the students who must be responsible for teaching at Columbia.

Clearly, looking at Merton's theory from a systematic point of view, we have already drawn attention to enough confusion of categories to raise doubts as to whether the theory deserves serious attention at all. But there is still one other major problem which the theory raises. This is whether it is intended as a sociological, a cultural or psychological theory. Clearly it is important to know whether we are discussing a series of situations in which individuals make adjustments *ad hoc* from situation to situation, or whether it is being suggested that individuals develop a trained response, or a response based upon ego sickness, which leads them, once conditioned, always to approach social relations in these typical ways. Significantly Parsons, advancing an avowedly psychological theory of the genesis of deviance, arrived at virtually the same categories as Merton. Probably Merton would claim that his theory is a sociological one and it has been hailed as such, but much ambiguity remains, and it is treated sometimes as a psychological, sometimes as a sociological, sometimes as a cultural theory.

A shorter comment may be made about the effect of the work of George Mead and what has come to be called symbolic interactionism on sociological theory and on deviance theory. Clearly Mead is a philosopher and the problems with which he was dealing were essentially philosophical problems, which he dealt with within the tradition of pragmatist thought. Like Dewey before him, Mead was concerned with the continuities as well as the discontinuities and emergents in the evolution of man within the animal kingdom. Against this background, he saw the crucial importance of language, and of the fact that an individual could understand his own gestures, as well as being able to 'take the role of the other'. This led on to the notion that the notion of the self was something which arose within the context of symbolic interaction. All of this was extremely important within the context of philosophical argument. It certainly injected a sociological element into the study of language and the study of the self. But to say this is not to say that Mead's formulations help us to formulate explicit hypotheses or even to indicate the range of possibilities within social interaction. In fact, if Meadian concepts are to be of use in sociology, they have to be demystified and unpacked. If we do this, we are bound to spell out, as has been done above, the various elements which are involved in what is very loosely and confusingly called taking the role of another, just as it becomes necessary to get beyond the simple problem of consciousness of identity to the problem of what it means to say that an individual gives meaning to his behaviour, or responds to a demand. It would be better if deviance theorists were to try to do this instead of simply repeating the Meadian phrases in an incantatory way. If they did they would find that many present conflicts and ambiguities in deviance theory could be readily resolved.

We should not, of course, be too harsh in our criticism of Mead or Merton: Mead was, as we have said, a philosopher, while Merton was a sociological theorist concerned with many issues other than those of deviance. The point which has been made here, however, is that deviance theory could benefit from relating itself to broader sociological theories, and it has been suggested that there is a certain way of looking at the epistemological problems of sociology, its conceptualizations and its vocabulary, to which deviance theory could profitably affiliate itself.

20

The domestication of sociology

Introduction: statement of the problem

The professionalization of the sociologist's role proceeds apace, and this, for many sociologists, is a matter for rejoicing and self-congratulation. What is not commonly recognized, however, is that the actual nature of this professionalization is ambiguous. Most commonly what is aimed at by sociologists is that they should have recognition as men performing the same kind of function as natural scientists. Only rarely does anyone suggest that in seeking professional recognition sociologists should seek recognition as being a separate profession subject to distinct logical, methodological, moral and social norms: but even if we were to confine ourselves to the attempts which sociologists have made to gain recognition as though they were natural scientists, some ambiguity would remain. For while sociologists might seek to affiliate their self-images to an ideal type of scientist ('ideal', it might be said, in a double sense, i.e. a both methodologically and morally pure type), far more commonly they would be likely to emulate the behaviour of actual flesh-and-blood scientists, whom one could capture for analytic purposes only in a series of empirical types, but all of whom, despite their variety, had been subject to the temptations of what Kingsley Davis and William Moore have so nicely called 'things that give sustenance and comfort', 'things that contribute to humour and diversion', and 'things that contribute to self-respect and ego-expansion' (Davis and Moore, 1945).

What we hope to do in this chapter is, first to indicate what the professionalization of science is thought to mean both in its ideal and in its actual empirical form, and then to show what it means to say that the role of the sociologist is to be institutionalized in our society as though he were a scientist. To this end we must

243

outline (a) the ideal image of the scientist's role, (b) possible 'pathological' deviations from that ideal, (c) the gap between the goals of sociology as they have been formulated by sociologists and the aims which sociology is likely to pursue if it is institutionalized as science and (d) the effect on sociology of the adoption of various pathological elements of scientific professionalization.

The ideal definition of the scientist's role and its institutionalization

We may take as a basis for discussion here, the presidential address of Professor Shils to the British Association for the Advancement of Science, in September 1967 (Shils, 1968). The actual occasion of such an address is not without significance and may justify this prefatory comment. The Association for the Advancement of Science is by definition an organization in which scientists meet, free of the entangling restraints imposed on them when their roles as scientists are merged with those of professor or business and government consultant. Moreover, the occasion has a certain ritual quality which almost requires that what should be affirmed should not be the day-to-day norms of scientific expediency but rather those norms, subscription to which gives the scientist a special sense of moral worthiness. All of this, however, is likely to be exaggerated in the sociology section of the Association, when the social institution of science is discussed. Sociology is a late-comer in the Association. Its very arrival there is a part of the process of its institutionalization, and the section meetings are likely to be attended especially by those sociologists who see the institutionalized destiny of the subject as being a scientific one. Finally, since acceptance of the section's legitimate membership is far from universal amongst other scientists, the likelihood is that the section's public thoughts on this matter will be marked by over-conformity to the ideal of science. None of this, of course, means that argument will not occur or that speakers in the section will not honourably seek to assert the truth as they see it. What it does mean is that the terms of the argument are to some extent set by the situation in which it occurs.

Professor Shils's presidential address tackles three fundamental problems about the scientific profession. These are (a) the differentiation of scientific activity as a separate activity, having its own identity, (b) the institutionalization of this activity through the creation of legitimate and largely full-time roles which permit and encourage it and (c) the control of the activity both in terms of selection procedures with regard to admissions to the scientist's role and in terms of the determination of priorities amongst scientific projects and between scientific and non-scientific projects.

The differentiation of the activity of science is described by Shils, when he talks of the scientific profession as follows:

> [The scientific profession] is constituted by all those for whom research or research and teaching are a full-time occupation in the exclusive performance of activities, which derive directly from an elaborate body of intellectual tradition, and admission to which is conditional on the demonstrated and certified meeting of that tradition. It is self-governing in the sense that it determines its own criteria of valid accomplishment and its own hierarchy of eminence and authority; it creates and applies such rules as it needs for determining its membership and the conduct of its members. It is disinterested in the sense that it is not leaned on for pecuniary gain alone and that whenever the prospect of pecuniary gain is an important criterion in any decision as to whether it should be performed in any particular instance, its actual performance is governed by conditions beyond the anticipation of pecuniary gain. It is concerned not only with the interests of its members, but with the transcendent interests of the discovery of truth as well.
>
> (Shils, 1968, p. 472)

The crux of the matter clearly lies in the closing sentence. It is not merely that science, like other professions, sets other goals at least on the same level as pecuniary gain. Its particular goal is a transcendent interest in the discovery of truth as well. And if artists or theologians were to claim that such a goal was not specific to scientists, some further differentiation might be suggested in terms of the employment of empirical criteria to establish propositions. Clearly the recognition of this differentiation of this kind of activity is an important historical event. To this Shils would add that to a much higher degree than in any other profession the performance of the practitioners is judged, not by a lay client, but by his fellow-practitioners. Whereas 'the older learned professions have in common the performance of sciences for the laity as their chief object. . . . What is cultivated in scientific communities is the incessant awareness that one's peers will scrutinize everything one does' (Shils, 1968, pp. 472–3). This indeed is the institutional expression of the goal of a transcendent interest in the discovery of truth. The scientist is not simply out to please. He has to convince colleagues trained in a certain set of procedures of enquiry that he has adhered to accepted standards of objectivity, accuracy and so on.

An activity such as this does not easily gain the recognition which institutionalization requires. Priests, kings, politicians, and others might well find its growth threatening to their own interests. One possibility is that it will be carried on only as a part-time pursuit and for pleasure by those whose social position is so secure that their right to do what they like with their spare time is unquestioned. But to bring science into the centre of things it is necessary that it should be performed within the framework of established and recognized organizations and probably in conjunction with some other role enjoying high prestige and legitimacy. Thus:

> In England, where science came slowly into the universities
> and last into those of relatively low prestige, the scientific
> role had to stand alone and unaided by association with
> honorific institutions. [While] in the German-speaking
> parts of Europe when the scientist's role was first
> appreciated, both for itself and for the economic benefits
> which it made possible, the scientist's role was enshrouded
> in that of the university professor, who was a teacher and
> civil servant at the same time as he was a scientist.

Nonetheless, 'this condition of the fusion of multiple roles was an advantage for science because it enabled it to enjoy the prestige of the other roles of professor and civil servant' (Shils, 1968, p. 470). It did not mean that the role itself was suppressed. Rather the new role of scientist with all its special features was built into the structure of society.

Control of scientific activity within the scientific profession turns on the question of selection of scientists and the financial support of projects. Selection takes place first through the fact that to be heard a man must publish, a fact which selects out those capable of expressing their ideas in a convincing form, and second through the agencies which control publication and appointment to paid posts in institutions. Shils believes that their selection procedures 'reinforce the integrity of universal submission within the community to the standards of scientific truth' and that:

demagogy and the display of personality might well exist in the temperament of scientists, but every scientist knows that these will count for nothing in the establishment of his good name as scientist.

(Shils, 1968, p. 473)

Thus:

Practically no one in the scientific community believes that anyone else has attained such eminence as he possesses by any practice other than a severe devotion to the traditions and standards of his discipline.

A research worker's reputation depends entirely on his own accomplishments and has nothing to do with his kinship or his class origins or affiliations. . . . He might be stimulated to high achievement by his relations with colleagues in a particular institution but the fact of his membership as such in that institution does not have anything to do with his reputation away from his scientific work. Colour, race, nationality, all yield before the quality of scientific achievement.

(Shils, 1968, p. 474)

One cannot, however, simply defend science as a self-governing profession without recognizing the fact that a majority of scientists do not work within the cloistered institutional seclusion of the university. Many work in industry and are 'less concerned with the advancement of knowledge as such and much more concerned with the advancement of knowledge for the sake of a more efficient means of production (or destruction) and a more profitable or otherwise more devisable material product' (Shils,

1968, p. 475). Not merely this, but, as the scale of scientific work and its demand for resources increases, governmental intervention is inevitable.

Shils suggests that the control of science by scientists can be maintained despite this situation:

> much of the scientific role remained—what was changed was the setting of the task to which the scientist directed his knowledge of skill and imagination, the criterion by which he selected his problems for enquiry and his freedom to communicate the results of his research to all other scientists working on his problem. The scientist's procedure remains and with it the ethos which inhered in the procedure. The intellectual self-discipline remained. [Indeed] certain of the greatest industrial scientific institutions have permitted so much of the full scientific role to function that its incumbents have not felt themselves to be different in any significant way from those who perform their scientific roles in wholly scientific institutions.
>
> (Shils, 1968, p. 475)

In the control of science in the modern industrial state, however, there are three sorts of decisions to be made: (a) those which involve selecting for support those projects which have the maximum prospective scientific relevance and fruitfulness; (b) those which concern the relative usefulness of projects for industry or social welfare, and (c) those involving political questions, e.g. the importance of investment in science instead of, say, the relief of poverty.

The pattern of scientific institutionalization with regard to these problems is not yet wholly determined. The likelihood, according to Shils, is that scientists will continue to take responsibility for the first type of decision and are at the moment patently unqualified to do so for the third. But there does seem some reason to suppose that forms will be found which will permit scientists to control the second area where there is still considerable uncertainty and, given success there, may move on to play a larger role in the third.

Pathological forms in the institutionalization of science

It is not intended here to deny the value and importance of Shils's ideal type of scientific institutionalization. Any fruitful work in the sociology of science presupposes a conceptual construction of this kind. If we can be clear what sort of structures and what sort of institutional relations a pure type of development such as this would imply, we may use the resulting model of a social structure as a standard against which existing cases should be measured. The claim that one is refuting Shils by showing that actual scientific institutions deviate from this type is as misplaced as that which deems that Weber's pure type of bureaucracy is refuted by empirical studies of particular governmental or industrial organizations.

Ideal types, however, are most useful if used in pairs. Weber's ideal type of bureaucracy becomes far more significant when it is seen as being at the opposite pole to any sort of patrimonial or charismatic administration. Similarly the pure type of scientific activity and of scientific institutionalization serves better as a yardstick when we recognize the various pathological forms which might arise. We therefore suggest that it is worth considering the other alternatives which are opened at each point in the process of the institutionalization and professionalization. The result may appear a caricature, just as Shils's outline appears as an idealization, but the effect will be to provide a better idea of what the main variables in scientific institutionalization are.

The first question one would raise is about Shils's definition of the activity of science. His emphasis is upon the transcendent importance of the quest for truth. Yet men calling themselves scientists have often had other goals. One has only to go back to the foundations of sociology to see that this is so. The campaign which St-Simon's useful class waged against their 'useless' adversaries was carried on in the name of science and the positive philosophy from which sociology emerged was far from being an unambiguous search for truth. And, in more recent times, Western sociologists have noted that Marxism as a political ideology of a ruling class or a revolutionary class seeks to justify itself as being scientific. Moreover, if they were more critical of themselves they might recognize that much that is called scientific is in fact ideological and that the claim to scientific status is nothing more than a weapon in the political struggle.

But whether science becomes detached from ideology or not, its institutionalization in universities and other institutions might well result in the emergence of a different pattern of social relations surrounding it than that which Shils suggests. In the first place, the activity of the scientist might be just as 'client-oriented' as any other, and, in the second, even if it is not the result of the continuous search for the approval of his peers, might very well retard rather than facilitate scientific discovery.

It is true, of course, that, so far as natural science is concerned, it is more likely that the patrons, sponsors and users of research will influence the selection of problems much more than they will the process of scientific discovery. But it would be a shallow view of the problem of objectivity which held that the actual conclusions of scientific investigation were never influenced by consumer or employer demand. It is less likely to be the case that the investigator will produce false conclusions to please his masters, it is true, though even this might happen, but he might more readily be prepared to suppress findings which conflict fundamentally with their ideology or interests. And in so far as the need to do this is sustained, what may occur may be not merely the suppression of this or that fact, but the maintenance of misleading and ideologically loaded theories and concepts. This is what Mannheim once referred to, in his discussion of the problem of objectivity as the 'lie in the soul'.

This suppression of conclusions or even of the commencement of an investigation in scientific research is, however, facilitated by the 'internal' structure of social relations which results from the professionalization of science. Two points need to be noted here. One is that the creation of a 'job' for the scientist has important social and cultural consequences. The other is that, in a highly competitive struggle for recognition, a level of feudalism is likely to develop.

There appears to be an internal tension between the notion of wage-earning or salaried employment and truly creative work of any kind. A parallel case to that of science is that of art. An artist who accepts employment will either run the risk of being told by his employer that he produces work too irregularly to justify the continuance of his job, or that of producing a certain norm of output which is of dubious intrinsic value. Artists, however, are usually salaried only for short periods and may be prepared to sacrifice security for creativity. Scientists who look to a career with increments are likely to suppress their more radical ideas until they have convinced their superiors that they are capable of doing a good job as measured by formal criteria.

It is strange that the important general concepts advanced by Robert Merton in his essay 'Social Structure and Anomie' (Merton, 1957, pp. 125–33) have not been applied to the sociology of science. If we say that the good scientist is expected to prove himself and to rise to the top of his profession by adhering to the goal of scientific discovery and the means of formally correct procedures, then two at least of Merton's categories of deviance apply, namely those of the 'innovator', who sticks to the goal but uses illegitimate means, and that of the 'ritualist', who abandons the goal but is meticulous about method. What seems to have happened here is that the innovator has been recognized and is quite regularly the object of attack by his fellow scientists. (One suspects that Shils has him in mind when he says that 'demagogy' and 'display of personality' must count for nothing in the establishment of the good name of a scientist.) But there is little exposure of the ritualist, the man who never puts a foot wrong, whose methods and particularly his provable quantitative methods are impeccable, but who never ever discovers anything of any significance at all.

The feudal structure of universities and other scientific institutions encourages this kind of ritualism. In a highly competitive world only those at the top may take risks. Others must seek their protection. In commending themselves to academic protectors, therefore, young scientists must be able to point to formally correct pieces of work and to qualifications and references which indicate that they have done such work. So the masterpiece and the doctor-piece take a ritualistic form. The more established the subject, the more certainly will the scale, the type, the methods and even the content of the work required to pass the test be laid down. And, of course, the journals in which such pieces of work are reported will increasingly remain unread for their sole function tends to become that of registering who has published and in what field.

The individual who amasses completed projects and journal articles of this kind is praised for his objectivity, his detachment and his professionalism, whereas the innovator who fails to publish is thought to be either a chiseller or a rate-buster—just as much as were the men described in the Hawthorne experiment. Simmel, it may be remembered, noted that academics on social occasions avoided talking to colleagues about their work, because such talk might lead to conflict which would damage the solidarity of 'pure sociability' (Wolff, 1964, pp. 51–3). It has been insufficiently noticed how far this social and psychological process affects the structure of academic work itself.

The young scientist who is wise, then, will seek to acquit himself well in formal terms and then commend himself to a more highly placed protector. The protector will act as his refuge and use his contacts with *his* protectors to ensure his protégé's preferment. And, if he is wise, the protégé will try to find himself as highly-placed a protector as possible with whom he can establish a direct personal link. Most hope lies in service in the retinue of the truly great. Promotion and independent power may then be won on the death of the master. In such circumstances the most that can be hoped for is that there will be a large number of powerful barons. Out of their contention there might ensue that real dialectic which is impossible between any one of them and his dependents.

The profession of science, then, can be so organized that any potential threat to the other established institutions of the society is neutralized. Parsons (1952) and Shils (1968) have both drawn attention to the fact that institutionalization reassures the public that the new forms of investigation are not threatening, but they conclude from this that institutionalization is the essential prerequisite of the advancement of science. Surely there is also another possibility. Institutionalization is essential because it is the necessary condition for the suppression of scientific and other forms of creative endeavour.

It may, of course, be asked why advanced societies should spend so much on scientific activity in universities and research institutions, if it does not make an important contribution to the advancement of knowledge and to human happiness. The answer to this is, of course, that in the real world it does. But in our ideal or pure type what we are trying to do is to explain that part of the expenditure which does not yield such a result. What we would say about this is that modern industrial society must spend large

sums on the advancement of science because it is of the essence
of its myth and charter that it is always increasing human welfare
by the use of science.

Finally, we have to look at the question of applied science.
Here it will be remembered in Shils's ideal type, the applied
scientist working in private industry, still remained a scientist,
loyal to the procedures and the ethos of his profession, even
though his problems might be selected for him and his employer
might have a property in his findings. The true locus of the
scientific profession lay not in industry but in the universities,
in pure research institutions and in professional associations.
But there is no reason why this should necessarily be the case:
at the other extreme is the type of situation in which not merely
problems but methods, construct, and even conclusions, of
research are determined by the researcher's employer, while at
the same time the universities modify their teaching and their
research programmes to suit industry's needs. Far from it being
the case that universities provide a professional base within
which the applied scientist can find support against his employers, very often the science departments of universities go out
to industry seeking its approval and, much more, its endowments
to help along departmental growth. It is true that many applied
scientists would prefer to work in universities which are, on the
whole, more prestigious places than factories, but this high
prestige could follow from the legitimating function of the
university in relation to industrial practice, rather than because
of the superior scientific value of the work conducted there.

Nor need we hope that the intervention of governments will
do much to change the situation created by the internal social
relations of science or its external relations with its industrial
sponsors. In order to sponsor research, in order to back one
project rather than another, in order to intervene and innovate,
the government must appoint committees to scrutinize the
proposals put up by scientists. But there are rarely available men
who combine the necessary knowledge with a portion of neu-
trality. Thus the government must fall back on trusting the
process of decision-making either (a) to a powerful group of
scientific barons with a predominant interest in the field, or (b)
to a committee of competing 'barons' who might serve to neutra-
lize one another and ensure that nothing is done, or (c) to an

outsider to the immediate field under consideration, at the risk of his not understanding the issue, or (d) to what can best be called a methodologically refined ignoramus, who can ensure that the ritualistic standards mentioned above are adhered to, whether or not the projects concerned are of any value to science or society.

In summary this model of the pathological extreme of the institutionalization of science posits its neutralization as a means to mastery of the environment or welfare—at least beyond what is necessary in the interests of those who control the society. What it does, however, is to create well-paid positions for those who claim to practise science, so that they will appear to be putting the society's affairs on a 'scientific basis' while they actually do no more than go through ritualistic motions. Both the internal aristocratic control of the profession and the external control exercised by sponsors, consumers and government are largely directed to maintaining this state of affairs.

Of course this is a caricature. But as we have said the opposite ideal type advanced by Shils is an idealization. The truth in any concrete society lies somewhere between the two extremes. What we should be clear about, however, when we talk of the professionalization of the sociologist as a scientist is that the process is as likely to show features outlined in our negative caricature as it is to show those of Shils's idealization.

Sociology as a vocation

There is far less certainty as to what is the vocation of sociology than there is regarding the vocation of natural science. Moreover, we cannot simply assume that the sociological practice of our universities and research institutes at the present day provides us with the necessary evidence to answer this question. For what we do today is the result of the process of professionalization and we must at least keep open the possibility that in the process of professionalization the activity itself has been emasculated or at least fundamentally transformed.

The first thing to be said about the vocation of sociology as it first appeared historically is that, for all its claims to be the new *science* of politics or of society, it was not an activity wholly distinct from ideology or for that matter from religion. Positivism meant not merely the application of scientific method to the study of society; it meant also the attempt to deduce moral and political injunctions from that study. And the other major nineteenth-century attempt to move from philosophy to science, dialectical and historical materialism, was also directed towards not merely interpreting the world but changing it. Further the positivists at least saw sociologists as nothing less than a priesthood who would impose a new scientific religion on society.

Clearly this kind of preoccupation has disappeared from contemporary sociology. Most sociologists today would agree with Karl Popper that the so-called laws of development in terms of which unexperienced futures were predicted had no scientific validity, and, with our own hindsight, it appears clear that what appeared inevitable *and* morally right to the founders of sociology was by no means unquestionably so. This does not necessarily mean, however, that all the preoccupations of nineteenth-century sociology were misguided or that sociology must be reduced to the sort of low-level empiricism which Popper's (1957) 'piecemeal social engineering' appears to imply. In the first place the general emphasis of sociology, within the range of possible emphases which can be made in scientific procedure, may be different from natural science. And second, the nature of the sociological subject matter might be such as to suggest a method different from that which is set out on most of the paradigms of natural-science method.

This is no place to embark upon an extended discussion of models of scientific method and scientific explanation. The point may be made, however, that whatever model we do accept, the manner of its use and the object of its use in sociology might be different from that in natural science. Thus though we may accept some version of the hypothetic-deductive method as the basic method of scientific explanation, we need not place quite the same emphasis upon the falsifiability principle as Popper does. The falsifiability principle should play an important part in scientific thinking when what is at issue is the testing of a particular law. But a major part of sociological thinking has to be devoted to the construction of general scientific models, i.e. of trying to find sets of laws or theories which may serve as a general guide for structuring social experience. In part this is because sociology is a young science. In part it is because such general models of what a social system is like are what men who call themselves sociologists are seeking.

It should be noted here that we are not entering into the argument as to whether the falsifiability principle is essential to science or not. The position put forward in the previous paragraph is quite compatible with the view that in order to qualify as science sociology must submit its propositions to the test of non-falsification. But with this said, it is important to draw attention to the logic of the procedure which is involved before the question of falsification arises. At this stage the sociologist is concerned with the meaningful relations of a number of theoretical propositions and with developing models of social structure which have numerous rather than single empirical implications. Our criticism of those who emphasize the falsifiability principle at every stage is that they too often avoid the problem presented by the creation of such models of social structure.

Most of the truly creative thinking in sociology has in fact been concerned with the development of ideal types of social structure. It is only against the background of such ideal types that useful empirical work can begin. Lack of progress in modern sociology has often been due to the fact that while old ideal types have been rejected new ones have not been found to take their place and sociological research as a result lacks any sense of direction, particularly when it comes to comparing one society with another. An interesting recent development in this respect is what Glaser and Strauss (1968) have called *The Discovery of Grounded Theory*. One of the points which they make is that new insights are sometimes gained in sociology as a result of the juxtaposition of situations which apparently have little in common. Such a procedure may well be necessary simply because insufficient attention has been given in the first place to the development of ideal types.

But we have yet to note the most fundamental difference between the activity of the sociologist and that of the scientist. Sociologists have never been entirely willing to accept purely meaningless correlations, causal sequences or theoretical constructs. They have gone beyond prediction and explanation in the usual scientific sense to seek 'understanding', i.e. to explain social structures in terms of subjectively formulated concepts, rather than as purely external and non-human things. This is not

merely a matter of a dispute between the Weberian and phenomenological tradition on the one hand and the Durkheimian one
on the other. All sociologists invite us to see whether their
explanations work on the level of meaning. The only question is
whether they do so implicitly or explicitly. Even Durkheim, who
made so much of the externality of social facts, invites us again
and again to think through his models of social structure from
the standpoint of a hypothetical participant actor.

There are, of course, very important epistemological as well as
methodological consequences which follow from the Schutzian
insight that whereas natural science involves having concepts
about things, social science involves having concepts about
things which have concepts (Schutz, 1964). At very least it must
be said that the implications of this situation are simply ignored
by scientistic sociology. But we need not even press this point
here. All that we need to do is to make the point that the goal
of sociology, implicitly or explicitly, has often been conceived
during the brief history of the discipline as the creation of models
which will explain how societies or institutions work, and that
these models, if they have had any great explanatory power, have
been cast in terms of the motivation of hypothetical actors and
their interaction with one another, rather than in terms of observed internal behaviour.

Conceivably sociologists who pursued this goal were misguided. Conceivably, also, it is not ultimately possible to create a
sociology of this kind which can be completely separated from
ideology. Whether this is true or not, however, there can be no
doubt that such goals as these are abandoned when sociologists
come to defend themselves as scientists and come to defend
science in terms of the falsifiability principle, empiricism,
operationalism and quantification, and social science as the study
of regularities in human behaviour. If this happens, no matter
how closely the professional situation outlined by Shils is approximated, sociology will have altered and narrowed the goals
which it once set itself.

If sociology is thought of as having had the aims which we
have mentioned, then of course its institutionalization and
professionalization (one might be tempted to say its domestication) as one of the sciences would have a very important social
function. For the search for new models of the social order which

make sense to the participants in that order is potentially far
more disruptive an activity than the relatively simple exercise
which Shils calls the transcendent interest in the discovery of
truth. Newly discovered facts taken in isolation have little
impact on ideology, no matter how fair the method by which they
have been collected. New ways of looking at the social order,
however, are highly productive of ideological agnosticism. The
first step, therefore, in neutralizing the sociologist lies in defining
him as a scientist and thereby denying him the right to re-
structure ideological models. It is hardly surprising that not
merely the defenders of the *status quo* but those who wish to
commit their fellows to a single revolutionary ideology have
insisted on defining sociology as science and thereby confined it
to a more limited role than it has claimed.

Sociology in its pathological scientistic form

The process whereby sociology came to be defined as a science
and thus won for itself house-room in the universities is a process
which has gone on over a period of a hundred years or more.
Paradoxically whereas, as Parsons rightly points out, science had
to win an institutionalized place, by being located close to the
study of the humanities, sociology which has strong links with
the humanities, now seeks, as proof of its respectability and
harmlessness, to show that it is a science. But this by itself is not
enough. A new phase of professionalization set in after 1945. In
this phase sociology sought to identify, not merely with science as
such, but with science in its more harmless domesticated and
ritualistic form. It is this phase which is often referred to when
we are told that the subject has now become more professional in
character.

The same process as that which is undergone by individual
scientists seeking professional recognition is undergone by
sociology as it seeks entry into the university or makes any
kind of claim on publicly provided research funds. Above all a
discipline with a past, such as sociology has, must prove its
respectability. And in an atmosphere when success in discovery
is hard to come by and to seek success through creative and
imaginative work means exposure to ruthless competition, the
likelihood is that the newcomer will seek to prove himself by

ritualistic adherence to formal standards with regard to research techniques.

What sociologists are required to show is that they can undertake typical pieces of work of a scientific kind. To show at the moment of entry into the university community that one's methods of enquiry are fundamentally different and the normal criteria of the scientific masterpiece are inappropriate would be to imperil one's application for entry. What has to be shown is that one's discipline does not merely measure up to standard criteria as well as any other science, but surpasses them all in the purity of its method.

The best evidence which sociology can offer of its attainments in this regard is to be found in the majority of its professional journals. The more perfect the statistical and mathematical techniques become, the more closely tied the data are to particular empirical subject matters; the less the general significance of articles for the understanding of society, the better it is for sociologists seeking respect and recognition amongst their scientific colleagues.

One of the consequences of this is that the proportion of time spent by sociologists in writing books which can be read by laymen, or by those who must take the important decisions about our social future, decreases. In fact a radical split opens up between sociologists who write books and those whose main effort takes the form of journal articles. This process reaches its logical conclusion when we hear it suggested that what is needed for teaching purposes is a good reader based upon the key journal articles.

Those who have contemplated producing such a reader will be fully aware, however, just how difficult the enterprise is. There is no principle in terms of which the articles can be integrated into a meaningful whole. They refer to each other and produce results which are of cumulative significance only in the shortest possible sequences. They reflect in an extreme form the anomie which Emile Durkheim was perceptive enough to see as the hallmark of professionalized and institutionalized science. If their findings ever have an impact on public policy this usually takes the negative form of throwing doubt on an existing policy assumption rather than on the provision of a new one.

The assumptions lying behind social, political and economic policy are, of course, often complex. Thus the social scientist who attempts to discuss them finds himself up against an initial difficulty. Even if he extends his methods to the maximum to take account of a variety of 'variables' the problem which he elucidates is simpler than that which confronts the policy-maker. The outcome of all this then is that the policy-maker must continue to work in terms of his own untutored insights, intuitions and ideologies.

Now it will be remembered that the claim of Parsons, Shils and others was that the institutionalization of the scientist's role in the universities had the effect of protecting him and enabling him to raise questions of a potentially disruptive kind. It will also be remembered that we raised the question even in the case of natural scientists of whether what actually happened was that the price of the scientist's institutionalization was that he refrained from reaching such disruptive conclusions. Clearly the latter is much more likely to be the case so far as sociologists are concerned. What is at stake very often is that the conclusions of the sociologist might challenge ideological assumptions. Hence it is not merely necessary that the sociologist should be prevented from venturing into the ideological field. His work must be so directed that it does not impinge, or impinges only in the most minimal way, on the field of policy-making.

A clear illustration of what happens may be gleaned from the field of race relations. If a sociologist in Britain or the United States seeks to analyse racial conflict in terms of a model which begins by seeking to make an objective estimate of the likely behaviour and motivation of all the participants in the situation, including not merely that of the white racist extremists and various negro groups, but also of those in governmental positions and those holding so-called 'liberal' views, one is bound to impinge on what is an ideological field. If, however, one accepts that what one can do *qua* sociologist and scientist is to analyse small-scale correlations and causal sequences, then one is likely to find oneself engaged on a project estimating, say, the effect on public attitudes of fair practices procedures. A sociologist, salaried in a university or a research institute, is far more likely to be supported in the latter type of work than he is in the former.

The feudalism of the institution of science which we noted earlier is even more likely to apply amongst sociologists. The field of anarchical power relations which institutional feudalism has to tame amongst scientists includes primarily other scientists. But the boundaries of this field of anarchy for the sociologist merge with the political field. Thus it is not merely desirable from a career point of view to seek the protection of a highly placed professor. It is best to seek one who enjoys a high measure of political security. To imagine that in such circumstances sociologists will be motivated solely by a transcendent interest in the truth is naïve to a degree. Skill, in empirical demonstrations of propositions and lucidity of argument, may be admired and may be central to the norms to which the profession confesses. But to suggest that this is likely to amount to a transcendent respect for truth is wide of the mark.

So far as the applied field is concerned most of the problems which arise for natural scientists arise for sociologists too. But what is perhaps most striking in the case of sociology is that the amount of applied research is as small as it is. Thus there will be a great deal of work done in fields such as that of market research where the sociologist is employed purely as a technician. But the problem of institutionalizing 'scientists' engaged in more fundamental work hardly arises since in most cases such work, if it exists at all, has been institutionalized in the universities where it cannot do any harm to anyone.

The promotion of sociological research in these circumstances has come to depend upon government agencies and foundations. But this relationship is even more problematic than its equivalent in the natural sciences. Who is to decide what projects shall be backed? Foundations have their terms of reference set for them. Government agencies, even if they have more liberal scope, depend upon and are controlled by their often politically appointed heads. It would be surprising indeed if such bodies were capable of preventing the sociological profession from following its own pathological inclinations. Broadly speaking, such grant-giving bodies are likely to adopt one of four alternatives in recruiting the personnel who will decide what projects should be supported. They may include overtly political personnel, who will ensure that the work at issue does not transcend ideological limits. They may rely on social science administration with a policy brief as to the areas which should be investigated. They may call upon the known barons drawn from the profession itself, or, playing safe, they may produce their own 'statistical ritualists' who will ensure that while standardized research techniques are adhered to, no fundamental questions are asked. The last alternative is in some ways the most destructive, because it ensures the elimination, not merely of what is ideologically dangerous, but, through its non-disciplinary and sub-disciplinary approach, the exclusion of sociological questions.

What is likely to emerge in the advanced societies, according to this model, is a set of institutions such as universities, trust funds and research agencies which serve to assure the populace that a part of the society's surplus is being spent upon social projects through which science is advancing the welfare of mankind, yet at the same time ensure that these projects do not undermine the society's ideological foundations. This is what the institutionalization and domestication of sociology is likely to mean.

Fortunately, it may be pointed out in conclusion, the organization of sociology has not yet reached this point, and, in the opinion of the present writer, at least, it has gone less far in this direction in the Western democracies than it has in the Communist countries. For one thing the institutionalization of liberal political values does still ensure that the sociologist whose researches and opinions impinge upon the political field will get a hearing. For another the fact that the sociologist's role is also institutionalized as that of a teacher in higher education ensures that he is continually being challenged to answer more far-reaching questions. The point of this chapter, however, is that the goal of professional recognition in the scientific community might push the sociologist in another and 'pathological' direction. Such a view will not be popular amongst professional sociologists. It may, however, be sustained by a 'liberal' journal editor.

Bibliography

ALTHUSSER, LOUIS (1970), *For Marx*, trans. Ben Brewster, London: Allen Lane, The Penguin Press.

APTER, DAVID ERNEST (1965), *The Politics of Modernisation*, Chicago: University of Chicago Press.

BALDAMUS, W. (1966a), *The Category of Pragmatic Knowledge in Sociological Theory*, University of Birmingham Faculty of Commerce and Social Science, Discussion Papers Series E, No. 1.

BALDAMUS, W. (1966b), *The Role of Discoveries in Social Science*, University of Birmingham Faculty of Commerce and Social Science, Discussion Papers Series E, No. 2.

BALDAMUS, W. (1967), *Notes on Stratification Theory*, University of Birmingham Faculty of Commerce and Social Science, Discussion Papers Series E, No. 5.

BALDAMUS, W. (1969a), *Alienation, Anomie and Industrial Accidents: an essay on the use of sociological time series*, University of Birmingham Faculty of Commerce and Social Science, Discussion Papers Series E, No. 12.

BALDAMUS, W. (1969b), *On Testing Hypotheses*, University of Birmingham Faculty of Commerce and Social Science, Discussion Papers Series E, No. 13.

BALDAMUS, W. (1971), *Cross-Classification*, University of Birmingham Faculty of Commerce and Social Science, Discussion Papers Series E, No. 16.

BECKER, HOWARD (1963), *Outsiders: Studies in the Sociology of Deviance*, New York: Free Press.

BECKER, HOWARD and BARNES, HARRY ELMER (1961), *Social Thought from Lore to Science*, New York: Dover Books.

BELL, DANIEL (1960), *The End of Ideology*, Chicago: Free Press.

BENDIX, REINHARD (1960), *Max Weber: An Intellectual Portrait*, London: Methuen.

BERGER, PETER L. (1966), *Invitation to Sociology: A Humanistic Perspective*, Harmondsworth: Penguin.

BERGER, PETER L. and LUCKMANN, THOMAS (1967), *The Social Construction of Reality: a treatise in the sociology of knowledge*, London: Allen Lane, The Penguin Press.

BERLIN, ISAIAH (1939), *Karl Marx: his life and environment*, London: Oxford University Press.

BEVERIDGE, WILLIAM (1945), *Full Employment in a Free Society*, London: Allen & Unwin.

BOOTH, CHARLES (1902), *Life and Labour of the People of London*, London: Macmillan.

BOTT, ELIZABETH (1957), *Family and Social Network*, London: Tavistock.

BOTTOMORE, TOM (ed.) (1963), *Karl Marx: Early Writings*, London: Watts.

BRYANT, CHRISTOPHER G. A. (1970), 'In Defence of Sociology: a reply to some contemporary philosophical criticisms', *British Journal of Sociology*, Vol. XXI, pp. 95–106.

BURY, JOHN BAGNALL (1932), *The Idea of Progress: an enquiry into its origins and growth*, New York: Macmillan.

CARR-SAUNDERS, ALEXANDER MORRIS, JONES, D. CARADOG and MOSER, C. (1958), *A Survey of Social Conditions in England and Wales, as illustrated by Statistics*, Oxford: Clarendon Press.

CICOUREL, AARON V. (1964), *Method and Measurement in Sociology*, New York: Free Press.

CLINARD, MARSHALL B. (ed.) (1964), *Anomie and Deviant Behavior*, New York: Free Press.

COLE, G. D. H. (1954), *History of Socialist Thought*, London: Macmillan.

COLE, G. D. H. (1955), *Studies in Class Structure*, London: Routledge & Kegan Paul.

COMTE, AUGUSTE (1853), *The Positive Philosophy*, 2 vols, trans. Harriet Martineau, London: Trubner.

COMTE, AUGUSTE (1966), *System of Positive Polity*, New York: Franklin.

COSER, LEWIS (1956), *The Functions of Social Conflict*, London: Routledge & Kegan Paul.

DAHRENDORF, RALF (1959), *Class and Class Conflict in Industrial Society*, London: Routledge & Kegan Paul.

DAHRENDORF, RALF (1968), 'Out of Utopia: towards a reorientation of sociological analysis', in *Essays in the Theory of Society*, London: Routledge & Kegan Paul.

DAVIS, KINGSLEY (1948), *Human Society*, New York: Macmillan.

DAVIS, KINGSLEY (1959), 'The Myth of Functional Analysis', *American Sociological Review*, Vol. 24, pp. 757–73.

DAVIS, KINGSLEY and MOORE, WILBERT E. (1945), 'Some Principles of Stratification', *American Sociological Review*, Vol. 10, pp. 242–9.

DURKHEIM, EMILE (1915), *The Elementary Forms of the Religious Life*, trans. Joseph Ward Swain, London: Allen & Unwin.

DURKHEIM, EMILE (1933), *The Division of Labor in Society*, trans. George Simpson, Chicago: Free Press.

DURKHEIM, EMILE (1938), *The Rules of Sociological Method*, (ed.) George Catlin, trans. Sarah Soloway and John Mueller, Chicago: Free Press.

DURKHEIM, EMILE (1952), *Suicide: a study in sociology*, (ed.) George Simpson, trans. John A. Spaulding and George Simpson, London: Routledge & Kegan Paul.

DURKHEIM, EMILE (1959), *Socialism and St-Simon*, (ed.) Alvin Gouldner, trans. Charlotte Sattler, London: Routledge & Kegan Paul.

EASTON, LLOYD D. and GUDDAT, KURT H. (eds), (1967), *Writings of the Young Marx on Philosophy and Society*, New York: Doubleday Anchor.

FEUERBACH, LUDWIG (1957), *The Essence of Christianity*, trans. George Eliot, New York: Harper & Row.

FLORENCE, SARGANT (1953), *The Logic of British and American Industry*, London: Routledge & Kegan Paul.

FRANK, ANDRE GUNDAR (n.d.), *Sociology of Development and the Underdevelopment of Sociology*, Copenhagen: Zenit Reprint.

GARFINKEL, HAROLD (1967), *Studies in Ethnomethodology*, Englewood Cliffs, N.J.: Prentice-Hall.

GERTH, HANS and MILLS, CHARLES WRIGHT (eds) (1948), *From Max Weber: Essays in Sociology*, London: Routledge & Kegan Paul.

GERTH, HANS and MILLS, CHARLES WRIGHT (1954), *Character and Social Structure: the psychology of social institutions*, London: Routledge & Kegan Paul.

GLASER, BARNEY G. and STRAUSS, ANSELM L. (1968), *The Discovery of Grounded Theory: strategies for qualitative research*, London: Weidenfeld & Nicolson.

GLASS, DAVID V. (ed.) (1954), *Social Mobility in Britain*, London: Routledge & Kegan Paul.

GOLDMANN, LUCIEN (1969), *The Human Sciences and Philosophy*, trans. Hayden V. White and Robert Anchor, London: Cape.

GOLDTHORPE, JOHN H. (1964), 'Social Stratification in Industrial Society', in Paul Halmos (ed.), *The Development of Industrial Societies*, Sociological Review Monograph No. 8.

GOLDTHORPE, JOHN H., LOCKWOOD, DAVID (1969), (with BECHHOFER, FRANK and PLATT, JENNIFER), *The Affluent Worker in the Class Structure*, Cambridge: Cambridge University Press.

GOODE, WILLIAM J. (1963), *World Revolution and Family Patterns*, New York: Free Press.

GOULDNER, ALVIN (1970), 'The Sociologist as Partisan: sociology and the welfare state', in Jack Douglas (ed.), *The Relevance of Sociology*, New York: Appleton-Century-Crofts.

HOBHOUSE, LEONARD TRELAWNY (1952), *Morals in Evolution*, London: Chapman & Hall.

HODGES, HERBERT ARTHUR (1944), *Wilhelm Dilthey: an introduction*, London: Routledge & Kegan Paul.

HODGES, HERBERT ARTHUR (1952), *The Philosophy of Wilhelm Dilthey*, London: Routledge & Kegan Paul.

HODGKIN, THOMAS LIONEL (1958), *Nationalism in Colonial Africa*, London: Mueller.

HOOK, SIDNEY (1962), *From Hegel to Marx*, Michigan: Ann Arbor.

HYNDMAN, HENRY MAYERS (1890), *Socialism and Slavery: being an answer to Mr. Herbert Spencer's attack on the Social Democratic Federation in the Contemporary Review, April, 1884, under the title, 'The Coming Slavery'* (3rd edn), London: William Reeves.

KORNHAUSER, WILLIAM (1960), *The Politics of Mass Society*, London: Routledge & Kegan Paul.

LAING, R. D. (1965), *The Divided Self: an existential study in sanity and madness*, Harmondsworth: Penguin.

LAING, R. D. (1967), *The Politics of Experience and the Bird of Paradise*, Harmondsworth: Penguin.

LANDIS, J. T. and LANDIS, M. G. (1953), *Readings in Marriage and the Family*, Englewood Cliffs, N.J.: Prentice-Hall.

LAZARSFELD, PAUL and OBERSCHALL, ANTHONY (1965), 'Max Weber and Empirical Social Research', *American Sociological Review*, Vol. 30, pp. 185-98.

LAZARSFELD, PAUL and ROSENBERG, MORRIS (eds) (1955), *The Language of Social Research*, Chicago: Free Press.

LEACH, EDMUND (1970), *Lévi-Strauss*, London: Fontana Books.

LEMERT, EDWIN M. (1951), *Social Pathology*, New York: McGraw-Hill.

LEMERT, EDWIN M. (1964), 'Social Structure, Social Control and Deviation', in Clinard, M. B. (ed.) (1964).

LERNER, DANIEL (1967), *The Passing of Traditional Society*, New York: Free Press.

LICHTHEIM, GEORGE (1961), *Marxism*, London: Routledge & Kegan Paul.

LICHTHEIM, GEORGE (1970), *Lukács*, London: Fontana Books.

LIPSET, SEYMOUR MARTIN (1959), *Political Man: the social bases of politics*, London: Heinemann.

LIPSET, SEYMOUR MARTIN and SMELSER, NEIL J. (eds) (1961), *Sociology: the progress of a decade*, Englewood Cliffs, N.J.: Prentice-Hall.

LOCKWOOD, DAVID (1964), 'Social Integration and System Integration', in George Zollchan and Walter Hirsch (eds), *Explorations in Social Change*, Boston: Houghton Mifflin.

LUNDBERG, GEORGE A. (1939), *Foundations of Sociology*, New York: Macmillan.

MCKINNEY, JOHN C. and TIRYSKIAN, EDWARD A. (eds) (1970), *Theoretical Sociology: Perspectives and Developments*, New York: Appleton-Century-Crofts.

MALINOWSKI, BRONISLAW (1944), *A Scientific Theory of Culture and Other Essays*, Chapel Hill: University of North Carolina Press.

MALINOWSKI, BRONISLAW (1966), *Coral Gardens and Their Magic: a study of the methods of tilling the soil and of agricultural rites in the Trobriand Islands*, London: Allen & Unwin.

MANNHEIM, KARL (1960), *Ideology and Utopia: an introduction to the sociology of knowledge*, trans. Louis Wirth and Edward A. Shils, London: Routledge & Kegan Paul.

MARCUSE, HERBERT (1955), *Reason and Revolution: Hegel and the rise of social theory* (2nd edn), London: Routledge & Kegan Paul.

MARCUSE, HERBERT (1964), *One-Dimensional Man*, London: Routledge & Kegan Paul.

MARSHALL, T. H. (1950), *Citizenship and Social Class and Other Essays*, Cambridge: University of Cambridge Press.

MARX, KARL (1939–41), *Grundrisse der Kritik der Politischen Oekonomie*, Moscow: Institute for Marxism-Leninism.

MARX, KARL (1956), *Economic and Philosophical Manuscripts of 1844*, Moscow: Foreign Languages Publishing House.

MARX, KARL (1961), *Capital*, Moscow: Foreign Languages Publishing House.

MARX, KARL and ENGELS, FRIEDRICH (1953), *Selected Correspondence*, Moscow: Foreign Languages Publishing House.

MARX, KARL and ENGELS, FRIEDRICH (1962a), *Selected Works*, 2 vols, Moscow: Foreign Languages Publishing House.

MARX, KARL and ENGELS, FRIEDRICH (1962b), 'The Communist Manifesto', in *Selected Works*, Moscow: Foreign Languages Publishing House.

MARX, KARL and ENGELS, FRIEDRICH (1964), *The German Ideology*, Moscow: Foreign Languages Publishing House.

MATZA, DAVID (1964), *Delinquency and Drift*, New York: Wiley.

MATZA, DAVID (1969), *Becoming Deviant*, Englewood Cliffs, N.J.: Prentice-Hall.

MEAD, GEORGE HERBERT (1934), *Mind, Self and Society*, Chicago: University of Chicago Press.

MERTON, ROBERT KING (1957), *Social Theory and Social Structure* (revised edn), Chicago: Free Press.

MILLS, CHARLES WRIGHT (1948), *The New Men of Power: America's Labor Leaders*, New York: Harcourt Brace.

MILLS, CHARLES WRIGHT (1951), *White Collar*, New York: Oxford University Press.

MILLS, CHARLES WRIGHT (1956), *The Power Elite*, New York: Oxford University Press.

MILLS, CHARLES WRIGHT (1958), *The Causes of World War Three*, New York: Simon & Schuster.

MILLS, CHARLES WRIGHT (1959), *The Sociological Imagination*, New York: Oxford University Press.

MILLS, CHARLES WRIGHT (1960), *Castro's Cuba*, London: Secker & Warburg.

MILLS, CHARLES WRIGHT (1963), *The Marxists*, Harmondsworth: Penguin.

MILLS, CHARLES WRIGHT (1966), *Sociology and Pragmatism: the higher learning in America*, New York: Oxford University Press.

MILLS, CHARLES WRIGHT et al. (1967a), *Puerto Rican Journey*, New York: Russell.

MILLS, CHARLES WRIGHT (1967b), *Power, Politics and People: the collected essays of C. Wright Mills*, ed. Irving Louis Horowitz, New York: Oxford University Press.

MYRDAL, GUNNAR (1958), *Value in Social Theory: a collection of essays on methodology*, London: Routledge & Kegan Paul.

PARK, ROBERT E., BURGESS, ERNEST W. and MACKENZIE, RODERICK D. (1925), *The City*, Chicago: University of Chicago Press.

PARKINSON, HARGREAVES (1951), *The Ownership of Industry*, London: Eyre & Spottiswoode.

PARSONS, TALCOTT (1937), *The Structure of Social Action: a study in social theory with special reference to a group of recent European writers*, Chicago: Free Press.

PARSONS, TALCOTT (1952), *The Social System*, London: Tavistock/Routledge & Kegan Paul.

PARSONS, TALCOTT (1964), Introduction to Max Weber, *The Theory of Social and Economic Organization*, New York: Free Press.

PARSONS, TALCOTT et al. (eds) (1965), *Theories of Society*, New York: Free Press.

PARSONS, TALCOTT (1966), *Societies: Evolutionary and Comparative Perspectives*, Englewood Cliffs, N.J.: Prentice-Hall.

PARSONS, TALCOTT (1971), *The System of Modern Societies*, Englewood Cliffs, N.J.: Prentice-Hall.

PARSONS, TALCOTT and BALES, ROBERT F. (1956), *Family: Socialization and Interaction Process*, London: Routledge & Kegan Paul.

PARSONS, TALCOTT, BALES, ROBERT F. and SHILS, EDWARD A. (1953), *Working Papers in the Theory of Action*, Chicago: Free Press.

PARSONS, TALCOTT and SHILS, EDWARD A. (eds) (1951), *Toward a General Theory of Action*, Cambridge, Mass.: Harvard University Press.

PARSONS, TALCOTT and SMELSER, NEIL J. (1956), *Economy and Society:*

A Study in the Integration of Economic and Social Theory, London: Routledge & Kegan Paul.

PEIRCE, CHARLES SANDERS (1958), *Collected Papers*, Cambridge, Mass.: Harvard University Press.

PICKERING, W. (1958), 'The Place of Religion in the Social Structure of Two English Industrial Towns, Rawmarsh (Yorkshire) and Scunthorpe (Lincolnshire)', unpublished Ph.D. thesis, University of London.

POPPER, KARL RAIMUND (1957), *The Poverty of Historicism*, London: Routledge & Kegan Paul.

POPPER, KARL RAIMUND (1959), *The Logic of Scientific Discovery*, London: Hutchinson.

RADCLIFFE-BROWN, A. R. (1952), *Structure and Function in Primitive Society*, London: Cohen & West.

REX, JOHN (1961), *Key Problems of Sociological Theory*, London: Routledge & Kegan Paul.

REX, JOHN (1968), 'The Sociology of the Zone of Transition', in R. Pahl (ed.), *Readings in Urban Sociology*, London: Pergamon Press.

REX, JOHN (1970), *Race Relations in Sociological Theory*, London: Weidenfeld & Nicolson.

REX, JOHN (1971), 'Typology and Objectivity in the Work of Max Weber: a comment on Max Weber's Four Sociological Methods', in Arun Sahay (ed.), *Max Weber and Modern Sociology*, London: Routledge & Kegan Paul.

REX, JOHN (1972), *Race, Colonialism and the City*, London: Routledge & Kegan Paul.

RICKERT, HEINRICH (1962), *Science and History: a critique of positivist epistemology*, trans. George Reisman, Princeton: Van Nostrand.

RICKMAN, HANS (1967), *Understanding and the Human Studies*, London: Heinemann.

ROCHE, M. (1973), *Phenomenology, Language and the Social Sciences*, London: Routledge & Kegan Paul.

RODRIGUES, OLINDE (1832), *Oeuvres complètes de Saint-Simon*, Paris.

ROTH, GUENTHER (1968), 'Introduction to Max Weber', in *Economy and Society*, New York: Bedminster Press.

SCHUTZ, ALFRED (1964–67), *Collected Papers* (3 vols), (eds) Maurice Natanson, Arvid Brodersen and Ilse Schutz, The Hague: Martinus Nijhoff.

SCHUTZ, ALFRED (1967), *The Phenomenology of the Social World*, trans. George Walsh and Frederick Lehnert, Chicago: Northwestern University Press.

SHILS, EDWARD A. (1959), *The Torment of Secrecy*, London: Heinemann.

SHILS, EDWARD A. (1968), 'The Profession of Science', *Advancement of Science*, Vol. 24, pp. 469–80.

SIMMEL, GEORG (1959), 'How is Society Possible?', in Kurt Wolff (ed.), *Georg Simmel 1858–1918: a collection of essays with translations and a bibliography*, Columbus, Ohio: Ohio State University Press.

SJOBERG, GIDEON (ed.) (1969), *Ethics, Politics and Social Research*, London: Routledge & Kegan Paul.

SMELSER, NEIL J. (1959), *Social Change in the Industrial Revolution: an application of theory to the Lancashire cotton industry, 1770–1840*, London: Routledge & Kegan Paul.

SMELSER, NEIL J. (1962), *The Theory of Collective Behaviour*, London: Routledge & Kegan Paul.

SMELSER, NEIL J. (1963), 'Mechanisms of Change and Adjustment to Change', in Bert F. Hoselitz and Wilbert E. Moore (eds), *Industrialisation and Society*, Paris: UNESCO Mouton.

SPENCER, HERBERT (1896), *Principles of Sociology*, London: Williams & Norgate.

SPENCER, HERBERT (1915), *First Principles* (6th edn), London: Williams & Norgate.

TITMUSS, RICHARD (1962), *Income Distribution and Social Change*, London: Allen & Unwin.

TÖNNIES, FERDINAND (1955), *Community and Association*, trans. Charles P. Loomis, London: Routledge & Kegan Paul.

TÖNNIES, FERDINAND (1967), 'Estates and Classes', in Reinhard Bendix and Seymour Martin Lipset (eds), *Class Status and Power: social stratification in comparative perspective* (2nd edn), London: Routledge & Kegan Paul.

TOWNSEND, PETER (1963), *The Family Life of Old People*, Harmondsworth: Penguin.

TROELTSCH, ERNST (1931), *The Social Teaching of the Christian Churches*, trans. Olive Wyon, London: Allen & Unwin.

TUCKER, ROBERT C. (1961), *Philosophy and Myth in Karl Marx*, Cambridge: Cambridge University Press.

VEBLEN, THORSTEIN (1931), *The Theory of the Leisure Class*, New York: Random House.

WARNER, W. LLOYD and LOW, J. O. (1947), *The Social System of the Modern Factory*, New Haven: Yale University Press.

WARNER, W. LLOYD and LUNT, PAUL (1941), *The Social System of a Modern Community*, New Haven: Yale University Press.

WEBB, SIDNEY (1962), contribution to *Fabian Essays* by George Bernard Shaw et al. (6th edn), London: Allen & Unwin.

WEBB, SIDNEY and BEATRICE (1932), *Methods of Social Study*, London: Longman.

WEBER, MAX (1949), *The Methodology of the Social Sciences*, ed. and trans. Edward A. Shils and Harry A. Finch, Chicago: Free Press.

WEBER, MAX (1951), *The Religion of China: Confucianism and Taoism*, ed. and trans. Hans Gerth, Chicago: Free Press.

WEBER, MAX (1952), *Ancient Judaism*, ed. and trans. Hans Gerth and Don Martindale, Chicago: Free Press.

WEBER, MAX (1958), *The Religion of India: the sociology of Hinduism and Buddhism*, ed. and trans. Hans Gerth and Don Martindale, Chicago: Free Press.

WEBER, MAX (1961), *General Economic History*, trans. Frank H. Knight, New York: Collier Books.

WEBER, MAX (1967), 'Class, Status and Party', in Reinhard Bendix and Seymour Martin Lipset (eds), *Class Status and Power: social stratification in comparative perspective* (2nd edn), London: Routledge & Kegan Paul.

WEBER, MAX (1968), *Economy and Society: an outline of interpretative sociology*, 3 vols, eds Guenther Roth and Claus Wittich, New York: Bedminster Press.

WEBER, MAX (1971), 'Socialism: speech for the general information of Austrian officers in Vienna 1918', trans. D. Hÿtch in J. E. T. Eldridge (ed.), *Max Weber: the interpretation of social reality*, London: Michael Joseph.

WHYTE, WILLIAM F. (1960), *The Organization Man*, Harmondsworth: Penguin.

WILLIAMS, RAYMOND (1961a), *Culture and Society 1780–1950*, Harmondsworth: Penguin.

WILLIAMS, RAYMOND (1961b), *The Long Revolution*, London: Chatto & Windus.

WILSON, EDMUND (1940), *To the Finland Station*, London: Fontana Books.

WINCH, PETER (1958), *The Idea of a Social Science and its Relation to Philosophy*, London: Routledge & Kegan Paul.

WITTGENSTEIN, LUDWIG (1961), *Tractatus Logico-Philosophicus*, trans. D. F. Pears and B. F. McGuinness, London: Routledge & Kegan Paul.

WOLFF, KURT (ed.) (1964), *The Sociology of Georg Simmel*, New York: Free Press.

YOUNG, MICHAEL and WILLMOTT, PETER (1957), *Family and Kinship in East London*, London: Routledge & Kegan Paul.

ZWEIG, FERDINAND (1950), *The British Worker*, Harmondsworth: Penguin.

Index

272